...this relic of barbarism—the Queen was rather portly, of medium height and plainly dressed...with a full round face, broad across the cheeks, thick lips, rather dull expression, and a countenance indicative of a severe temper and strong determination. She was darker than the ordinary native, showing evident traces of negro blood.

— Lt. Lucien Young, U.S.N.

To Steal A Kingdom

Michael Dougherty

Island Style Press
Waimanalo, Hawai‘i

Cover Design: Doug Behrens   Photo: Archives of Hawaii
Dougherty, Michael, 1924 -

To Steal A Kingdom by Michael Dougherty
Includes bibliographical references and index.
Hawai'i History and overthrow of monarchy A.D. 375 - 1903.

ISBN 0-9633484-0-X
LC 92- 90654

Island Style Press
P. O. Box 296
Waimanalo, Hawai'i 96795
(808)259-8666

Who controls the past controls the future;
who controls the present controls the past.

— George Orwell

In commemoration of the one hundredth
anniversary of the tragic overthrow of the Kingdom
of Hawai'i.
January 17, 1893 - 1993

CONTENTS

Probing Hawaiian History

In 1968 I was commissioned to write the narrative for an historical documentary to be filmed on the Island of Hawai'i. Researching a mountain of locally published material, I was dismayed to discover that much of the material was poorly documented and lacked the credibility I had encountered while researching history elsewhere. I told the producer I had misgivings regarding the accuracy of the sources and advised him to abandon the project. He did.

Although I disagree with certain views expressed by the erudite Lawrence Fuchs regarding Hawai'i in 1992, in 1968 I was impressed by his book *Hawaii Pono*, dealing with the 1900 to 1960 period in Hawai'i. It was carefully documented and crisply written. It challenged me to write the same sort of book dealing with the period from 1778 to 1900.

During the years that followed, I dug deep into the debris of Hawaiian history to discover that the research had taken a route of its own. It drove me to places that I had not intended to visit and to people whom I had not expected to meet. It opened my mind to questions which had not occurred to me when I began.

Since Hawaiian history began at least 1400 years before Captain Cook "discovered" the Sandwich Islands in 1778, it is clear that in order to reach a modicum understanding of Hawai'i one must trace the origin and culture of the Hawaiian people as far into the past as possible.* Their story begins with a brief, up-to-date anthropologically documented chapter on when humans first entered Oceania and of how they arrived at and settled far-flung islands and of what led one small group to migrate to Hawai'i.

Since Captain James Cook is generally recognized as the first European to observe Hawaiians in 1778 and since many contemporary Western beliefs regarding Hawaiians are still based upon observations by Cook and his crew, it seemed obligatory to put Cook and his sponsors under a magnifying glass. Research led me to the premise that Royal Society spin-doctors had altered the accounts of Cook's logs and the journals of his crew, as well. When I found documented evidence validating that premise, the question became, how did these sanitized accounts affect Hawaiians?

---

* The late dean of Hawai'i's historians, Dr. Ralph S. Kuykendall wrote *The Hawaiian Kingdom*, a three-volume, 1527 page history of Hawai'i. As an introduction to Volume I, he gives the reader "A Glimpse of Ancient Hawaii" in eleven pages.

Dr. Gavan Daws devoted 494 pages of his work *Shoal of Time* to the 190-year postcontact period of Hawaiian history. He failed to mention fourteen centuries of precontact Hawaiian history.

The ensuing chapters spotlighting principal players in Hawai'i's history are chronologically arranged. However, since it was not my intention to write an orthodox narrative history, I encourage these characters to speak for themselves, leaving less room for errors of interpretation on my part. As Havelock Ellis observed, "It is the little writer...who seems never to quote, and the reason is that he is never really doing anything else."

Robert Louis Stevenson hailed Melville as "...the first and greatest writer to touch the South Seas with any genius." Although Melville's outrage against Hawai'i's missionaries is expressed in *Omoo*, a work of fiction, Melville states "There are passages in the ensuing chapters which may be thought to bear rather hard upon a revered order of men. Such passages will be found, however, to be based upon facts admitting of no contradictions, and which have come immediately under the writer's cognizance."

Hawai'i's all-time best-selling histories, *The Hawaiian Kingdom* and *Shoal of Time,* ignore Melville. With the benefit of 150 years of hindsight enabling us to rate Melville's credibility against that of Gerrit P. Judd and his missionary contemporaries, I devote a chapter to Melville, enabling him to air his on-the-scene views.

When Hawai'i's isolation was penetrated in 1778, it became highly vulnerable to the diseases and greed of foreigners. To better understand these foreigners and their role in engineering the overthrow of the Queen in 1893, it is necessary to understand something of the cultures of their homelands. Therefore, we tag along with Damon, Judd, Alexander Liholiho, Lot Kamehameha, David Kālakaua, and others as they journey to many lands and mingle.

My hope is that this book will provoke readers into a thoughtful reexamination of this period in Hawaiian history.

— Michael Dougherty
Waimanalo, Hawai'i
September 1, 1992

Chapter One

EXPLORATIONS
250,000 B.C. - A.D. 1758

When man first settled Asia's off-shore islands almost a quarter of a million years ago, encroaching ice packs had lowered water levels in oceans and rivers. Land masses between China and Malaysia, separated by water today, were likely to have been connected. Land-bridges of that time made possible walking migration of men and animals. Conjecture leads to the idea that populating of the islands of Indonesia, New Guinea and Australia occurred before the ice thaw submerged those land-bridges. With the disappearance of land-bridges, millennia later, sailors, perhaps from Africa and/or the Middle East, arrived to turn the Pacific into an avenue of exploration. The following account traces their migrations eastward to the far corners of the South Pacific and, then north, to Hawai'i.

NEW GUINEA

The Pacific Ocean encompasses 64,186,000 square miles, an area exceeding the total land surface of Earth. Its mean depth is 14,500 feet; in the Marianas Trench, where greatest ocean depths have been recorded, it plunges more than seven miles to 37,800 feet. Oceania includes the islands of west, central and south Pacific. It embraces the far-flung islands of Melanesia, Micronesia and Polynesia.* Archaeologists tell us that the first human settlement of this vast area occurred more than 200,000 years ago.[1] Little is known about these settlers, but it is thought that their migrations from continental Asia were inspired by famines and tribal wars. Land-bridges and crude rafts made their migrations possible.

The second phase of South Pacific settlement occurred about 150,000 years later at New Guinea, when the sea barriers between

* Definitions of unfamiliar terms are given in the Glossary Page 194.

1

these Asian islands and Australia and New Guinea were crossed in relatively more sophisticated dugout canoes.

Twenty thousand years later, according to evidence based on isotopically dated coral reefs, New Guinea appeared as a frozen peninsular extension of the great island continent of Australia.[2] New Guinea was fused to Australia by a huge glacier, perhaps three or four miles high, a product of Earth's last Ice Age.

They remained joined until a great thaw occurred more than 20,000 years later, when the swelling seas rose and land disappeared, resulting in new shorelines. With the retreat of the last glaciers, coastal sea levels were raised dramatically, some as high as 400 feet, leaving New Guinea's settlers isolated from other humans for the next 5,000 years.[3]

In 1975, scientists at the University of Miami reported that they had found evidence supporting the idea that melting glaciers caused a great surge down the Mississippi River 11,600 years ago, raising sea levels and perhaps causing the destruction of Atlantis and the Great Flood of the Bible. During this era, ancestral Australoids developed the languages still spoken among today's dark-hued, wooly-haired aborigines of Australia and New Guinea.[4] Upon their arrival in New Guinea, they lived as food gatherers and hunters. Six thousand years later, Pacific civilization took a giant step forward, when newcomers settled islands and emerged as Oceania's first farmers and began producing food surpluses, necessitating a primitive trading system involving long-distance sea voyages.

Their isolation was broken again in about 3300 B.C., when yellow-skinned Mongoloids from Indonesia and the Philippines appeared upon their beaches. These migrants, a different breed than their hosts, were already skilled enough in sailing and navigating to leave passengers on a new shore and then to return to their original port and repeat the process.[5] The first of their kind to penetrate Melanesia, they spoke an Austronesian language traceable to that spoken in Indonesia and in the Philippines.[6] In the third millennium B.C. a people made up of Caucasoid and Mongoloid races sailed into the edge of Oceania. When they mixed with the previous settlers some skin tones gradually changed, adding a bronze hue.[7] In about 2000 B.C. the descendants of earlier immigrants to Indonesia, a mixture of several groups, hoisted their matted sails and set out in their canoes to begin explorations into the South Pacific, where thousands of specks of land created by tiny sea creatures and volcanoes lay exposed to tradewinds and storms.[8] These remote islands of Oceania were separated from each other by hundreds, and frequently thousands, of miles of blue Pacific. Improving on sailing skills that had delivered their ancestors past the shores of the Malayan Peninsula and down the coastal islands near to what is now Indonesia and farther on to the coast of the Philippines, these multiracial sailors traversed the storm-swept seas surrounding New Guinea. By day they navigated by the sun, with careful observation of waves and the direction of birds in flight. Overcast skies meant following prevailing winds and ocean currents. After the sun had set they found their course by reading the moon and stars. They sometimes carried caged frigate birds, and when the navigator lost direction, he would release the birds and follow their course to the nearest land.

In their voyages from the Philippines to New Guinea, these navigators of antiquity sailed against prevailing winds while running against ocean currents.[9] Employing these same techniques and utilizing the force of northwest monsoons and southeast trade winds, they quickly expanded their overseas vistas to include the Bismarck Archipelago, the Admiralty Islands, New Britain, the Solomons, New Ireland, New Caledonia, and ultimately New Hebrides.[10]

Ethnographic evidence supports the opinion that by 2,000 B.C. they had already begun successful explorations beyond the edges of Melanesia and on into the vast blue of Micronesia.[11] Thirty-four hundred years later common Western man still feared that he would sail off the edge of earth upon reaching the endless line of the horizon. Columbus dared to sail across the Atlantic in 1492, thanks to an invention of his day—the magnetic compass. Until then, the ships of the white man stayed close to the great land masses for even the longest voyages. Oceanic man sailed through those far horizons to discover a new world for himself.

Yet another group of Austronesians, the potters of a distinct style of ceramic called Lapita by contemporary archaeologists, occupied a number of coastal niches in Melanesia in about 1500 B.C.[12] These newcomers, better sailors than their predecessors, soon headed eastward to break a 2,000 mile barrier of unknown seas. They occupied Fiji on the eastern border of Melanesia and settled nearby Tonga in Western Polynesia. Evidence relating to this point in time substantiates the conclusion that today's Polynesians are the direct descendants of these early Lapita ceramicists and that Tonga became the first permanent settlement for Oceania's people in Polynesia and subsequently became the birthplace of the people we call Polynesians.*[13] The date was approximately 1300 B.C. With Fiji as a jumping off point to western Polynesia, these seaborne people began in earnest the colonization of the huge geographical triangle of Polynesia, stretching 3,600 miles south to New Zealand, 3,000 miles eastward to lonely Easter Island, and then 2,600 miles northward to its apex, Hawai'i. This triangle encompasses twice the area of the continental

* Some scholars contend that oral history honors Samoa's claim as the birthplace of Polynesia.

United States.[14] Within 3,000 years, these restless voyagers settled 278 habitable islands in Polynesia and became the most widely spread people on Earth.

To the Northwest their cousins, the Micronesians, were slowly populating the necklace-like atolls and volcanic mountain chains of islands that comprise the Marianas, Carolines, Marshalls and Gilberts.[15]

FIJI

The most unique island group in all of Melanesia is Fiji. It lies on the eastern border of Melanesia, adjacent to the western border of Polynesia, about 400 miles west of the Polynesian island cluster called Tonga. Fiji has produced an historic amalgamation of culture, language and physical likeness to Melanesia and Polynesia.[16] It stands by itself as an apparently unclassified product of many influences, a result of the flow of Oceanic migrants who sailed to, and sometimes through, her during their eastward occupation of the Pacific islands. Anthropologists believe that the population of Fiji was about 250,000 before the arrival of Abel Janszoon Tasman in 1643. More than half that number perished during the 1800's due to the importation of diseases and weapons by the Europeans.

Researchers have been so bewildered in their efforts to categorize Fiji, first settled by man in about 1300 B.C.,[17] as being either a Polynesian or Melanesian culture that one renowned anthropologist, W. W. Howells, dubbed them "Melanesianized Polynesians."

Early discoveries point out that Fiji was historically cut up into several chiefdoms whose boundaries were frequently changed by the victors in a series of tribal wars. Pottery of the Impressed Tradition found in Fiji supports the view that Fijians are Melanesian.[18] On the other hand, the Fijian language displays a basic affiliation to the Polynesian language and not to the languages of eastern Melanesia to which the Pacific Impressed pottery tradition would naturally be linked.[19] Linguists contend that Tongan is the single language to which noticeable borrowing by Fijian can be observed; however, this borrowing does not affect the primary vocabulary of the Fijians.

Melanesians first occupied Fiji more than 3,000 years ago, according to radiocarbon-dated charcoal found there on several sites containing Lapita pottery at its earliest levels.[20] Both Melanesians and the newcomer Mongoloids settled Fiji more than a thousand years before the birth of Christ.[21] At approximately that same time, Babylon was a thriving city, while Egypt was already sliding into its decline and the first Olympic games in Athens were 300 years ahead. Plundering Vikings were sailing their broad-beamed longships on distant runs of 750 miles between Norway and Iceland.[22] At that same time Polynesian man, with his enormous knowledge of the sea passed on to him through ancestral chants, was embarking on well-planned seasonal voyages of more than 2,000 miles across vast, empty seas. They sailed from Asia's offshore islands to Samoa and the Marquesas, to Easter Island, to Hawai'i, to Tahiti, and finally to New Zealand.

Pinpointed by archaeologists as the primary junction for the settlement of the eastern Pacific, Fiji had a population that rose and fell between 150,000 and 250,000. One of the largest groups in the Pacific, the 300 Fiji islands cover an area of more than 7,500 square miles.[23] Among the most talented and ferocious of all Pacific people, the Fijians developed to a sophisticated degree every art form known to the Polynesians and other arts unknown to Polynesians.[24] They built large, well-constructed houses for their chiefs, adorning them with imaginative designs. Their early pottery was beautifully shaped with undulating patterns and hand rubbed to a near flawless finish. Fijian weapons were intricately ornamented, and their cutting tools approached razor sharpness.[25] They prided themselves on the design of their canoes, which ranked as the swiftest and most seaworthy to survive the towering waves of Pacific Ocean storms. Some say Fijian chiefs hired Tongans, who had better technology, to build their canoes and to fight their wars.

In an attempt to recreate the product of their earlier technologies, the Fijians began building a 118-foot long and 24-foot wide double canoe in A.D. 1842.[26] Six feet deep from the weather deck to keel, it could transport 250 warriors and their weapons on long voyages. On peaceful journeys it could carry 30 people and ample enough cargo to settle new lands. Built of heavy planking cut from wedge-slit logs, this canoe was fitted with hand-cut lugs and stiffening ribs. Utilizing precision-cut joints which needed little caulking, its hulls were joined with sturdy timbers on which the deck was laid. Topside they added a deckhouse and a platform to shelter its passengers. It carried a huge, lateen-type sail with boom and yard each half as long again as its 50-foot mast. Upon completion it maintained a speed of seven knots. When the conditions were ideal, it could move along at a 16-knot clip.

A teacher to those who reached its shores, and then traveled on, Fiji had something for everyone. Highly skilled in the Stone Age art of surgery, Fijians also developed skill in the realm of pharmacology through their experiments with herbal medicines. They built irrigation systems with grids of canals and bridges to water their vegetable patches on terraced hillsides.

As physical specimens, the Fijians were taller and more ferocious appearing, with bushier hair, than their Polynesian neighbors, and their physiques were thinner.[27] Fijian warriors were widely feared for their frequency of human sacrifices and appetites for human flesh. Their armies were small in number, seldom having more than a thousand warriors, and disputes were frequently negotiated away before the clash of battle.[28] It has been estimated that the early Fijians lost fewer than 2,000 lives annually to human sacrifices and war.

TONGA

The first large island group thought to be settled from the junction of Fiji was the Tonga group, 400 miles to the southeast. It was there its settlers created the most aggressively stratified society in Polynesia and in all likelihood first produced the people who came to be known as Polynesians.[29] Tongatapu, its largest island, is 25 miles by 10 miles. It is the site of Nukualofa, the capital of the oldest inhabited island group in Polynesia, with radiocarbon dates as early as 1140 B.C.[30] The earliest radiocarbon date found, so far, on Samoa is 940 B.C.[31] Most scientists agree that Tonga's first settlers, makers of Lapita pottery, were the first true Polynesians. Linguists concur, having traced this migration through the spoken word back to Fiji, forward to Samoa, and then eastward to the Marquesas, where the oldest sites in East Polynesia have been located. The cultural foundations we recognize as Polynesian today were laid in Tonga during the millennium period after their first landing. As the western gateway to Polynesia, Tonga was the likely departure point for many explorations to other Polynesian islands, certainly including the Marquesas group. Currently, it is postulated that the archipelagos of Fiji, Samoa and Tonga were discovered and settled by a closely related people more than 5,000 years ago.[32] The analysis of similar Lapita pottery in all three island groups has provided the vital clue that gives substance to this claim.

Tongan studies trace the Lapita ceramic trait that likely covers more than a thousand years but almost fades from sight after the birth of Christ.[33] The ceramic evidence pleads the case that Tonga was settled initially and that the eastern and northern areas of Polynesia were occupied from bases in Tonga. Bone tattooing chisels, unearthed in early deposits along with arm rings, beads of small shells, shell rings and other personal items, were probably introduced to Tonga by its earliest settlers. Radiocarbon dated charcoal gives evidence of their early presence on Tonga.[34] Most items found in later Polynesian civilizations were carried to Tonga by its first settlers from Fiji.

The early Tongans preferred coastal living to inland villages, and small quantities of human bones have been discovered spread along its rocky shores. One skull, that of an old man, suggests that he died as the result of a frontal blow to his face.[35] Other human bones found nearby suggest cannibalism. Evidence leads to the assumption Tongans abandoned pottery making before A.D. 100 and that groups of them set out to explore the unknown seas of eastern Polynesia. The discovery of stone pavements, fences and hearths suggests that a well-organized, functioning society had already been created on Tonga. Pictured by historians as an idyllic, well-cultivated, and well-landscaped group of islands, Tonga boasted of dispersed villages connected by stone paths and well-laid-out clusters of shelters. After the visits of Captain James Cook in 1774, the Tongans radically altered their living pattern by concentrating their population in large fortifications for lengthy periods of time.[36]

The most formidable of prehistoric Polynesian civilizations, Tonga is made up of six inhabited islands out of a group of 160 islands, with Tongatapu and Uta Vava'u being its principal islands. Having a land area of approximately 260 square miles and an early population spread of 27,000 to 30,000, Tonga's islands were blessed with grassy plateaus and lush valleys lying in the shadows of towering lava pinnacles. According to the logs of early European explorers, Tonga appeared as "one of the most fertile plains in Europe ... nature, assisted by a little art, nowhere appears in a more flourishing place ... joy and contentment is painted in every face ..."[37] Its farms were laid out precisely with elaborate terraces, and its plantations were fenced off by massive stone walls designed as tide pools to catch food from the sea-washed shore by the changing tides. The level of artistic accomplishment among early Tongans is preserved in relics of wooden bowls and weapons aesthetically shaped and polished to glossy finishes with elaborately muted ornamentation.

Evidence portrays the early Tongans as a group who enjoyed peace and unity for longer periods than any similar island people. They lived in a near blissful calm with each other and their neighbors for a period of 600 years, beginning in about A.D. 1200. Tui Tonga, who bore the title of supreme chief, controlled all of Tonga's acreage and the commoner women of his choice were happy to comply with his sexual peccadillos. He wielded absolute power over his subjects. Those who disobeyed his wishes were summarily executed. During this period, ordinary Tongans lived out their lives within the pattern of an orderly civilized society. Relatively free of attacks from the outside, perhaps because of their reputation as merciless warriors and staunch defenders of their islands, the Tongans were among the tallest and best-proportioned people on Earth. The epitome of handsome Polynesians, with their copper-colored complexions, strong features and sculptured lips, the Tongans basked in the respect of other islanders.

One early European visitor to Tonga was the legendary Will

Mariner, who in 1804, at the age of 13, left London as a cabin boy aboard the British privateer *Port-au-Prince*. Upon the death of the captain, the ship dropped anchor off Tonga. Tongans attacked her, and Mariner was among a small group whose lives were spared. Adopted by the powerful Chief Finau II, Mariner spent the next four years gaining the confidence of his benefactor. Upon return to London, Mariner wrote an account of his stay in Tonga. Buried in this account is the documentation that Finau's father, Finau I, who was in control of the island of Ha'apai when Captain James Cook arrived there in 1777, had a well-laid plan to kill Cook and to seize his ships.[38] Cook departed several days before his announced sailing date, fondly remembering Tonga as the "Friendly Islands."

Tonga, the only populated island group in the entire Pacific which has never been completely under foreign control, seems a fitting place for the birth of the proud Polynesians.

THE MARQUESAS

Similarities in language and other anthropologic evidence enables us to trace the route of ancestral Polynesian migration from Tonga through Samoa in about 940 B.C., and then eastward to the Marquesas in about 100 B.C., where the oldest archaeological sites in East Polynesia have been found.[39] Located about 2,300 nautical miles from Tonga, the eight volcanic Marquesas Islands have no protecting reefs and lie in the path of the cool Humboldt current. Its principal islands, Nukuhiva and Hivaoa, are near the equator and uncomfortably humid.

The early population of the Marquesas, estimated at about 80,000, is easily identified, by culture and physical aspect, with the populations of Tonga and Samoa. The old culture is thought to have collapsed due to constant tribal wars and to the introduction of European guns and diseases. By 1930 there were a scant 2,000 Marquesans left. When first settled in 100 B.C., the lonely Marquesans occupied coastal acres where hook and line fishing flourished. Charred bones with radiocarbon dates of 100 B.C. have been unearthed, suggesting a degree of cannibalism in almost every valley of the Marquesas, where the density of population may have been greater than estimated.[41] That population probably achieved its high mark in about A.D. 1600. The scarcity of coastal plains and the surrounding high cliffs leading to extremely rugged mountains limited farming to the valley floors and isolated islanders from each other. With islands far apart and a population too strung out to become integrated, the Marquesans found their land was not adequate enough to support its population.

Judged by scholars to rank along with the finest sailors in Polynesia, the Marquesans lived on islands considered to be the least hospitable of all Pacific groups.[42] Farming was hindered not only by inadequate land, but also by steep cliffs and narrow valleys, a climate that produced long, searing droughts, and fishing was dangerous and difficult due to the lack of surrounding reefs. Needing to support a population that varied between 50,000 and 100,000, the Marquesans depended on open-sea fishing in order to catch enough seafood to survive. Marquesans, as Herman Melville would learn, were dispersed in lush isolated valleys and kept apart by the sheer walls of densely wooded mountains. Trapped in an unfriendly land and plagued by the elements that caused a continuing economic instability, the Marquesans engaged each other in a strong and frequently bitter competition. Although they stored away twenty-five percent of their annual breadfruit harvest against future hard times, the Marquesans found a way to destroy that prudent custom. Following a tribal war, the Marquesan victors ate the vanquished and then destroyed the breadfruit orchards of their newly digested rivals. This tradition created in the Marquesans the strong desire to fight to the death rather than to surrender and be eaten or to face a slow, painful death by starvation. The winners destroyed food supplies needed to nourish them through future droughts. With the odds of survival weighted against them, it is in many ways remarkable that they became the hub of East Pacific Polynesian culture. Perhaps it is understandable that they were to successfully complete at least two of the most prodigious sea voyages ever undertaken by man. These people reached out to more distant lands than those of any other islanders in the Pacific. Their craftsmen added to Polynesian culture by building huge ceremonial *heiau** while other Marquesans enriched the art of tattooing to a high degree of aesthetic perfection and chiseled out wood carvings of their tribal ancestors, some looming eight feet high.

In the words of historian Andrew Sharp, the Marquesans were "... heroes of the sea, whose likes may never be seen again."[43] Although New Zealander Sharp debunked what he called "the modern mythology of Polynesian migrations," he retained great admiration for the sailors of the Marquesas and their voyages. He agreed with the accepted west to east theory of settlement of the Pacific and challenged Thor Heyerdahl's view in *Kon Tiki* that Polynesian canoes could not have sailed the Pacific from west to east against the tradewinds and ocean currents. Heyerdahl concluded that Pacific settlement must have come from the American shores by Peruvian sailors drifting and sailing rafts from east to west, assisted by ocean

---

* See Hawaiian Glossary, Page 195 for Hawaiian word definitions.

currents and tradewinds.[44] Sharp countered that Pacific settlement came from west to east and that settlement was achieved more by accident than by design. He chalked it up to settlement by random drift and exile voyages. Drift occurred when a vessel was blown off course while on a short interisland trip and ended up weeks later on an uninhabited island. Exile settlement came about when islanders were forced to leave their island and, in the process of wandering aimlessly over the sea, they discovered, by happenstance, a new island home. Sharp reasoned that Polynesians could purposely sail between islands which were 300 miles apart, but he held the opinion that their navigational techniques and the limitations of their canoes excluded the possibility of longer-range voyages being accomplished.[45]

Other scientists, including Ben R. Finney and David Lewis, soon took to the open sea to prove or disprove the beliefs of Sharp.[46] Lewis covered 13,000 miles of the western Pacific, 1,680 of them on the open sea sailing without instruments, under the direction of Pacific island navigators.[47] In May of 1976 he was to join Finney and a master navigator from Micronesia, Pius Mau Piailug, on the famous *Hokule'a* voyage from Hawai'i to Tahiti. Based on data gathered on this successful voyage, they concluded that certain long-range voyages by the early Polynesians were clearly planned and successfully completed.[48]

It is likely that the Marquesans began preparing for the most spectacular of these long voyages shortly after A.D. 300. In the beginning their migrations could easily have been encouraged by their harsh surroundings, where famines caused by droughts, combined with great leaps of population, forced them out to sea. They began their preparations for such voyages by accumulating the rations needed to sustain life on their new island. They carried just enough food aboard to nourish themselves for a short trip, living on dried breadfruit, shellfish, coconut meat, dried bonito, *pandanus* flour, drinking coconuts and bamboo stalks filled with fresh water.[49] Months earlier they dried food under the equatorial sun and compacted it into small packets bound with *ti* leaves. Their canoes held items for future planting: sugarcane, *taro* roots, banana shoots, breadfruit roots, sweet potatoes, saplings, choice coconuts and divine food to appease their god—dried fish, whole yams and dried coconuts. Their livestock may have included dogs for baking, a rooster, hogs for breeding, chicken, and impregnated sows. They also carried replicas of their gods to ward off angry seas. An inventory of their equipment for the trip would list sail mats, bailing buckets, seashell scrapers, basalt stones for cooking, kindling for fires, spears and nets for catching fish, snares for catching sharks, paddles, a kit of stone adzes, food pounders, slingshots, stone anchors, fish hooks of pearl shell and bone, gourds, *tapa* beaters, *hau*-bark cordage for fishlines and waterproof mats.

Recent evidence concludes that the Marquesans were expert in both canoe building and in navigation. Aware that a year was 365 days, their religious celebrations were arranged around a moon month of twenty-nine and a half days. The Polynesian year was based upon the phases of the sun, and they acknowledged each phase of the moon cycle and named each so they could recognize it easily.[50] They knew exactly where the sun would position itself in the sky six months in advance and could take their directions from the position of the sun. "He also had to sail by the 'shape of the sky,' constantly tracking his course in relation to the bearings of major stars and the moon to the right or left of his course."[51] Unable to determine their latitude from the sun, they depended upon the stars and their constellations, which they had memorized. When the stars were obscured by overcast skies, the early Polynesian navigator monitored his course by observing the dominant ocean swell and the prevailing winds. He had the ability to alter a nearly true course under heavy cloud cover even when the moon and stars could not be observed for several days. With the knowledge of how to steer by following the direction of the prevailing wind, the Polynesian navigator stayed alert to changes in wind directions that might lead him off course. He was a student of the wind and unforgiving cross-currents and knew about seasonal variations and of wind changes caused by passing weather fronts and ocean storms. He knew a wind blowing against the direction of a tide would quickly produce a chop of hard, irregular waves whipped up on the surface and soon thereafter he would be riding a heavy sea. Using his direction finders—the sun, moon, stars and wind—in combination with his ability to understand the equatorial and counter-equatorial currents common to most Polynesian islands, the navigator was able to detect changes in that current and make adjustments to correct his star course. A seasoned navigator could steer his course by the feel of the ocean's long swells. Navigators followed the sea with the help of complex navigational information handed down generation to generation. Their minds were intricate storehouses of land signs, ocean condition, star courses, and they were keenly perceptive about their orientation at sea. "... their application demanded not only memorization, but also patient and discriminating observation of natural signs. Training was rigorous and prolonged over many years and it involved instruction both ashore and afloat."[52]

Constantly predicting the moods of the open sea, the Marquesans sailed farther east than any before them.[53] Adapting their double canoes to sail greater distances, they enlarged them to carry heavier cargos. As they journeyed southeastward against prevailing winds and currents, they took advantage of seasonal shifts in the wind to speed them eastward when westward trades were diminished and replaced by easterly winds.

Some experts on early Polynesian voyages speculate on the possibility of their sailing beyond the limits of the Polynesian triangle. They theorize that their capabilities included voyages between Hawai'i and the North and South American coasts and a crossing over the Tasman Sea to Australia. Although there is no evidence of Polynesian explorations in those areas, the possibilities of such voyages are being investigated.

In spite of the dangers of the sea, Polynesian men and women embarked on voyages which were certain to test their courage. They settled all of the major islands of Polynesia and often paid the price with a watery grave in the greatest ocean on earth. In about A.D. 350 these Marquesan sailors were preparing to embark upon two voyages of epic proportions.

EASTER ISLAND

Easter Island is far and away the most remote spot in Polynesia. A microscopic dot surrounded by a million square miles of blue ocean, it is one of the most isolated places on Earth. Like a lonely cork in the ocean, it lies 2,200 miles west of the coast of Chile and more than 2400 miles southeast of the Marquesas Islands.

Easter Island's nearest neighbor is Pitcairn, refuge for the mutineers of the *H.M.S. Bounty*, lying about 1,200 miles to the northeast. Being a scant fourteen miles long and seven miles across at its widest point, Easter Island has few blessings, no lush vegetation, no harbors, no palm trees, no sleepy lagoons and no coral reefs. It has tall brown waving grass, gigantic stone memorials to its dead chiefs and priests, and few trees spread out over its forty-eight square miles.

The odds that a primitive double-lashed canoe manned by Polynesians would land on its narrow rocky shores after a voyage of more than 2,400 miles over unknown seas are too astronomical to calculate. Luck played an important role in its discovery. According to radiocarbon evidence, it is highly probable that Polynesian settlers from the northern shores of the Marquesas did arrive on Easter Island perhaps around A.D. 400.[54] They found a barren land, harsh, hilly and without streams or lakes. Extinct volcanic craters acted as water reservoirs, while the soil elsewhere was composed of volcanic ash, causing rainfall to quickly seep away. Rolling hills toward the center of the island poke through clouds riding on strong sea winds. The climate is semi-tropical and its weather is ever-changing. One part of this small island may enjoy blissful sunshine, while another part may be cooled by a cloud burst. The island is bordered by menacing palisades of black basalt rock which seem at the ready to repel intruders. With little land suitable for producing food and a turbulent ocean without the buffer of a coral reef, the Polynesians were hard pressed to avoid starvation. Despite such obstacles, they survived to create one of the most complex and puzzling cultures in Polynesia.[55] Having a pre-European population peak of about 7,000, Easter Island became the most densely populated island in the Pacific.[56] They distinguished themselves by developing what appears to have been an authentic form of ideographic and pictographic writing found nowhere else in Polynesia. They also became the most prolific megalithic stone masons in the Pacific.

Centuries later, on April 2, 1722, Jakob Roggoveen, a Dutch sea captain aboard the *Arend*, sighted uncharted land and chronicled it in his log "a low and flattish island lying away to starboard."[57] It being Easter Sunday, he named the island in honor of the holiday and promptly led a landing party ashore. An assistant pilot panicked in a brush with an islander and shot a native who, he claimed, had tried to take away his musket. Other sailors and marines opened fire, killing a dozen islanders and wounding a score more.

When Captain James Cook anchored off Easter Island at Hangaroa Bay on March 13, 1774, he found "... a fair number of sweet potato gardens and plantation walks, some sugarcane, taro and yams were seen, a few gourds, but not a coconut, a few bushes four or five feet high, not a hog, not a dog ... and low miserable huts."[58]

Cook was awed by the product of their stone masonry: 1,000 stone images ranging in height from four to seventy feet with an average weight of approximately eighteen tons. He noted in his journal, "It was incomprehensible to me how such great masses could be formed by a set of people among whom we saw no tools. We could hardly conceive how these islanders, wholly unacquainted with any mechanical powers, could raise such stupendous figures, and afterwards place the large cylindrical stones upon their heads."[59]

Two hundred of these sculptured wonders had been placed on large stone platforms flanked by long paths of stone. These stone figures resemble no other statues ever fashioned.[60] Vertically the heads are rectangular-shaped and elongated. Eye sockets are deepset and shadowed, with brows sloping back. Carved out of volcanic tuff or limestone, with small crude picks of hard black obsidian, their characteristic form has a torso without legs, a head carved as a quadrilateral, with the chin being broader than the forehead. Their lips are thin and disapproving as they turn down at the ends. Eyebrows are emphatically ridged. Their arms, barely indicated and foreshortened, hang stiffly at their sides, while the pectoral muscles are well defined. Some are crudely made, while others are more precise, with designs on their backs which represent elaborate tattooing. They appear on altars staring out to sea and convey a mood of tragedy, a foreboding sense of calamitous endings. Among these stone figures are those that soar sixty feet into the sky and weigh as much as ninety tons.[61] Since the Easter Islanders were the only Polynesians to produce such great works out of stone, speculation runs rampant as to the reasons why they created these spectacular monuments. On the practical side, some theorize that, because trees were scarce, the Easter Islanders used stone, which was plentiful. More fanciful explanations include the theory that these stone figures portray astronauts from outer space who, with superhuman powers, helped the islanders carve the images in volcanic crater quarries miles across the island and then carried them down the steep cliffs to the stone altars on the plain below.

Easter Island legends simply say that the statues were "walked" from the quarries through the powers of great chiefs. Why were 200 nearly completed statues left at the Rano Raraku Crater site? It is believed that the unfinished work represents a tragic chapter in the collapse of a well-structured Polynesian system and that it came about suddenly when the Easter Islanders became unable to meet the physical challenges of their harsh environment.[62] As the population grew to its peak of 7,000, the marginal resources of the land and the surrounding sea became overtaxed and famine swept the island. Intertribal warfare developed as the culture declined and cooperation among the stone masons came to an end. Relics of that ancient period of decline are carved in the form of small wooden statues with meticulous detail of the human figure. These carvings depict gaunt faces and bodies with protruding ribs, bloated stomachs and goitered necks. They appear to represent people in the final stages of starvation. Stone giants reflect prosperous periods on Easter Island, while the wooden images mirror the catastrophe that soon followed. Later, when Cook landed there in 1774, he brought fame to the lonely isle by publishing a story about it. According to his account, the islanders were hospitable and in good physical shape. They were, in fact, the survivors of previous misfortunes, with more to follow.

In December of 1862, eight Peruvian ships appeared on the horizon.[63] Eighty armed slave traders came ashore and, upon departing, carried a cargo of more than a thousand manacled Easter Islanders, including the High Chief Kai Makoi and six of his heirs. Among the islanders taken were their priests, whose trained memories held the history of their people, the total knowledge of the centuries spent on Easter Island. None of them survived this disaster. Disembarking at Peru's offshore "guano islands," they were forced to labor, mining the droppings of sea birds used as fertilizer. Many died of foreign diseases. Months later, the Bishop of Tahiti intervened with the Peruvian government, ordering that the islanders be returned to Easter Island. When their rescue ship arrived, only one hundred remained alive. They were dying of smallpox. Fifteen reached home alive. They limped ashore to infect those left on the island.

HAWAI'I

It is probable that the Hawaiian Islands were first settled by Polynesian sailors from the southern shores of the Marquesas Islands sometime prior to A.D. 400. Artifacts unearthed in Hawai'i have given anthropologists the opportunity to travel back in time and piece together the story of what life was like then. Those same artifacts reveal a remarkable resemblance to those of archaic Marquesas Island artifacts. This same scientific time clock tells us that the Marquesas were settled in about 100 B.C. and that settlement of an archaeological site called Bellows on the Island of O'ahu at Waimanalo, Hawai'i, may have occurred as early as A.D. 375.[64]

Leaving the Marquesas, these people sailed over millions of square miles of ocean surrounding Polynesia. During the voyage they learned more about the seasons of the winds, the routes of constant tradewinds and the current and tide vagaries of the Pacific, both north and south of the Equator.[65] Long before reaching the shores of Hawai'i, they were on intimate terms with the northeastern trades that filled their plaited *pandanus* sails. They followed the signs of the moon, the Milky Way and the clouds across 2,500 miles of uncharted sea. Hawai'i's original settlers, who may have been isolated from other Polynesians for a period of up to nine hundred years, founded a unique society on their own. Oral records of this early voyage embodied in chants are obscured beneath the stratifications of the societies which followed. Consequently, the number of people and vessels involved initially will never be known.

Evidence suggests that their numbers were small and gives credibility to the idea that a single voyage beginning in the Marquesas in about A.D. 350 could account for the beginning of the Hawaiians.[66]

Knowledgeable Pacific sailors concur in the opinion that it would have been extremely difficult for those Marquesans who first settled Hawai'i, to make a return trip to the Marquesas[67] "because direct return to the Marquesas against strong steady winds and current would have been virtually impossible for any type of Polynesian voyaging vessel."[68]

"The only practicable way of reaching the Marquesas from Hawai'i would have been to head south to Tahiti-Tuamotus and then north-eastward toward the Marquesas—a laborious undertaking, which one would hesitate to postulate without some confirmatory evidence."[69] These same modern-day sailors agree with yesterday's historians that there is strong support for the supposition that a two-way contact of substantial volume was maintained between Tahiti and Hawai'i during the twelfth, thirteenth and fourteenth centuries.

Although the first Hawaiians had a calendar based on the stages of the monthly moon and a yearly cycle that counted from the positions of Pleiades, they had no written alphabet and no metal.[70] They did have an "alphabet" of sounds that were beyond the reach of Western ears. Their artwork, with a loose, unmarked sense of time, was carved on large, flat rocks with symbols in the form of line drawings called petroglyphs. These drawings depict men, gods, lizards, canoes, turtles and other objects in a clean, simple style. Despite the fact that they failed to develop a written language, it is widely believed among scholars that the Hawaiians, too, created a highly stratified society.

The eight populated islands of Hawai'i, with their green mountain tops wreathed in clouds, cover an area of 6,435 square miles, making Hawai'i larger than any other Polynesian group, with the exception of New Zealand. The entire Hawaiian archipelago, made up of hundreds of islands, is the product of thousands of sea floor lava flows, which first broke through the surface of the Pacific Ocean before the origin of man, more than six million years ago.

The Hawaiian Islands are the peaks of a great volcanic submarine mountain range. They were formed by a "hot spot" on the ocean floor, and subsequently moved into their present locations by the geogphysical process called plate techtonics. Mauna Kea on the Island of Hawai'i is the highest peak in the Pacific Basin at 13,796 feet. If you were to measure Mauna Kea from the floor of the Pacific Ocean, it would become the world's loftiest mountain with a height of about 30,000 feet.

In the beginning the high chiefs controlled all of the land. The common people, called *maka'āinana*, gathered together on the shore in small villages close to good fishing waters.[71] As time passed and the population multiplied, the chiefs divided the land into pie-shaped sections called *ahupua'a*, with boundaries often running from the top of the mountains to the sea. Those who lived and toiled there shared what was produced.

They were an extended family called an *'ohana*. Hawaiians were unique among Polynesians because they turned to the soil for their basic livelihood and consecrated their sons to *Lono*, the god of rain, agriculture and peace, rather than to *Kū*, the god of war.* Uncovered artifacts give us an insight into a society where common-

---

*Hawaiian gods *Kū*, *Lono*, *Kāne* and *Kāna Loa* had many overlapping forms and functions; strict distinctions were not always evident.

ers busied themselves with an assortment of tasks. Some toiled inland using simple sticks carved from hardwood to plant and harvest crops. Some played the role of civil engineers, designing and building elaborate irrigation systems. Some were fishermen, while others became canoe builders, bird catchers and house builders. The men of the society cooked using underground ovens, while the care of the very young was left to the women, along with the tasks of plaiting mats and the making of cloth from the inner bark of the paper mulberry tree.

As the society expanded, each domain produced its own chiefdom ruled by a high chief called *ali'i 'ai-moku*. He was responsible for enforcing a system of thou-shall-nots, called *kapu*, which controlled the lives of all within the society. Hawaiian historian David Malo, who was born in about 1793, and whose "mind had been impregnated with the vivifying influence of the new faith from across the ocean ... so entirely turned against the [old Hawaiian] whole system ... that his judgements often seemed warped causing him to confound ... the evil and the good ... the harmless and the depraved in one sweeping condemnation,"[72] explained "The condition of the common people was that of subjection to the chiefs, compelled to do their heavy tasks, burdened and oppressed ... the life of the common man was one of patient endurance, of yielding to the chiefs to purchase their favor."[73] Commoners did all the work on the land and part of their product belonged to the chief and his court. Ideally, a good chief was one who took care of his people. However, if a chief became overbearing to the extreme, he could be replaced. The dissatisfied commoner had the freedom to move about the island searching for a more suitable chief under whom to live and cultivate food crops.*

Education came by observing and participating in tasks, rather than by studying a subject and asking questions about it. At a very young age a Hawaiian *ali'i* learned that there was a spark in his being called *mana*. It was the spark of the god from whom he had descended. All things about him, his clothes, crumbs from his food, his hair, his body waste, and even his saliva, were imbued in this spiritual power. He had a high regard for his god and feared that foes would use objects containing his *mana* to harm him. In order to protect his spirit, he buried those items containing his *mana* in secret places. That ritual and their regular habit of swimming and surfing in the sea kept Hawaiians among the most hygienic people on Earth.[74]

The Polynesians of early Hawai'i were better developed physically and larger than the various Melanesian and Asian types from which they sprang. The combination of diet including *poi*, *taro* tops, coconuts, sweet potatoes, bananas, mountain apples, seaweed,

---

Great men became chiefs, great chiefs became gods and gods took many forms.
— Te Rangi Hiroa.

sea foods and, occasionally, chickens, pigs and dogs, along with their daily exposure to sunlight and exercise, gave the Hawaiians everything they needed for outstanding physical development.[75] They maintained their physiques by rough-water paddling in canoes where they also learned about harmony and cooperation as a way of life, rather than one of domination and competitiveness.

Artist-researcher Herb Kane explains how the shape of the canoe helped to shape the people. "Its design favored the survival of persons with stamina, muscle and ample fat to insulate the body from the deadly chill of wind evaporation upon spray-drenched skin. Rigorous selective pressures, oft repeated, may explain the physique and large size that distinguish Polynesians from other equatorial peoples."[76] Hawaiians of antiquity considered aggressiveness, possessiveness and acquisitiveness as undesirable behavior.

The early tillers of Hawai'i's soil and her fishermen were a peaceful sort who concentrated on producing enough food to feed their extended families.[77] The labor of cooperative systematic cultivation gave Hawai'i's commoners a gentleness of temperament uncommon in other Polynesian societies and an efficiency that soon created a surplus of crops. They gave thanks to *Lono*, the god "who caused things to grow and who gave plenty and prosperity to the country."[78]

This surplus food was the product of commoners who engineered agricultural gardens amid low, terraced plots with retaining walls of small stones, and by fishermen who built stone-walled fish ponds for *ali'i* beside rivers and at the shore to facilitate the natural gifts of Hawai'i. Such fertile lands, with their well-constructed terraces, watered by a network of irrigation ditches and streams combined with the wealth of the sea, gave early Hawaiians a bounteous living. The surplus allowed them to build temples for the glorification of their gods who were bestowing this bounty, as well as to create more gardens and irrigation ditches to produce even larger surpluses in a cycle of increasing production and increasing population which never utilized all of Hawai'i's available land.

They honored *Lono* with an annual four-month series of festivals called the *makahiki*, which was described by Malo as "a time when men, women and chiefs rested and abstained from all work, either on the farm or elsewhere. It was a time of entire freedom of labor."[79] The *makahiki* began in November after the harvest and continued into the month of February. The people left their fields and fishnets behind to celebrate and to pay homage to the gods and their chiefs by sharing their bountiful harvest. After the priest had acknowledged their gifts, he said, "We have accepted the offering to the god, the rest of the food is free, the rest of the mats, feathers and *kapa* [tapa cloth] is free to the people."[80] During the *makahiki,* the

Hawaiians, like the Athenians, forbade war, while boxing, wrestling, foot racing, chest pushing, hand gripping, spear throwing, dart throwing, sliding, stone bowling, *hula* dancing, and all other games that strengthened the body, were held. Spectator interest in the games was heightened by laying bets on the outcome of each event.

Unearthed artifacts and oral records translated from ancient chants have left us with a picture of the Hawaiians as a well-organized, highly skilled, self-sustaining group.[81] The method of learning from doing in old Hawai'i gave its people the ability to master many of the complicated skills of the craftsmen upon demand, as well as to assimilate the knowledge left by their erudite ancestors. The sons of chiefs learned not only about agriculture and fishing, but also about astronomy, herbal medicine, history, genealogy and navigating. The sons of commoners were taught the necessary skills for livelihood: farming, fishing, canoe building, house building, self-protection and hygiene. Hawaiians did not distinguish between work and play. Pounding *poi* and fishing were necessary, but pleasant, activities. Preventive habits were the key to health. "There was no loafing about all day and then later going to the gym to work out. They didn't get in the car and drive to the store for a loaf of bread and then jog for miles."[82]

Ancient Hawaiian chiefs practiced customs judged by "civilized" observers to be immoral and barbaric. The ideal royal marriage in Hawai'i was one where the high chief's son married his full or half sister, the daughter of his father.[83] It was believed that the offspring would concentrate the *mana* of both parents to produce a powerful heir, a superior chief. Prior to foreign contact, Hawaiian society encouraged spontaneous, casual sexual couplings as a prerequisite to permanent unions.[84] Consequently, they were bewildered by Christian moral teachings that forbade indiscriminate sexual relationships.

Human sacrifices were offered on special occasions. Christian missionaries condemned Polynesians for such excesses. The Mormon leader Brigham Young expressed feelings demanding human sacrifices. "As it was in ancient days, so it is in our day. There are sins that the blood of a lamb, of a calf, or of turtle doves cannot remit. They must be atoned for by the blood of the man." *

Compared to "civilized" Roman Catholic clergy who attempted to suppress heresy by torture and murder during the Inquisition, ancient Hawaiians appear as innocent choirboys.

---

* Brigham Young speech at the Mormon Tabernacle, September 21, 1856. See Thomas B. H. Stenhouse, p. 305.

Also Bringhurst, Newell, G. *Brigham Young,* p. 130.

When we consider their isolated position, the absence of a written language, their lack of metal and other tools essential for industry by Western standards, the Hawaiians enhanced the skills of their forefathers and came to a remarkably advanced stage of development long before the Europeans arrived.[85] They were manufacturing adzes from fine-grained basaltic stone, knives from sharks' teeth, and farming tools from hardwood. They produced *kapa* cloth from tree bark, fish hooks from bone and pearl shells, mats, fans, fish nets, rope-woven baskets, spears, javelins, slingshots of coconut fiber interwoven with human hair, bows and arrows, canoes—some as long as one hundred feet, with outriggers and masts for hoisting sails made of woven mats. They were self-sufficient, producing what they needed. Further evidence points out that pre-historic Hawaiians had an extraordinary knowledge of plants, including many different varieties of bananas, sugarcane, *taro* and sweet potatoes. According to the late anthropologist E.S.C. Handy, "There is every reason to believe that, as in the case of taro, the sweet potato, the breadfruit, coconut and sugarcane, new varieties of bananas were created consciously and purposefully by the skilled Polynesian horticulturists of the old days."[86] They were farmers with a wealth of botanic and agricultural talent, gifted artists and builders, warriors of great tactical skill and high courage, astute and creative in politics as well.

Since ancient Hawai'i was free of noxious insects, poisonous snakes, predatory animals and warlike tribes, the people had little occasion to fear their surroundings. Free from terror, they were able to develop other traits. One scholar observed that Hawaiians had the abilities for inquisitive dispositions, acuteness of sense, powers of observation, nimble, intellect, considerable imagination, mirthful hospitality and frankness of nature.[87] They could follow logical processes to the end, were capable of great sustained exertion and had the power to mimic, as well as to memorize. After the arrival of the white man, they easily acquired the skill to read and solve mathematical problems and displayed a decided poetical ability.

As centuries passed, the population of Hawai'i, isolated from foreigners and nourished by abundance, grew enormously.* The objects of Hawaiian worship were multiplied, its forms diversified, and the feudal system was developed and refined. The chiefs of its several islands emerged as a sharply defined upper class and the various *ali'i*, ambitious for more power and more possessions, turned upon each other and war replaced tranquility in Hawai'i. This evolution followed that found in Tonga, the Marquesas, Tahiti, Samoa and other Polynesian islands in terms of environment, technology and the

---

*Evidence supports the idea that Tahitians reached Hawai'i in the 1200's and made significant contributions to Hawai'i's culture.

productivity of its culture. A stratified society, with a sacred chief as its head, emerged to preside over a well-defined hierarchy of sub-chiefs, advisors, priests, craftsmen and commoners. Warfare became common in Hawai'i. Warriors armed with spears, slings and stones were killing each other in the long shadows of the giant mountain, Mauna Kea, on the Island of Hawai'i, when a woman of *ali'i* blood gave birth to a son. Chants say that the year was probably 1758. Later he would be called Kamehameha.

Chapter Two

INVADERS
1769 - 1779

Even though there is some evidence to support the view that Portuguese or Spanish sailors adrift from a sunken galleon between the coast of South America and the Philippines landed in Hawai'i at an earlier date than Captain James Cook, most historians discard that possibility. Or, if there was a chance landing made by foreigners, their impact is considered negligible. It is more generally believed among scholars that prior to 1778 the only explorers to reach Hawai'i were Polynesians and they became Hawai'i's original inhabitants fourteen hundred years earlier.

CAPTAIN JAMES COOK

On February 16, 1769, Captain James Cook, bound for Polynesia, completed the traverse of Cape Horn and declared that "... sooner or later degradation, despoliation and disaster would follow." Then, he asked, "In what other light can they look upon us but as invaders of their country?"[1]

Cook was born in a thatched hut in Yorkshire, England, in 1728. His father was a Scottish laborer and his English mother a domestic. As a youngster, James bartered herd tending for lessons in reading, writing and ciphering. Into his teens he became a stockboy, a sweeper and a package wrapper. In 1746, he apprenticed himself to John Walker, a Quaker shipmaster in the Yorkshire port of Whitby. Leaving drabness behind, he reveled in his first voyage aboard the *Freelove* to London, across the North Sea to Norway, and later to ports on the Baltic and Irish Seas. Between trips he taught himself navigation, memorizing charts that depicted the dangerous English coast. He learned the hazards of wind, tide and harbors from journeymen sailors. Industrious and quick of mind, he was rewarded for these qualities in 1752, when Walker gave him the rank of mate aboard a new vessel, the *Friendship*. He spent the next three years honing his skills.

Cook was 27 when Walker offered him a captaincy and command of his own ship. Cook rejected Walker's proposal and instead joined the Royal Navy as a common seaman.

In June of 1755, while General Braddock was fighting a losing battle as commander-in-chief of the British forces in the New World, Cook was assigned to duty aboard the 60-gun ship *Eagle* at Plymouth. His talents did not long go unnoticed, and in a month he was promoted to Master's Mate.

As England and France prepared to expand their American skirmishes into a wide-ranging war, the *Eagle* set sail in August to cruise between the Irish coast and the Scilly Islands off the southwestern tip of England. A tedious year passed before the *Eagle* was dispatched to the French coast, where she engaged enemy warships in battle. Bitter fighting and adverse weather took a toll aboard the *Eagle*. She sailed home to Plymouth for refitting in June, with the bodies of 26 crewmen aboard and 130 others with critical wounds.

In May 1757, back on Atlantic patrol, the *Eagle* engaged a French warship of 1,500 tons and 50 guns and, in a 40-minute running battle, captured her. That encounter was the most spectacular of Cook's combat cruises. On the eve of his twenty-ninth birthday, Cook was a battle veteran who had proved his coolness amidst death, suffering and incredible hardships, and he was recognized by his superiors as having attained an enormous knowledge of the sea. He had reached the top grade for an enlisted man in record time, but his lowly social credentials made it seem impossible that he would ever achieve officer status.

Late in October, Cook was assigned as master of the 64-gun *Pembroke* and set sail for Canada to help the badly mauled British force in its effort to storm the fortress city of Quebec.

The key to Quebec lay in the control of its lines of communication. The French and their Indian allies had already demonstrated their mastery over the English in guerrilla warfare, but their ability to hold Quebec was dependent upon their skill in moving replacement troops and provisions in and out over the St. Lawrence River. The British strategy was to cut these key lanes by sea and then to attack by land. When Cook disembarked from the *Pembroke* at Kennington Cove in July 1758, he was taken to a river bank to observe surveyor Samuel Holland at work. Already fascinated by navigation, Cook soon learned Holland's surveying technique and put it to practical use, in combination with his knowledge of navigation, when the English finally sailed up the St. Lawrence to close in on Quebec.

The following spring, the British succeeded in piercing the French defenses up the St. Lawrence to within five miles of Quebec, where they became stymied at the Traverse. This crossing, bristling with navigational obstacles, had been rendered even more hazardous by the enemy having cut loose their guide buoys. Two hundred British ships, crowded between the river banks, were stalled at the Traverse. Cook and two young apprentice surveyors were given the task of recharting and marking the tortuous passage. Working under heavy fire from French shore batteries, they completed their assignment in 23 days, and 200 warships passed through the Traverse without a casualty. When Quebec fell soon thereafter, Cook was given credit for the remarkable feat of getting the ships through safely and making that victory possible.

As the war in North America drew to a close, Cook charted the shallows of Nova Scotia, as well as the Newfoundland shoreline. By December of 1762, he was back on English soil packing his gear as he prepared to leave the last warship of his career. Before the month had ended, he married 21-year-old Elizabeth Batts. They were together until May, 1763, when he sailed aboard the *Antelope* to continue surveying for Thomas Granes, Governor of Newfoundland. Although he was officially carried on the Royal Navy books as an enlisted man, Cook was being paid a captain's salary.

Three years later, Cook's curiosity led him to observe a solar eclipse at Newfoundland. When the Admiralty checked his observations against those of the Royal Astronomer in London, they were astounded by Cook's accuracy. They recalled him to England to await a new assignment. Cook had become England's most innovative cartographer, the foremost navigator and one of her ablest seamen. Gentleman geographer Alexander Dalrymple, a powerful influence among his peers in the Royal Society, had earlier sailed out to Madras, where he had mastered the intricacies of the British spice trade and had become enchanted with the history of Spanish explorations in the Pacific. Dalrymple believed in the existence of an undiscovered land mass located somewhere in the Pacific.

In 1764, Dalrymple sailed aboard the schooner *Cuddalore* to Borneo and the Philippines. When he returned to England the following year, he was burning with the desire to return to the Pacific in search of what he called the Southern Continent. Three years passed before he was able to persuade his wealthy friends among the Royal Society to finance such a costly expedition. Dalrymple's dream of commanding that voyage collided with reality, when the Lords of the Admiralty overruled his peers at the Royal Society and plucked from its own ranks the man that they deemed most fitted to command such a prodigious expedition—James Cook. Lieutenant Cook sailed out of Plymouth Harbor on August 8, 1768, as Captain of the *Endeavour,* bound for the South Pacific.

The official rationale for the voyage was to transport and

assist Royal Society astronomers in their observation of the transit of Venus in Southern Hemisphere skies, from the Island of Tahiti. The underlying reasons were for Cook to chart new routes to lay claim to virgin territories for England and, if possible, to give substance to Dalrymple's Southern Continent.

The *Endeavour*, a 103-foot, three-masted coal schooner, with a speed of less than seven knots, ran low to the sea as it cleared the harbor with 94 men and enough provisions to last two years. Cook made a special effort to avoid the crippling seaman's disease of scurvy by including 7,000 pounds of sauerkraut among his supplies. In order to impress his crew with the importance of proper eating, Cook ordered two men flogged early in the voyage, when they failed to finish their daily ration of sauerkraut.

The *Endeavour* plowed its way across the Atlantic, around the Horn and into the Pacific, where Ferdinand Magellan, Pedro Fernandez de Quiros, Abel Janszoon Tasman, Captain Samuel Wallis, Sir Francis Drake and Louis Antoide de Bougainville had already left their wakes. Cook would soon surpass the efforts of the entire lot because he was the only one among them who combined the talents of seamanship, scientific navigation, surveying and cartography. Cook was uniquely equipped to succeed where others had failed because he was fully versed in the skill of longitude determination and was carrying those editions of the Royal Society Almanac, which plotted astronomical changes that would occur in South Pacific skies for the duration of his voyage. He could also correct compass errors by utilizing those same astronomical observations. He always knew where he was and how to get to where he wanted to go. He knew exactly where he had been and could tell others how to get to those same places.

On January 24, 1769, as the *Endeavour* began its traverse of Cape Horn, Cook charted, sounded and surveyed the sea and its shores. Having sailed from the Horn on a northwesterly tack, searching for Dalrymple's continent, Cook sighted his first uncharted Pacific isle, Vahitahi, on April 4. Nine days later he sailed into Matavai Bay, Tahiti, having completed the first leg of the voyage more than seven weeks ahead of the Admiralty schedule. He detailed his men ashore to build a fort to protect the crude observatory for observing the position of Venus during the eclipse. When the transit was taken on June 3, overcast skies blotted out Venus and prevented an accurate reading. Cook, having satisfied the official reason for the voyage, was now free to explore at his own discretion.

Ten days later two pieces of barnacled wood and seaweed were brought aboard. Looking ahead toward a huge land mass, some were convinced that they had found Dalrymple's "Continent." However, it was the east coast of New Zealand, and a truculent group of islanders awaited ashore waving clubs and jabbing the air with spears to prevent the landing party from reaching shore. Cook's marines immediately loaded their muskets, took aim and, upon his command, fired, killing three of the group. The following day Cook went ashore. When one of his reluctant hosts became frightened and bolted for cover in the nearby woods, Cook, fearing that the savage was fleeing to gather reinforcements, ordered a fusillade from his marines and the aborigine fell dead.

Later that same day Cook, Joseph Banks, a patron of the Royal Society, and seven crewmen came upon a native canoe. When its occupants headed menacingly in their direction, Cook ordered another fusillade, killing three and wounding three others. Cook explained, "I can by no means justify my conduct in attacking and killing the people in this boat who had given me no just provocation..."[2] Banks, who had fired his musket killing one man, wrote, "Thus ended the most disagreeable day my life has yet seen, black be the mark for it and heaven send that such may never return to embitter future reflection."[3]

The pattern was set for Cook's encounters with Pacific Islanders.

In April the *Endeavour,* whipped by a driving rain, headed out of New Zealand waters toward the east coast of Australia where Cook's courage and judgment would be tested. On June 11, Cook wrote of "... an alarming and I may say terrible circumstance ..." The *Endeavour* had run aground on the Great Barrier Reef. The sea was depicted as calm and silvered by moonbeams.

It was high tide and the *Endeavour* was held rock fast with water rushing through her bottom. Cook ordered all nonessentials thrown overboard and then had his men prepare a sail, to stretch diaper-like under her bottom, in case they were able to free her. The alternative was disaster, since they were 20 miles off land without enough lifeboats to carry them ashore.

Huge combers breaking across the treacherous reef forced more water through her starboard side than could be pumped out. Using an anchor, capstan, windlass and the moon for illumination, the embattled crew was barely able to budge the vessel into deeper water, saving her from the swells before they tore her apart. Finally, on the roll of a gigantic wave, the distressed ship tilted, gave a mighty lurch and slid off the coral, refloating herself. The crew quickly secured the bottom in the sling as a shore party nursed her through a groin in the coral heads to a beach where repairs could be made. Two months later, the refurbished *Endeavour* crept past shoals and reefs and found clear blue sea ahead.

Home was halfway around the world to the west as Cook headed for Batavia where the *Endeavour* could be made seaworthy enough to complete the circumnavigation. During the 70-day passage to the tip of South Africa the Royal Astronomer and the Royal Artist died, along with 22 crewmen. All were buried at sea, victims of the twin scourges of the Dutch Indies—malaria and dysentery.

On July 12, 1771, the *Endeavour* made port at Dover. Its voyage had taken almost three years. Cook carried a letter to the Admiral. Its final paragraph read, "You will herewith receive my Journals containing an Account of the Proceedings of the whole voyage, together with all the Charts, Plans & Drawings I have made of the respective places we have touched at, which you will be pleased to lay before their Lordships. I flatter myself that the latter will be sufficient to convey a Tolerable knowledge of the places they are intended to illustrate, & that the discoveries we have made, tho' not great, will apologize for the length of the Voyage."[4]

SECOND VOYAGE

No instant fame awaited the great sailor-explorer. His efforts were eclipsed in the glare of publicity given his Royal Society passengers, who had enriched civilization by cataloging thousands of plants, insects, fish and animals heretofore unknown to man.

Cook was already making plans for his second Pacific voyage. The Lords of the Admiralty, who expressed their confidence by promoting him to Commander and saddling him with no official orders, encouraged Cook to explore on his own initiative.

A year after the *Endeavour* had returned to her home port, the *Resolution,* in the company of her sister ship the *Adventure*, sailed south out of Plymouth Harbor. By October 30, 1772, they had reached Cape Town on their way around the southern tip of Africa, bound for Antarctica, still searching for Dalrymple's Continent. The weather kept Cook and his ragged men on the edge of frostbite, feeling their way through thick, low-hanging fog, sleet and driving snow in a porcelain-like maze of 100-foot icebergs. When they were only 75 miles north of Antarctica and could go no further, Cook ordered his helmsman to come about. As the ships sailed north, they were buffeted by foul weather and became separated. Cook's contingency for such an occurrence was that the ships would rendezvous in New Zealand at Queen Charlotte Sound. Enroute he scanned the Indian Ocean watchful for the Southern Continent. On the morning of May 18, the Resolution returned cannon fire to answer the *Adventure's* signal and then eased into Queen Charlotte Sound. In three weeks, both vessels were ready to resume their travels.

On July 23, as they sailed toward the equator, the mess cook aboard the *Adventure* died of scurvy. Cook dispatched a boat to

Furneaux's ship to learn that 20 other sailors were critically ill with the same disease. Angry that his dietary rules had been ignored and concerned for the lives of his men, he altered course and headed for Tahiti, where fresh fruit and vegetables, the remedy for scurvy, were plentiful. Two weeks later, they dropped anchor at the bay near Tautira, Tahiti, where the ailing crewmen slowly regained their strength. When the long, lazy August days dissolved into September, the surgeon's mate advised Cook his men were fit for duty. On October 1, they arrived at Tonga, where Royal Astronomer William Wales was inspired to write, "... affords without exceptions the most beautiful & variegated prospect I ever beheld."5 Cook exclaimed, "I thought I was transported into one of the most fertile plains of Europe ... Nature assisted by a little art, nowhere appears in a more flourishing state than at this isle."6

He described the Tongans as having surpassed all other societies of the Pacific in that they were clean, healthy, industrious and gave more than they expected in return. Their land was fertile, overflowing with an abundance of crops and livestock. Cook's party replenished their stores and, when they sailed away a week later, the Tongans bade farewell to the first white men they had ever seen.

As Cook headed back to the frozen vastness of Antarctica, the *Resolution* and the *Adventure* became separated again. But Cook went on to sail his craft farther south in that particular longitude than any other ship in history, a noble but futile last attempt at finding Dalrymple's Continent.

Thwarted by solid ice on January 30, 1774, Cook confided, "I whose ambition leads me not only further than any other man has been before me, but as far as I think it possible for man to go, was not sorry at meeting with this interruption."7

Always protective of his men's health, Cook often neglected his own. Now, after the strain of the vigorous weeks just past, he collapsed. George Forster, the *Resolution's* 18-year-old historian and artist, noted, "The Captain was taken ill of a fever & violent pain in the groin, which terminated in rheumatic swelling of the right foot: ... pale & lean, entirely lost his appetite, and laboured under a perpetual costiveness. He seemed to recover as we advanced to the northward."8

Cook recovered quickly when he added fresh baked Tahitian dog to his diet, exclaiming, "Few there were of us but what allowed that a South Sea dog was next to an English lamb." Strong enough to be on the bridge when the *Resolution* neared Easter Island and her telescopes brought into focus its awesome monumental stone idols, Cook tested his strength by leading a party ashore the following day. The gigantic, mournful figures caused Cook to conclude that, "The stupendous stone statues erected in different places along the Coast are certainly no representation of any Deity or places of worship; but most probably Burial Places for certain Tribes or Families."9 Struck by the similarities of Polynesians on other islands with those living on Easter Island, Cook explained, "... it is extraordinary that the same Native should have spread themselves all over the isles in this Vast Ocean from New Zealand to this Island which is almost a fourth part of the circumference of the Globe, many of them at this time have no other knowledge of each other ... never the less a careful observer will soon see the Affinity each has to the other."10

The Marquesas afforded Cook the opportunity to observe what he described as the most beautiful people he was ever to encounter. Cook and his men lolled in the Marquesan countryside for several days and then on April 22 set sail for Tahiti.

Soon they were skirting New Hebrides and heading for the central Pacific. While charting 500 miles of central Pacific sea dotted with a vertical chain of 91 islands, Cook and his marine shore parties encountered a different breed of island man. He was stocky, muscular, wooly headed, blue-black in color, courageous and fiercely protective of his domain. Cook's first confrontation with these Melanesians resulted in an aborted landing attempt, when two marines suffered flesh wounds from stone-tipped spears. The Englishmen retreated, regrouped and returned to kill 13 islanders with musket fire at close range.

On the return trip to New Zealand, Cook sailed into the harbor of an island with a 250-mile whaleback silhouette and marked it on his chart as New Caledonia. Soon after, they arrived in New Zealand, hoping to find their sister ship. When it was discovered that the *Adventure* had gone, Cook ordered full sails hoisted and plotted a course for Plymouth via Cape Horn and the Atlantic. He arrived home safely on July 30, 1755. The total elapsed time was three years, 18 days and four hours.

Out of the *Resolution's* original complement of 112 men, 108 returned hale and hearty. Of the four lost along the way, one began the voyage suffering from a terminal disease and three were lost overboard.

COOK'S THIRD AND FINAL VOYAGE
1776 - 1779

Having received a token of the recognition due him, Cook was shunted to a desk job at Greenwich Hospital. Disappointed, he wrote to John Walker, his first mentor, "As I have not now time to draw up an account of such occurrences of the Voyage as I wish to communicate to you, I can only thank you for your obliging letter and kind enquiryes after me during my absence; I must however tell you

that the *Resolution* was found to answer on all occasions even beyond
my expectations and is so little injured by the Voyage that she will
soon be sent out again, but I shall not command her, my fate drives
me from one extream to another. A few months ago the whole
Southern hemisphere was hardly big enough for me and now I am
going to be confined within the limits of Greenwich Hospital, which
are far too small for an active mind like mine, I must however confess it is a fine retreat and a pretty income, but whether I can bring
myself to like ease & retirement, time will show." [11]

Cook was nominated as a fellow of the Royal Society and
awarded the Copley Medal for his paper on combating scurvy at sea.
Soon it was rumored that the Admiralty had a third voyage in mind.
Now almost 48 years old, Cook volunteered and was accepted. Eight
days after the American colonies had declared their independence, he
boarded the *Resolution* to sail for the Pacific. His goal this time, to
explore the Pacific coast of North America in order to determine the
existence or nonexistence of a Northwest Passage that could open up
a direct trade route from England to the Far East. As he cleared
Portsmouth, with Commander Charles Clerke's *Discovery* following
in his wake, Cook crossed the path of a 52-vessel convoy escorted by
three British men-of-war. They were transporting hired Hessians to
North America to aid Sir William Howe in his vain attempt to beat
Washington's troops at New York. Here, in a rare outspoken mood,
Cook expressed the paradox of that moment, "It could not but occur
to us as a singular & affecting circumstance that at the very instant of
our departure upon a voyage, the object of which was to benefit
Europe by making fresh discoveries in North America, there should
be the unhappy necessity of employing others of his Majesty's ships,
and of conveying numerous bodies of land forces, to secure the obedience of those parts of that continent which have been discovered &
settled by our countrymen in the last century ..."[12]

Rounding the Cape of Good Hope, Cook sailed east across
the South Indian Ocean to Van Timpanis Land [Tamarind], where he
was urged to intercede in an intertribal war. He refused, explaining
later that, "If I had followed the advice of our pretended friends I
might have extirpated the whole race, for all the people of each hamlet, or village, by turns, applied to me to destroy the others, a most
striking proof of the divided state in which they live."[13]

Cook did an emotional flip-flop. Overnight he grew arrogant
and assaultive in his dealings with islanders and his crew. He personally hacked off the ears of a Tahitian in Huahine who was suspected
of stealing an armorer's tongs. "At Moorea," according to Cook's
painstaking biographer, Dr. J.C. Beaglehole, "he tried a different
plan, to get back a wretched goat, staging a regular punitive expedition burning houses, smashing and burning canoes threatening not to

leave a canoe on the island."[14]

John Forster, who represented the Royal Society aboard the Resolution, remembered Cook during this time as "A cross-grained fellow who sometimes showed a mean disposition and was carried away by a hasty temper ... giving vent to his passions, which in fact, became so detrimental to himself, as to occasion his destruction."[15]

Cook took hostages who had nothing to do with offenses he was trying to rectify. "He tried all sorts of ways, from kidnapping chiefs to flogging—a dozen lashes, two dozen, three, four, five, six dozen. When that failed, he ordered ears cropped, and had men's arms slashed cross-wise with a knife. There were those among his own men who were distressed and baffled. Was this the Captain of whose humanity they had heard so much?"[16]

Beaglehole, the most eminent Cook scholar, and Forster, the sharp-eyed witness, agree that Cook had suffered an ugly personality change.* Official Royal Society accounts of Cook's character omit any reference to such aberrant behavior, following the line that he was always in control, moderate, humane and gentle. Perhaps the reason for such a wide discrepancy lies in the explanation scholar Walter Besant gives for using the uncensored log of the *Resolution's* Lieutenant George Gilbert in his research as a cross-check on the official journals compiled by the Royal Society. Writing in London in 1888, Besant states, "The account of this voyage was published from the log-books and journals of Captain Cook, and by Captain King ... C.R. Douglas, Bishop of Salisbury, edited the work. Unfortunately he also *doctored* it and though he says in his introduction that Cook's journal was faithfully adhered to, he also owns to incorporating a quantity of matter .... In fact, a large number of eminent hands assisted in the production of the work, and if, after so much assistance, there is still much of the original journal left, we ought to be thankful ...."[17] Besant went on to explain that he decided to follow the account in Gilbert's Journals, after comparing the text of both accounts, because the Royal Society's official account "had been so much *edited* and *doctored* by the Bishop and his friends."** Many details, omitted in the official journals, have been preserved in Gilbert's unexpunged log. For example, at the Friendly Islands "These Indians ... stole several things from us. Captain Cook punished in a manner rather unbecoming of a European, viz. by cutting

---

*According to Sahlins, *Islands...* (p. xiii) a recent historical diagnosis offered by a prominent English physician suggests that Cook was suffering from intestinal parasites.

**Jonathan Swift in *A Voyage to Laputa* parodies the British Royal Society saying "Rather than making their mathematics follow the natural shape of things, they change the shape of things to fit their mathematics."

off their ears, firing at them with small shot or ball as they were swimming or paddling to the shore, and suffering the people (as he rowed after them) to beat them with the oars and stick the boat-hook into them whenever they could hit them; one in particular he punished by ordering one of our people to make two cuts upon his arm to the bone, one across the other close below his shoulder; which was an act that I cannot account for ...."[18] Little wonder that Chief Finau of Tonga was plotting to kill Cook and to seize his ships.

On January 19, 1778, the *Resolution* and the *Discovery* were seen by Hawaiians on the coast of Oʻahu. Executive Officer John Gore, on the bridge of the *Resolution,* sighted Oʻahu and sang out for a new course. A green haven, perhaps, a port for fresh water and vegetables. Cook, hastening to the bridge, ordered, instead, a course toward the rose-blue haze that tinted the western horizon.

In 1778 there were eight populated islands in the Hawaiian chain, which were divided into several independent chiefdoms. According to estimates by men in Cook's company, there were between 250,000 and 500,000 Polynesians living on these eight islands. Today, knowledgeable demographers set the figures between 200,000 and 300,000.*

The *Resolution* and the *Discovery* sailed on past Oʻahu, riding a favoring wind. Cook's capable, but tart-tongued, master, William Bligh, age 21, shouted out commands to 45 able-bodied seamen, while six midshipmen raised telescopes for a better look at Kauaʻi. Aboard the *Discovery*, a 19-year old midshipman, George Vancouver, stood beside mate Nathaniel Portlock. They were awed by the beauty of the channel and aroused by the anticipation of discovery. Back aboard the *Resolution,* Third Lieutenant Williamson, who was shunned by his fellow officers as a coward, spoke harsh words to his charge of 20 marines. He would lead the landing party the next day.

When dawn came, Cook was close enough to hear swells breaking over Kauaʻi's reef.

Hawaiians ran to view the three-masted ships. They formed a throng of thousands along the sandy beach, chanting, laughing, waving, pointing, shouting at the explorers. When Cook's men returned their salutations, hundreds of canoes slipped into the sea and excited paddlers headed toward ships the likes of which they had never seen. Cook ordered Williamson ashore with his landing party. In the melee that followed, Williamson's quick trigger finger shot to death the first Hawaiian to make physical contact with a white man. After the killing, Williamson and his party went ashore, located fresh water and returned quickly to the *Resolution* as the sun was setting.

---

* Stannard, *Before the Horror* (p. 30) estimates the Hawaiʻi contact population to be in the range of 800,000-1,000,000.

Hawaiian historian Samuel M. Kamakau related "That night guns were fired and rockets flew into the sky. They thought this thing is a god and called it *Lonomakua*. The natives thought this was war."[19]

Missionary historian Sheldon Dibble, writing from translated Hawaiian chants, explained, "An impression of wonder and of dread having been made, Captain Cook and his men found little difficulty in having such intercourse with the people as they chose.* In regard to that intercourse, it was marked, as the world would say, with kindness and humanity. But, it cannot be concealed that here and now and at this time, in the form of loathsome disease, was dug the grave of the Hawaiian Nation; and from so deep an odium it is to be regretted, that faithful history cannot exempt the fair name of Captain Cook himself . .."[20]

Kamakau, retelling the story 56 years later, added, "After this, there was promiscuous living among the men of the ship and the people of the land, with the result that the vile diseases of the white people were quickly scattered over all the islands from Waimea, Kaua'i, to Hilo, Hawai'i, flying here and there like a pestilence, destroying the people, spreading sin and death all over the island."[21]

On the morning of the 21st, when Cook first went ashore, the chiefs prostrated themselves, their eyes lowered. He was afforded divine honors with the full ritual of chanting and anointing. Lieutenant James King noted that "... they certainly regarded us as a Superior race of people to themselves ... we must nevertheless own, that we durst never trust them with such entire confidence as we have done these people ... It is very clear ... that they regard us as a Set of beings, infinitely their superiors; should this respect wear away from familiarity, or by length of intercourse, their behaviour may change."[22]

A gusty *kona* storm blew the *Resolution* out of its anchorage before she was adequately stocked with fresh provisions. Cook attempted a landing on the west side of the nearby Island of Ni'ihau. Fresh water was found and transported through a boiling surf to the ships. The trades kept a steady pressure on the ships and as they were clear of the reef, Cook gave the order to weigh anchor. His Majesty's replenished ships bade *aloha* to Hawai'i.

Early in March the coastline of the great continent of North America came into view. It was a majestic sight, a vast and magnificent land back-dropped by distant snow-capped mountains.

---

*"The natives [in Eastern Kaua'i] though poor are kind even to extremes; they usually set before us the best of their foods, and as a mark of respect the husband offers his wife, the father his daughter, and the brother his sister. We have told them there is a God in heaven who has forbidden such inequity; they say it is good, but you are strange white men." Samuel Whitney, *Journal,* 27 May 1820.

Hampered by dangerous on-shore winds, Cook wisely kept out to sea, bearing north, all the while charting a running survey of what is now Oregon, Washington and British Columbia. By April the ships had sailed into Nootka Sound, on the windward side of the island named for Vancouver. Leaving this sound late in April for Alaskan waters, Cook again steered well out to sea, sighting and recording steep-sided gulfs, fiords and sea-doused valleys. The ships dogged the coast in fog, squalls, haze and strong winds until a sheltered cove was discovered where they put in for repairs. Curious, placid-appearing Eskimos ventured alongside in their kayaks. Then, without warning, six of the natives brandished long, curved, bone-knives and short tusk-like daggers and attacked. They were quickly repulsed by cutlass-wielding crewmen who, in a reversal of procedure, were forbidden by Cook to use firearms.

Repairs completed, the ships left their haven, running in seas where visibility was always poor and danger lurked in racing tides and half-hidden rocks awash in uncharted waters. Cook sailed on, mapping the Aleutian Sea and then crossed into the Bering Sea, up the Bering Strait to 71 degrees north, near the northernmost point of America, where ice packs nudged the vessels across to the Siberian side. In early October, the two ships battered again and, manned by bone-tired crewmen now two years at sea, headed south to Dutch Harbor. Reasonably sure that no northwest passage existed, Cook studied his choices and, with the vivid remembrance of sunshine, warmth and refreshment, he ordered the bow of the *Resolution* pointed south and set sail for Hawai'i.

The Island of Maui was sighted on November 26, 1778. Prominent among the tens of thousands of Polynesians who paddled out to welcome the visitors was a wrinkled, red-eyed, smiling old man, the High Chief of the Island of Hawai'i, Kalani'ōpu'u.

As Cook sailed about the rough, roiling waters seeking a safe anchorage, hundreds of beautifully hand-wrought canoes stroked themselves into formation. Cook noted the mood of his officers and men, "Few lamented our having failed in our endeavor to find a northwest passage ... To this disappointment we owed our having it in our power to revisit the Sandwich Islands, and to enrich our voyage with a discovery which, though the last, seemed, in every respect, to be the most important that had hitherto been made by Europeans throughout the extent of the Pacific Ocean."[23]

Cook brought his crew to the edge of an ugly mutiny by sailing tantalizingly close to the shores of Hawai'i's islands for eight long weeks before landing. Master's Mate Bligh, who was to become the Royal Navy's foremost expert on mutinies, helped Cook to avoid that particular uprising by finding a suitable anchorage on the leeward coast of the island of Hawai'i before the crew could implement their plan for taking over the ship. On January 17, 1779, Cook ordered the *Resolution* into Kealakekua Bay.

The ship's log noted that, against the background of the snow-capped summit of Mauna Loa, the setting was spectacular.

Again, the welcome was tumultuous; thousands of canoes splashed about as Cook and Clerke ordered their anchors dropped and a mass of cheering islanders surged forward on the beach. Many dived into the clear, blue waters and swam toward the ship.

When the welcoming celebration subsided, Cook set about restocking his depleted food stores amid the beat of the caulking hammer as the ships' carpenters made hulls watertight, while other seamen were busy patching sails, reinforcing masts and reweaving cordage.

When Cook boarded a shoreboat three days later, tens of thousands of adoring Polynesians awaited him on the beach. They had mistaken him for their God *Lono,* as he had arrived during the *makahiki* celebrating their harvest in tribute to him. Ship's log relate 10,000 islanders in 2,500 canoes came out to greet him, and hundreds more skimmed gracefully toward him on their surfboards. In Cook's words, "The ships very much crowded with Indians & surrounded by a multitude of canoes. I have nowhere in this Sea seen such a number of people assembled at one place, besides those in the Canoes all the Shore of the bay was covered with people and hundreds were swimming about the Ships like shoals of fish."[24]

In an elaborate ritual Cook was deified as *Lono.** Then, on January 24, the royal entourage paid a visit to Cook aboard the *Resolution* honoring him with gold and red feather helmets and cloaks. One member of that party, a savage-appearing young chief, towered over the English sailors. His curiosity about the ships and their armament brought him back several times. On one occasion he spent an afternoon in the company of Cook aboard the *Resolution.* Several days later he passed the morning aboard the *Discovery* to begin a friendship with Midshipman Vancouver. According to Vancouver, this young Polynesian chief took a special interest in the ship's cannon whose thunderous blasts had echoed off the black lava palisades ashore, bringing even the bravest of Hawaiian warriors respectfully to their knees. He was Kamehameha.

The Hawaiians entertained Cook by staging a series of spectacular athletic contests. Included among the games were surfboard riding, bare knuckle boxing, wrestling, spear hurling, marathon running and draught playing. Women were plentiful, affectionate, cooperative and uninhibited.

On February 4, their ships having been repaired and their

---

*"Captain Cook appears as an ancestral god to Hawaiian priests, more like a divine warrior to the chiefs, and evidentally something else and less to ordinary men and women.... people came to different conclusions ...." Sahlins, *Islands...*, p. x.

holds loaded with almost all the food available at Kealakekua, Cook sailed north, bound for Maui. As they approached Kohala, on the northern tip of the Island of Hawai'i, a fierce storm blew in, snapping the foremast of the *Resolution.* Since it would require a major repair, Cook was forced to act quickly. His choices were to limp on to Maui and hope for a safe port, or risk a dangerous channel crossing and put into Kaua'i, or come about for a return to the safe, sheltered harbor he had just left. Cook chose Kealakekua. When they sailed back into the bay, there was no joyous throng to welcome them. The following morning the hulking young chief Kamehameha came aboard the *Discovery* to renew his acquaintance and to trade an elegant crimson and gold feather cloak for nine crudely made iron daggers. When a party of ship's carpenters went ashore to begin repairs on the foremast and insisted upon enlisting a work force from among the Hawaiians, they were met by a hail of rocks. According to King, Cook ordered, "... that on the first appearance of throwing stones or behaving insolently, to fire ball at the offenders; this made me give orders to the Corporal, to have the Centries' pieces loaded with Ball instead of Shot."[25] Muskets loaded with shot would in all likelihood wound and slow a warrior—while a direct hit from a musket ball at close range almost always meant death.

It was late in the afternoon of February 13, when a Hawaiian came aboard the *Discovery* and seized a pair of blacksmith's tongs, along with a steel chisel. Coveted tools in hand, he dived into the bay, where he was quickly picked up by a waiting canoe. Hearing the commotion, Captain Clerke sprinted up on deck and, following Cook's orders, shouted for his marines to fire at the fast-disappearing canoe. Midshipman Vancouver, the *Discovery's* Mate, and two other sailors followed that canoe to the beach in a small cutter. As Vancouver's cutter neared the shore, Hawaiians in yet another canoe handed over the tongs and chisel to his crew. Meanwhile, a shore boat from the *Resolution,* having seen Vancouver in pursuit, hastened to his assistance. Cook and King, already ashore to oversee the carpenters' work, heard the initial gunfire from the marines aboard the *Discovery* and ran along the shoreline to intercept the culprit. They were in pursuit of the wrong man. Cook seized this fellow, brought him back to the *Resolution,* had him hoisted to the main shrouds and, when he was securely tied spread-eagle fashion, ordered that he be administered forty lashes. The innocent victim's shrieks carried across the bay as the whip was laid on again and again.

Vancouver resumed his pursuit of the canoe that was used in the theft. When he caught up to that canoe near the shore, a bumping and shoving match ensued, during which one of Vancouver's marines broke an oar over the head of the chief called Palea. This act enraged the crowd of Hawaiians who had gathered on the shore. They attacked the English party, pulling them from the cutter and beating them to the ground. Palea, the victim of the oar bashing, saved Vancouver's life by calling off the mob.

King described Cook as furious when Vancouver and his men returned to the *Resolution*, adding, "In going on board, the Capt' expressed his sorrow, that the behavior of the Indians would at last oblige him to use force; for they must not he said imagine they have gained an advantage over us."[26]

Later that night, Hawaiians cut the tether of the *Discovery's* largest cutter and towed it away. Cook awoke with the dawn on February 14, 1779 to find Captain Clerke already on deck, waiting to report the loss of his ship's cutter. Cook acted immediately. He ordered two heavily armed shoreboats to be stationed at convergent points on the mouth of the bay to prevent any vessels from leaving. When King arrived, he "... found them all arming themselves & the Capt loading his Barrell piece; on my going to acquaint him with last nights adventure, he interrupted me & said 'we are not arming for last nights affairs, they have stolen the *Discovery's* cutter it is for that we are making preparations."[27]

Large canoes were moving off shore all along the bay when Cook ordered cannon fire from his deck guns to drive them back. The blissful Sandwich Island visit was turning into a horrific nightmare. Cook climbed aboard a pinnace, intending to take Kalaniʻōpuʻu hostage until the missing cutter was returned intact. Cook's shore party, bristling with arms, included three boats, a small cutter commanded by Master's Mate Lanyon, a launch with Lieutenant Williamson in charge, and Cook's own craft, occupied by nine marines and their Irish Lieutenant, Molesworth Phillips. Cook, Phillips and his marines came ashore without incident at a small cove near the chief's village. Williamson, was on the launch, and Roberts, stayed aboard the pinnace, a few yards off shore.

Nine marines followed Cook and Phillips into the village. They came to a halt at the door of Kalaniʻōpuʻu's hut. The old chief, confused, wiping sleep from his eyes and noticeably trembling, emerged. Conversation quickly established that he had no knowledge of the missing cutter. When Cook invited him to come aboard the *Resolution,* the chief gravely nodded his acceptance. As they neared the shore, Kalaniʻōpuʻu's wife insisted that her husband stay where he was amid a gathering crowd of about 3,000 Hawaiians. She explained that he was in danger and that Cook meant to kill him. The chief sat down near the shoreline.

According to the carefully detailed eye-witness account of the *Resolution's* Lieutenant Gilbert, which differs in tone and in fact from the much more highly publicized Royal Society's official account, "This enraged Captain Cook very much, as he was not accustomed to have his intentions frustrated by any person, and had but little command over himself in his anger; at this instant a canoe came over from the other side of the bay, and brought the natives intelligence that a chief was killed there by one of our boats firing on shore; upon this they began to arm themselves with spears and pieces of the branches of trees that they broke up in a hurry instead of clubs; and some of the chiefs had the same iron daggers that we had given them; the Captain had with him a double barrelled piece, one loaded with small shot, the other with ball, and a dagger by his side. They now began to press together and grew rather tumultuous, and some in particular insulting him, he beat them with the butt end of his musket, which caused them to be still more so; Mr. Phillips, the lieutenant of marines, perceiving this, repeatedly told Captain Cook of the danger he apprehended they were in, and urged him to retire, which, as if Fate had determined he should fall, he took not the least notice of; but fired at one of them with small shot and wounded him; and a little afterward at a chief with ball; but missing him killed the man that stood next to him outright, and although this enraged them to the highest degree, yet they then did not dare attack them.

"At last, finding it was impossible to accomplish his design, he ordered the marines to retreat, and was himself following them, and possibly would have got safe off, had not the people in the boats very unfortunately on hearing the second report of his musket, begun to fire upon the natives, which threw them into a state of fury; the marines likewise on shore without orders followed their example; and Captain Cook, who could not swim, had no sooner got to the water side and waved to the boats to give over firing, when one of the chiefs, more daring than the rest, stepped behind and stabbed him betwixt the shoulders with an iron dagger; another at that instant gave him a blow with a club on the head by which he fell into the water; they immediately leaped in after and kept him under for a few minutes, then hauled him out upon the rocks and beat his head against them several times; so that there is no doubt that he quickly expired. The marines likewise at the same time, after they had discharged their pieces were closely attacked, and, not being able to load again, the corporal and three private men that could not swim were seized and killed upon the spot. The lieutenant, sergeant, and the other four leaped in the water, which was four or five feet deep close to the rocks, and escaped to the pinnace, which was lying within thirty yards of the shore; but by reason of the continual showers of stones that were thrown at them and the confusion of those people getting in, they could not afford the least assistance to Captain Cook, and very narrowly escaped from being taken. The launch that lay close without her, and the cutter, that was inshore at a little distance, both kept up a brisk fire for the space of ten or fifteen minutes till they were obliged to retire; having killed and wounded several of the natives, and caused the greater part of them to retreat; and we were informed by the gentlemen in the cutter, who were the last that left the shore, that very few of them remained by the dead bodies when the launch and pinnace came away. During the firing on the shore we saw a great number of natives running away up an adjacent hill, at whom we fired five or six shot from our great guns."[28]

According to Surgeon William W. Ellis, "... the sergeant of the marines was wounded in the neck, and received a severe blow upon the head from a stone; one of the private men had the point of a spear, which broke off, fixed under his left eye; Mr. Phillips was wounded in the shoulder, and a corporal and three privates were killed ... the Indians behaved with great resolution and intrepidity, and notwithstanding a severe fire was kept up for some time afterwards, they maintained their ground, and as soon as one fell, another immediately supplied his place."[29] The young warrior Kamehameha was close enough to Cook, at the time of the killing, to be injured in the scuffle.

Ellis eulogized Cook, "In every situation he stood unrivaled and alone; on him all eyes were turned; he was our leading-star, which at its setting left us involved in darkness and despair."[30]

That darkness and despair led to a dreadful carnage.

Captain Clerke was in command now.

Heinrich Zimmerman, who sailed with Cook as an ordinary seaman, was a German national. As such, he had no allegiance to George III and no obligation to submit his personal journal to the Royal Society or commission of the Admiralty for *doctoring*. He left this account of his experiences: "Early the next morning, 15th February, Captain Clerke sent Lieutenant King and Midshipman Wennkover ashore with five strongly-armed boats and a white flag. Lieutenant King was commissioned to endeavor to make friends with the Hawaiians, and to obtain from them the body of Captain Cook. The five boats stopped at a short distance from land, and the two officers, who both had a very fair knowledge of the language of the islanders, addressed their request to those who were on the beach. They in their turn held up a piece of white cloth as a sign of peace, but they mocked at us.

"Lieutenant King sent a boat back to report to Captain Clerke, and to ask whether we should fire upon them. The return orders were that we should not fire, but that we were to return to the ships. Early the next morning, 16th February, we made another like attempt, but the islanders mocked us still more, and some of them even danced about before us, clad in some of Captain Cook's clothes. As we had again received order to do the islanders no harm, we once more returned to the ships. Scarcely had we reached them when one of the chiefs followed us boldly in his canoe, cocked Captain Cook's hat over one ear before our very eyes, and then took it off and swung it round his head. Captain Clerke, becoming very angry at this, ordered that the *Resolution* should be taken closer in shore, and some shots were fired from the guns into the town where the king lived. The inhabitants there upon ran in thousands up the mountains, and got out of the way of the guns.

"On the 17th we made our way to the other side of the harbour to get a supply of fresh water from the spring close to the native town situated there. But the inhabitants, in spite of the treatment meted out to their neighbours on the previous day, concealed themselves behind their houses and behind the rocks, and threw spears at us and pelted us with stones, so that we were obliged to return to the ship without carrying out our mission. At our request, and because we were urgently in need of water, Captain Clerke, who was always afraid that our shore party would be cut off by the natives, who considerably outnumbered us, at last, though unwillingly, gave us his consent to our setting fire to the town and shooting down any of the inhabitants who should oppose us. We at once went ashore, set fire to the houses, and shot every person who came in our way. Where a number of the inhabitants had gathered together, the *Discovery*, which had been brought close in, opened fire upon them with her guns. In a short time not a single native was to be seen ... between two and three hundred of the inhabitants had been killed, and among these were thirty chiefs."[31]

While that site was still ablaze, the *Discovery* Surgeon's Mate David Servell, wrote that Williamson led a shore party to the center of a group of bodies, where "... our people cut off the heads and brought them on board. At this time an elderly man was taken prisoner, bound and sent on board in the same boat with the heads. I never saw horror so strongly pictured as in the face of this man."[32] Chief Kaireekeea, who had become friendly with the officers of the *Discovery,* came aboard to "... expostulate with us on our want of friendship and on our ingratitude. On coming aboard he had seen the heads of his countrymen, he was exceedingly shocked and desired with great earnestness that they might be thrown overboard." King, considered to be the most intellectual officer on the voyage, completed Cook's journal and wrote "Had I been present myself, I might possibly have been the means of saving their little society from destruction ...."[34]

Williamson, who had again displayed his cowardice by ordering his marines to fire prematurely and then by ordering his launch away from the shore when Cook needed him most desperately, was promoted to second lieutenant. Later he would be accused of cowardice and failure to obey orders for not responding to Cook's command. Subsequently, he was court martialed for a similar offense at the Battle of Camperdown.

Cook left his generous hosts shreds of his lifeless body, a few pieces of hardware, gonorrhea and syphilis.

Chapter Three

KAMEHAMEHA I
1779 - 1819

Before we became acquainted with these people we considered them as a ferocious and turbulent set of savages. This character they are by no means entitled to, as they are mild and tractable; uncivilized, unpolished, and in a true state of nature, they possess great courage and will not tamely bear an insult or an injury. Their few laws are strictly adhered to, and was their code more numerous, I conclude they would abide by them with equal promptitude. To each other they are free, easy and cheerful, and show more good nature than I have seen in better regulated societies.

During the whole of my stay I was never witness to a quarrel; they delight in jokes, which were never known to produce an angry blow or uplifted arm.

— Thomas Manby
1789

KAMEHAMEHA I

In 1780, following Captain Cook's aborted attempt to take Kalani'ōpu'u hostage, the old high chief, feeling death's breath near, summoned all of his chiefs to a council meeting where he proclaimed his son Kiwala'ō as heir to his kingdom, and his nephew, Kamehameha, as protector of *Kūkā'ilimoku*, a Hawaiian God of War. Kalani'ōpu'u traveled to the south of the Big Island, where an uprising had been quelled and the dead rebel chief's body was being prepared for sacrifice to the war god. Kamehameha usurped the prerogative of his cousin, Kiwala'ō, by picking up the body and offering it in sacrifice. Kamehameha was expelled from the Royal Court.

Two years later, when Kalani'ōpu'u died, Kiwala'ō provoked a quarrel with Kamehameha over the division of the kingdom. The issue was settled on the battlefield, where Kiwala'ō was killed. Kamehameha became high chief of the northwestern part of the Island of Hawai'i.

When High Chief of Maui, Kahekili, died in 1794, Kamehameha had already developed a plan to turn the weapons of the foreigners upon his fellow Hawaiians. Within the year Maui felt the impact of Kamehameha's new army. With the assistance of Isaac Davis and John Young, Englishmen who were stranded on the Island of Hawai'i in 1790, and fourteen other white men, Kamehameha used all available "civilized" war techniques and equipment, including the captured *Fair American* and a ship that Vancouver had built as a gift, plus cannons and muskets to overrun his native island. He then invaded and conquered Maui and, in April of 1795, landed an army of 16,000 warriors in 1,400 canoes at Waikiki and watched the last defenders of O'ahu leap off the lip of the 600-foot Nu'uanu precipice. The battle of Nu'uanu Pali is considered by many to be the greatest battle in Hawaiian history and the most important event in Kamehameha's struggle to unite the entire Hawaiian group under his rule.

Young and Davis were more than mere armchair advisors. They fought in key battles, manning cannons, directing small-arms fire and physically leading charges of Polynesian slingers and spearsmen. They were richly rewarded with chiefdoms of their own and *ali'i* brides. Young's first wife died after bearing him three children, and he subsequently married Kamehameha's niece. Later, he became the first European to hold high office in Hawai'i as Governor of the Island of Hawai'i.

The circumstances of Young and Davis landing on Hawaiian soil involved a fur trading sea captain named Simon Metcalfe. On July 14, 1789, John Young stood beside Metcalfe on the bridge of the schooner *Eleanora,* helping to supervise the loading of beaver and raccoon pelts off the coast of what is now Oregon. When the hold was packed with animal skins, Metcalfe ordered his helmsman to steer a course to Kealakekua Bay, Hawai'i. There he was to rendezvous with his 18-year-old-son, Thomas, Captain of the *Fair American,* and then continue out to China. Nearing the end of the first leg of his journey, the elder Metcalfe dropped anchor at Honua'ula, Maui, where he became angered when Hawaiians stole one of his shore boats and kidnapped a crewman. Upon learning his crewman had been killed, Metcalfe sailed on to Olowalu, Maui, and enticed Hawaiians who had nothing to do with the killing, to come alongside to trade. When they had completed their transactions and asked to be paid, Metcalfe, according to Young's account, shouted, "I'll give you more pay that you expected!" Then he ordered, "Barrage fire!" Innocent Hawaiians were cut down in clumps. Rows of dead and dying littered the red sea. Young reported that more than one hundred islanders died immediately and at least that many "screamed in pain from horrible wounds."

Metcalfe sailed on to Kealakekua Bay to await the arrival of his son. As the first few weeks there passed pleasantly, he found Kamehameha eager to barter fresh vegetables, pigs, water and women, all in a seemingly endless supply. Young went off to hunt wild boar on the slopes of Mauna Loa. A night passed and Metcalfe, who had grown impatient waiting for his son, sailed close to the shore and fired several rounds from his cannon, signaling Young to return. Since Metcalfe had placed a *kapu* on native crafts approaching the *Eleanora*, he in effect forced the abandonment of Young, who had no boat on shore.

On that same day, Metcalfe's son and his crew of five were attacked by a swarm of war canoes thirty miles north of Kealakekua Bay. The enraged chief Tamaahmotoo (Kame'eiamoku), leading the attack, was out to avenge an earlier insult inflicted by the elder Metcalfe. He ordered young Metcalfe and all his crew killed on the spot, save the first mate, Isaac Davis, who made an impassioned plea for his life. Davis and Young soon became the nucleus for Kamehameha's general staff, and young Metcalfe's tiny schooner, *Fair American*, became the flagship of the warrior king's growing fleet.

VANCOUVER RETURNS

By 1791, George Vancouver had risen to the rank of captain and become heir to Cook's place in the Royal Navy. When he returned to Hawai'i on three separate occasions between 1792-94, he boldly cultivated and rewon the friendship of Kamehameha and forgave chief Tamaahmotoo, "reputed to be the man who had stabbed Captain Cook." It was while reacquainting himself with Kamehameha that he met Young and Davis. In a letter to the Admiralty in 1794, he wrote, "And I likewise beg leave to recommend messers John Young & Isaac Davis, by whose service the persons under my command have been indebted for their good offices. I am convinced that through the uniformity of their conduct & unremitting good advice to Kamehameha ... that they have been ... instrumental in causing the ... civil ... behavior lately experienced by all visitors from the inhabitants of this island."[1]

Vancouver's view of Kamehameha after an absence of 13 years was altered, "I was agreeably surprised in finding that his riper years had softened that stern ferocity which his younger days had exhibited."[2] He added that Kamehameha appeared to be open, cheerful and sensible.

Earlier that same year, Vancouver, had upon the request of John Young, off-loaded Hawai'i's first cattle at Kawaihae Bay on the Big Island. A score of cattle, along with a few sheep, had made the crossing from Monterey in California and were presented to Kamehameha as a gift with the proviso that they be left unharmed to reproduce themselves for a period of ten years. Kamehameha placed the cattle under a *kapu* and released them to graze on the grassy upland range of Waimea.

After a passage to O'ahu, Archibald Menzies, Naturalist aboard the *H.M.S. Discovery* with Vancouver, described the sophistication of farming in Waikiki in 1792, "The verge of the shore was planted with a large grove of coconut palms, affording a delightful shade to the scattered habitations of the natives ... We pursued a path back to the plantation, which was nearly level and very extensive, and laid out with great neatness into little fields planted with taro, yams, sweet potatoes, and the cloth plant. These ... were divided by little banks on which grew the sugar cane and a species of Draecena [ti] without the aid of much cultivation, and the whole was watered in a most ingenious manner by dividing the general stream into little aqueducts leading in various directions so to supply the most distant fields at pleasure, and the soil seems to repay the labor and industry of these people by the luxuriancy of its production."[3]

•

A gigantic man of enormous appetites, disarming grace, surprising composure, articulate wisdom, sulking stubbornness and eruptive jealousies, Kamehameha found time for no less than 22 wives, nine of whom bore him 14 heirs.[4] Although he conquered Hawai'i with brute force and was "... as able to dodge a spear as any other man is to throw one," Kamehameha knelt as would a humble commoner in the presence of his sacred wife, Keopuolani. She towered above him on the Polynesian social ladder.

However, only one wife matched Kamehameha's fearlessness "... a handsome woman, straight and well-formed was Ka'ahumanu, without blemish, and comely .... Of Kamehameha's two possessions, his wife and his kingdom, she was the most beautiful."[5]

She, Kamehameha's 17th wife—daughter of Chief Ke'eaumoku who assassinated Keoua, Kamehameha's most powerful rival—would play a pivotal role in Hawai'i's history.[6] The gallant Vancouver was much taken with her in 1793, when he described her as "... about sixteen, and undoubtedly did credit to the choice and taste of Kamehameha, being one of the finest women we had yet seen on any of the islands. It was pleasing to observe the kindness and fond attention with which on all occasions they seemed to regard each other."[7]

After a separation from Kamehameha, because of an infidelity with his nephew, with Vancouver playing the role of peacemaker, Ka'ahumanu returned to the king when he solemnly promised "... that on her return to his habitations he would not beat her." Years later, she confided to missionary Bingham that Kamehameha often beat her brutally.

Most historians agree that Kamehameha's 24-year reign was successful. They praise him for having persuaded his people to follow his deeds as well as his decrees. In the midst of a famine, which was partially caused by his sandalwood trading, he took to the royal fields to plant, cultivate and harvest his own *taro* and refused to eat produce from another source. He set out to repair some of the damage his wars of conquest had caused and reestablished some of the almost forgotten tranquility among the ravaged islanders. With his strong Polynesian respect for the land, he anticipated twentieth century environmentalists by setting standards for the conservation of natural resources. He helped to lay the keel for Hawai'i's early shipbuilding industry. "The ... success of the first Kamehameha and his final domination over the group was due not only to unusual strength of character, but also to his readiness in adapting foreign ways of warfare and in following the advice of white men salvaged from the crews of looted foreign vessels by which qualities he proved himself a capable dictator."[8]

Others chronicled Kamehameha as being highly vulnerable to gaudy trinkets dangled before him like forbidden fruit. They say he mortgaged his kingdom to white traders and hastened the downfall of his people. Unaware of the law of diminishing returns, he was no match for the business acumen of encroaching whites.

On the eve of his final departure from Hawai'i, Vancouver wisely counseled Kamehameha to "... not permit foreigners to settle in Hawai'i. Two only should stay, Olohana [Young] and Aikake [Davis]. Most of the foreigners are men of very bad character, evil-hearted, desiring to secure lands, but not the right people to dwell thereon. They will lead you astray."[9]

SANDALWOOD

The origin of the Hawaiian sandalwood trade can be traced to the captain of the American clipper *Lady Washington*, John Kendrick, who was accidentally killed by cannon shot from a British warship saluting his arrival in Honolulu Harbor on December 12, 1794. However, the tragic effects of sandalwood trading were not felt in Hawai'i until 1812, when three Bostonians, Jonathan and Nathan Winship and William Davis, exercised their Yankee shrewdness by persuading Kamehameha to sign a 10-year monopoly agreement on the export of that wood. The agreement provided that the king would have the sandalwood gathered and waiting for their ships. They, in turn,would sail it to Chinese ports, sell it and, upon return, give Kamehameha one quarter of the net profits.

Other traders, including John Jacob Astor of New York, found the sandalwood trade appealing and, because of the War of 1812 and the British blockade of American ships, were able to break the Winship monopoly and enter the market. Wood from the sandalwood tree soon became the most valued item in the Hawaiian economy and it remained so until 1829.

Sandalwood, called *'iliahi,* is a parasite that attaches itself to the root of another tree. As it grows, it becomes an extremely hard, highly fragrant wood. It is still in great demand today in Asia, where it is used as incense, fuel for funeral rites, temple carvings, handmade boxes, medicine and as a basic ingredient in perfume. The list of items traded to the Hawaiian chiefs for sandalwood included beads, boats, silks, rifles, rum, wool suits, pistols, precision mathematical instruments, gilded candelabras, folio volumes of Hogarth, rosewood writing tables inlaid with mother of pearl, cutlasses, crystal goblets, billiard tables, stove pipe hats, mirrors, cannons, flowered satins, roofing slate, gin, lavishly mounted sabres, sterling services, globes, ammunition, crystal lamps and nails. Goods such as laced hats, beaver coats and sumptuous gowns rotted in dank caves and humid grass shacks as the forests were denuded.

Kamehameha attempted to maintain absolute control over sandalwood trading in Hawai'i. According to his rule, the chiefs were allowed to sell only with royal approval and the white man could not buy without it. "... he ordered men to go out in the mountains ... to cut sandalwood, and he paid them in cloth and bark for making native cloth, as well as with food and fish. Men were also detailed to carry the wood to the landings ... The chiefs also were ordered to send out their men to cut sandalwood."[10]

Some Yankee traders found a way to break the royal chain of command and deal direct. "... commerce has attracted to this place some Americans who, in the hope of speedily making their fortunes, established themselves here several years ago. I cannot say that they carry on any regular trade here, but rather contraband; they can obtain whatever they want at so cheap a rate. In the morning they take half a dozen bottles of wine to the Governor, and the good soul is soon stretched at their feet; they make presents of a few hatchets and muskets to the principal chiefs; all the rest of the population are then quite at the disposal of these gentlemen. Some strong and active men are sent to the mountains; the forests are examined, and some sandalwood trees are cut down; these are conveyed to the waters edge at night by about twenty women, who are paid for either carrying or dragging them along with a few ells of European cloth or linen; thence to be embarked aboard a vessel that is always stationed in the harbour. On the arrival of spring, their correspondents on the Northwest coast of America come here with a cargo of furs, to obtain provisions, and increase their rich ventures with acquisitions of their partners; and, sure of an immense profit, they push on to Macao, or Canton, to sell their cargos to lazy Chinese for dollars, sugars, or silks which they know how to transmit speedily to Europe."[11]

A letter from Bryant & Sturgis, postmarked Boston, August 31, 1818, instructed the master of their brig *Ann* to "... sell the king any articles of your cargo on advantageous terms, to receive your pay in Sandalwood when you return from the coast. Take as many stout Islanders as will increase your crew to 21 or 22 ... and when you return from the coast pay them off in such articles of trade you have left ... when you return from the Coast to the Islands, if you have any trade left endeavour to exchange it for Sandalwood, of which we hope you may obtain a full cargo, and to do this may be advisable to remain sometime at the Islands."[12]

When dawn came, thousands of commoners trudged up the slopes of valleys to the long-shadowed forests, where they would toil until the sun set. They hacked at sandalwood trees until their hands and arms throbbed with pain and they were overcome with exhaustion. Then they hacked on through their pain and exhaustion until they had filled a hole gouged in the forest floor as long, as wide, and as deep as the hold of a ship. They dragged the trees up and down and across the hilly terrain to the beach. There the prized logs were dried, trimmed and floated with guide canoes to foreign ships laying off shore. "It was through sandalwood that slavery replaced freedom to the people. Natives were treated like cattle. Up and down the treacherous mountain trails they toiled, logs and sandalwood strapped to their sweating shoulders. Men and women actually became deformed due to the tremendous weight of the logs on their backs. The forced laborers in the sandalwood forests had no time to farm—food grew scarce and famine came."[13]

Now in his 17th year as monarch, Kamehameha, who had ruled from his court on O'ahu during the previous nine years, made a grand tour of his kingdom and, upon visiting his beloved Kona, on the Island of Hawai'i, he came to the realization that sandalwood trading was inflicting a terrible hardship on his subjects on all islands. Many were broken physically and others who had begun life as the heirs of plenty were helpless and starving to death. As a small recompense for the suffering caused by the royal greed, Kamehameha put his court followers to work in *taro* and sweet potato patches. In fact, he himself returned to the soil, toiling in the fields of Kona.

Upon his death seven years later, sandalwood trading expanded and continued unchecked. Soon it brought Hawai'i to the brink of disaster. The greed of Americans who swarmed to Hawai'i, eager to profit from sandalwood trading, ultimately caused their own undoing when they inundated the Chinese market until supply far exceeded demand. The bottom fell out of the market.

American traders demanded immediate payment on all promissory notes held against island chiefs. When the chiefs pleaded for more time to pay, John Jacob Astor led the traders' lobby in complaining to the United States Senate that American missionaries were interfering with American business by channeling the energy of the Hawaiian people in religious services, school attendance and the building of churches. It was during the administration of President John Quincy Adams, with Secretary of State Henry Clay as spokesman, that the United States government, in an outrageous act of gunboat diplomacy, responded to the pleas of the traders by dispatching two warships to the islands to "render all possible aid to American Commerce."

Although the sandalwood forests were denuded by 1829, most debts owed by the Hawaiian chiefs to American traders were paid that year, or rewritten for payment by 1843.

A Russian naval captain who had established a relationship with Kamehameha in 1818 described the aging monarch as "... still strong, active, temperate and sober. He does not use liquor or eat to excess. We can see in him a combination of childishness and ripe judgement. Some of his acts would do credit to a more enlightened ruler. His honesty and love of justice have been shown in numerous cases. The petty faults which we may find in the old king will not obscure his great merits. He will always be considered as an enlightener and reformer of his people. One fact which shows his good sense is this. None of the foreigners visiting his country enjoy any exclusive privileges, but all can trade with his subjects with equal freedom. Europeans are not allowed to own land. They receive it on conditions that after death it shall be returned to the king, and during their lifetime it is not transferable from one to another."[14]

Six months later, Kamehameha's chiefs assembled at his bedside in Kona. Their spokesman stepped forward. "Here are we all: your younger brethren, your successor and your foreigner; give us your charge ...." The king haltingly replied, "Go on in my good way." Too feeble to say more, he embraced John Young, drew him closer, and bade him farewell by touching noses in the Polynesian manner. Kamehameha, eaten by sorrow for the misery that sandalwood trading had caused his people, died on May 8, 1819.

According to one account, Kamehameha was still grieving over the loss of his heir apparent and favorite son, Alexander

Stewart. In 1801, the tale begins, Kamehameha gave his blessing for his beloved teenage son Alexander to leave Hawai'i aboard the American trading ship *Perseverance* and to sail to Canton, China, under the command of Captain Amasa Delano. The king hoped that Alexander would gain knowledge through his travels which would enhance his leadership when he assumed the throne. When the *Perseverance* arrived in the port of Wampoa, China, Alexander left that vessel to visit an English ship. It is unclear what Alexander's intentions were in boarding that ship. He was never heard from again. When Captain Delano returned to Honolulu six years later, he explained the situation to Kamehameha and, although the king became distraught with grief, he did not hold Delano responsible for the loss of Alexander Stewart.[15]

•

According to the late Dr. Romanzo Adams, Hawai'i's renowned demographer, there was a population decline of more than 166,000 Hawaiians between 1778 and 1823.[16] If we attribute a loss of 70,000, as Adams did, to the *mai'eku'u,* the terrible [foreign pestilence] cholera epidemic in 1804, and another 30,000 to normal attrition and to European-style tribal wars, we can conservatively estimate that more than 65,000 Hawaiians lost their lives as a result of sandalwood trading and the naivete of the *ali'i.*[17] Adding those 70,000 cholera deaths to the sandalwood deaths, we arrive at the figure of 135,000 Hawaiian deaths—all during the first 45 years of exposure to the white man.[18]

Ralph S. Kuykendall, dean of Hawaiian historians, noted, "Besides their other gifts to the Hawaiians, the foreigners initiated them into the use of alcoholic liquors and tobacco, taught them the art of distillation, engrafted upon the primitive social order some of their own vicious habits and were the means which started the Hawaiian people on a toboggan slide down the slopes of depopulation."[19]

KA'AHUMANU

She is prodigiously fat, but her face is interesting ... her legs, the palm of her left hand, and her tongue, are very elegantly tattooed.[20]

— Jacques Arago
1823

To Hawaiians, feminine beauty has never included the sunken-cheeked, meagerbosomed, swallow-waisted mannequin product of Western fashion. The early Hawaiian beauty was a woman of flamboyant proportions and great physical prowess.

Women of rank usually had more than one official husband and as many lovers as time and desire would permit. They fished, ran foot races, and, when necessary, took spear in hand to fight in wars alongside their warrior lovers. While the common men did most of the cooking and the gathering of foodstuffs, fishing and farming, the common women were responsible for the rearing of children, fashioning what clothes were needed, weaving mats and pounding the *taro* root into *poi*.

After the arrival of Cook, the Hawaiian woman vigorously gave herself to the white man for a trinket and the pleasure it gave her. Soon Hawaiian love was sold on the weather decks of the foreign ships lying at anchor. And, because of the white man's diseases transmitted to Hawaiian women, the act of interracial sex became a death sport for Hawaiians.

The patriarch of the Hawaiian family would pack his canoe with giggling daughters, nieces, sisters, lovers and wives and paddle off to a ship. Sexual activity between native women and *haole* sailors had become a regulated government business, with a fee being paid in advance to an agent of the Hawaiian government before the *wahine* was allowed to board a ship. One ship's officer wrote, "At sunrise we fired two muskets and sent the women out of the ship, and at sundown did the same as a signal for them to come aboard."

In the eyes of the Hawaiian gods, the woman was not on a par with the man. A rigid set of *kapu* kept her in an inferior role. When menstruating, the woman was barred from sleeping in the same house as her husband or lover. If she disobeyed, the punishment was death. Women were never allowed to eat with men and were not allowed to partake of the Polynesian delicacies of turtle flesh, coconuts, bananas or roasted pig. A missionary teacher told of a five-year-old girl whose eyeball was popped from its socket for the offense of eating a banana.

Six months after having participated in an orgy celebrating the death of her departed spouse, Ka'ahumanu bedecked herself in his royal battle cloak, tilted his feathered helmet on her imposing head and brandished her departed husband's favorite spear toward the sea. She stood waist-deep in the Kailua-Kona surfline awaiting the appearance of Kamehameha's son and heir, the 22-year-old Liholiho. Ka'ahumanu had successfully enlisted the support of Liholiho's Queen Mother, Keopuolani, and was prepared for a confrontation with the young king. "It was clear to him what was going on at Kailua. He accordingly sent his messengers to fetch rum ... and for two days he and his chiefs sailed about the Kona Waters in his two masted canoe, sending every little while for rum ... When the wind died down Ka'ahumanu sent a double canoe and paddlers and towed the boat to Kailua."[21] She welcomed him on the beach, exclaiming, "Hear me, O Divine one, for I make known to you the will of your father. Behold these chiefs and the men of your father, and these your guns, and this your land, but you and I shall share the realm together."[22]

Liholiho agreed to her terms and Ka'ahumanu became *Kuhina Nui,* with powers greater than those of a prime minister. She appointed him as ceremonial ruler and herself as chief administrator for the kingdom. Her first official act was to destroy those parts of the *kapu* system that were humiliating to her and to the Queen Mother. Together they arranged a royal *lu'au* and invited the *ali'i,* with separate tables for the men and women. "After the guests were seated, and had begun to eat, the king took two or three turns around each table, as if to see what passed at each; and then suddenly, and without any previous warning to any but those in the secret, he seated himself in a vacant chair at the women's table "and began to eat voraciously, but was evidently much perturbed. The guests, astounded at this act, clapped their hands, and cried out, *'ai noa*—the eating *tabu* is broken.'" [23]

On November 5, 1819, Liholiho, obeying the wishes of Ka'ahumanu, commanded the destruction of all religious images and temples in the kingdom. This act ended official state rituals and their associated *kapu.* Many basic beliefs and practices remained.

Ka'ahumanu would rule Hawai'i for the next thirteen years as *Kuhina Nui* and then as Queen Regent. At that same time, having become a Christian, she would enact a code of laws for her loyal subjects based on the Ten Commandments.

Ka'ahumanu was 59 years old when she died in 1832. Herman Melville penned an epitaph,. "... Ka'ahumanu the giant old dowager queen—a woman of nearly four hundred pounds weight ... was accustomed, in some of her terrific gusts of temper, to snatch up the ordinary sized man who had offended her, and snap his spine across her knee. Incredible as this may seem, it is a fact ... at Lahainaluna the residence of this monstrous Jezebel—a humpbacked wretch was pointed out to me who, some twenty-five years previously, had had the vertebrae of his backbone very seriously discomposed by this gentle mistress."[24]

Albertine Loomis, great-granddaughter of Pioneer Company missionaries, points out that Ka'ahumanu "was only eight," when "Kamehameha had taken her to his train and shortly thereafter made her a consort."[25]

Chapter Four

HIRAM BINGHAM
1820

The clergy strives for the control of frightened men, women, and children; their ultimate ambition is to perpetuate themselves in positions of power, backed by civil law, for the everlasting glory of their particular denomination.

— Thomas Jefferson

HIRAM BINGHAM

Hiram Bingham was born in a farmhouse surrounded by the bleak countryside of Bennington, Vermont, on October 30, 1789. His father was a noncommissioned soldier who stalked the forest during the French and Indian wars hunting General Braddock's Redcoats. Hiram, one of seven boys in a family of 13 children, seemed content as a farmer on his father's acres until he was 22. Perhaps he felt the first tug of the "cloth" when he taught for a semester at the district school. At the end of 1811, he began to prepare for college under the tutelage of the Reverend Elisha Yale. He received his degree from Middlebury College, New York, in 1816, the year after Wellington withstood the charge of Napoleon at Waterloo.

Upon graduation from the seminary at Andover, Massachusetts, in 1819, Bingham became headmaster at a school founded for the education of American Indians and Pacific Islanders at Cornwall, Connecticut. When he was ordained a minister at Goshen, Connecticut, on September 29, he had already volunteered to lead a Christian mission of six or seven men and their children to Hawai'i. His superiors admonished him to "... aim at nothing short of covering those Islands with fruitful fields and pleasant dwellings and schools, and churches ... raising up the whole people ... a nation to be enlightened and renovated and added to the civilized world ...."[1]

The elders of the American Board of Commissioners for Foreign Missions, with headquarters in Boston, thought it imprudent to send bachelors into a heathen land. Hiram, who was handsome, with his heavy brow and lantern jaw, set out to find a suitable bride. In ten days he had met, wooed, and won wide-eyed, sober-faced Sybil Moseley. They "presented themselves in the broad aisle," of a brick church in Hartford and were married.

It was an apprehensive group that sailed from Boston six days later on October 23, 1819. In addition to Bingham and another ordained minister, Asa Thurston, the company included a doctor, two teachers, an apprentice printer, and a farmer, all with their wives. Most of the younger men were betrothed when they announced their intention to go to Hawai'i, but not all New England girls were ready for the rigors of missionary life. Several broke their engagements and had to be quickly replaced by other partners. Faith in the Holy Spirit would be called upon to sustain the purpose of the weaker members of the company. Since communications were extremely slow, there was no way for those on the east coast of the U.S.A. to know the pagan Polynesian gods had already been rejected by Hawaiian royalty. Consequently, Bingham's flock still harbored the fear of arriving in a hostile land and competing with a religious hierarchy of heathen priests among whom their lives would be in jeopardy. Although all in the company shared the same zeal, somber tenets, and absolute view of right and wrong, they were more strangers than friends when the rocky coast of Massachusetts dissolved in their wake.

The two ministers, Bingham and the full-bearded Asa Thurston, acclaimed at Yale for his feats on the playing field as well as the classroom, were acquainted, having studied together at Andover. The voyage was a test of strength—twenty-three weeks at sea under sail around Cape Horn, two families to a room, most on their honeymoon beds.

Samuel Ruggles, teacher and catechist, and Lucia Holman, destined to be the first American woman to circumnavigate the earth, were brother and sister. However, as members of an orphaned family, they had been separated most of their lives. Her husband, the company's physician, Thomas Holman, had wed her several months before he had agreed to join the mission. The remaining passengers, Samuel Whitney, Elisha Loomis and Chamberlain, were strangers to each other and newly acquainted with their wives. Led by Bingham, at sunup and sundown they knelt together on the swaying deck, praying earnestly to their savior.

As time passed slowly at sea, the admonitions of board member Samuel Worchester echoed in their ears, "Beware of the wounds of feeling, unkind debates, embittered strifes ... maintain brotherly love, constancy, strength, tenderness ... much vigilance, prayer ... much crucifixion of self."[2]

It was nearly April when they saw the peaks of Mauna Kea and Mauna Loa. Three days later their Captain, Andrew Blanchard, went ashore at Kawaihae and hurried back with the tidings that "the gods are no more. Kamehameha is dead; Liholiho is King; the *tabu* is broken." Bingham, the baritone, and Thurston, the tenor, stood on the deck at twilight leading their flock in singing, "Head of the church triumphant, we joyfully adore thee."

"How were our hearts surprised," entoned Bingham ... "some of our members, with gushing tears, turned away from the spectacle as the nude islanders, with wild cries, swam about the ship."

In the morning the sun rose behind the 13,680 foot summit of Mauna Loa. The Big Island of Hawai'i lay variegated green, shadowed beneath its cloud-wrapped peaks. Heavy woods ringed the rolling slopes of the great lava flows and a few fresh streams meandered down through taro and yam fields. The weary voyagers had come 18,000 miles in 164 days. It had taken their Puritan ancestors 100 days less to cross the Atlantic 200 years earlier.

The missionaries sailed down the coast to Kailua, at Kona, to ask permission to settle and build their churches. The men, garbed in their heavy wool suits, and the women, squeezed into corsets covered by layers of petticoats, were forced to remain on the vessel sweltering, while the young king and the old Englishman, John Young, decided their fate.

Bingham gazed toward the shore where "men, women and children, from the highest to ... lowest rank, including the king and his mother were amusing themselves ... swimming on surf boards, in canoes ... lounging... dancing ...."[3]

Young wished that Vancouver had kept his earlier promise to send English priests. Now Liholiho left to Young the decision of whether to allow the Americans to stay. Almost 76 years old, Young had mellowed in an adopted culture that took his word as law. He pondered, finally deciding in favor of their staying. Liholiho delayed his final edict, awaiting the approval of Ka'ahumanu, who had gone fishing. When she returned, she reluctantly agreed to follow Young's persuasion on the condition that the missionaries split up their group between the Big Island and O'ahu, and that they stay for only a year. Captain Blanchard took the Holmans and the Thurstons ashore at Kailua, providing Ka'ahumanu and Liholiho with their own private physician and minister. That evening the *Thaddeus* set sail for O'ahu.

In 1820, Honolulu was a town rife with sin. By night it was a dusty, brawling haven for ship deserters, fortune seekers, fly-by-night traders, sailors and whalers. Commerce hummed. One could buy not only the necessities, but also satisfy the instincts to pleasure. Pots and pans, rum, tents, gambling, brass beds, fresh meat and vegetables, dancing, singing, fiddle playing, porcelain, tea services and, not least, bevies of *da wahine*.

By day Honolulu was a gray, dusty plain dotted green by graceful coconut palms, some of which followed the shoreline to Waikiki's sun-drenched beach. It was a slumbering hamlet watched over by the distant silhouette of Diamond Head and a protective wall of coral reefs that turned rough seas smooth. There were barren flatlands stretching toward the gentle slopes of green foothills before the Ko'olau mountains. The air all around was soft, as tradewinds stirred up faint hints of tropical flower perfumes. Giant ferns swayed beneath wisps of clouds that lost their way in deeply-etched valleys amid the verdant snarl of grass and *kukui* trees. On the shore near Hawai'i's best still-water harbor stood a settlement of tired, slouching grass shacks. They leaned toward the gray wall of the waterfront fort, built in 1816. Fifty cannons poked their muzzles seaward, and Hawai'i's flag waved in the trades.

In order to find lodging for his flock, Bingham sought out the governor of O'ahu. Dark eyes flashing under a towering stovepipe hat, the minister resolutely strode down Fort Street, the tails of his somber claw-hammer coat riding behind. This New Englander had come to root the sin out of Honolulu. He was ready to condemn, pity, uplift and convert the heathen Hawaiian who was mired in adultery, murder, public fornication, whoring, incest, matricide, alcoholism, illiteracy, nudity and infanticide. Governor Boki swayed on his feet as he extended his hand to welcome this man of God. Reeking of rum, he greeted Bingham with a toothless grin and gifts of breadfruit and *taro*. When the subject of housing was broached, Boki ignored Bingham.

While in Boston, Bingham had become acquainted with sandalwood trader Jonathan Winship. Upon learning of Bingham's mission and his destination, Winship had offered him the use of his house in Honolulu should the need arise. Bingham, who was by all accounts the first American missionary in Honolulu, snatched at the offer. "Christianity civilizes in the broadest sense. Commerce, industry, science and literature all accompany her majestic march to universal dominion. Thus, while it denies the sufficiency of commerce alone to transform the savage, it encourages a legitimate commerce and even courts its alliance as one of the most important instrumentalities."[4]

Old Hawaiian customs previously bonded together by ancient Polynesian beliefs, now fractured by the overthrow of traditional religion, were collapsing at all levels. As a result of the void that appeared, self-esteem among the understandably bewildered Hawaiians plunged to a new low. Suddenly foreign missionaries were to sternly demand that a carefree people who lived for the day give up their immediate gratifications for a long-range chance at a mystical and mythical afterlife.

"It must be kept in mind," cautioned historian Kuykendall, "that the missionaries and others who professed an interest in the welfare of the Hawaiian people assumed without question that the pattern of Western culture with which they were familiar ... was superior to the culture of the Hawaiians and that the latter ... would be happier and better off ... if they acquired the foreign culture. But in order to effect that result, the habits of the people would have to be developed so that there would be products suitable for export, to exchange for useful and desirable goods brought from other countries. The missionaries believed that these changes, in cooperation with the Christian religion, would save the native race from extinction. In this very year, 1836, an estimate had been made of the population and the fact revealed that the Hawaiian people were decreasing at an alarming rate. Hence whatever was to be done needed to be done quickly."[5]

The 20-year period following the arrival of the Pioneer Missionary Company was the most crucial for the missionary, not because of disagreements with the Hawaiians, but rather because of opposition from American and other foreign business interests. Royal opposition to the missionaries was eliminated in 1825, when Bingham converted the volatile Ka'ahumanu to Christianity. At the outset, the island-hopping Ka'ahumanu played the role of part-time Christian, adding only a small measure of piety to her old, pleasurable sexual mores. Still the Polynesian, she took both the king of Kaua'i and his princely son as her lovers and then flaunted that relationship by riding to Bingham's church in a human-powered carriage with a prince on her left and a king on her right. "... she seated her immense stateliness in her carriage, which is a light hand-cart, painted turquoise blue, spread with fine mats and several beautiful damask and velvet covered cushions. It was drawn by half a dozen stout men, who grasped the ropes in pairs, and marched off as if proud of the royal burden. The old lady rides backward with her feet hanging down behind the cart ..."[6] Inside the church she sat at the head of a congregation attired in a bizarre array of costumes. One grizzled Hawaiian sat with his ample belly bursting the seams of a velvet waistcoat buttoned up the back, while another appeared in loin cloth and ascot.

During the week chiefesses, and sometimes chiefs, from all corners of O'ahu would gather at Bingham's mission house, asking the white women to fashion them American garments. As they awaited their turn to be measured for a Mother Hubbard, a ruffled shirt or frock coat, Bingham would appear, Bible in hand, urging them to repent their sinful ways. They sat patiently, eyes darting about the room, catching the flash of a needle and the glint in Bingham's dark eyes reflecting a sliver of sun, as he droned of hell and damnation and heaven and salvation. Hawaiians, conditioned to a benevolent feudal despotism, followed the lead of Ka'ahumanu and accepted the new religion. On the other hand, some white traders and shopkeepers, who had not yet discovered the advantages of making peace with the psalm-singing newcomers, regarded them as meddling do-gooders.

When Queen Mother Keopuolani died in 1823, her son Liholiho (Kamehameha II) and his wife, Kamamalu, began to prepare for a trip to England. The voyage had been arranged in order to discuss with the British the possibility of their taking over Hawai'i as a protectorate. The royal party set sail for England aboard the *L'aigle* on November 27, 1823, as the young queen spoke to her subjects from the deck of that ship. "Ye skies, ye plains, ye mountains and great sea. Ye toilers, ye people of the soil, my love embraces you." And then Kamamalu, who was the half sister of her husband, spoke. "To this land farewell! Yea, land for whose sake my father was eaten by deep sorrow, farewell! Alas! Farewell!" And finally, as though speaking directly to her dead father, "We both foresake the object of thy toil. I go according to thy command; never will I disregard thy voice. I travel with thy dying charge, which thou didst address to me."[7]

In the event of Liholiho's death, arrangements were made to have his nine-year-old brother, Kauikeaouli, succeed him and to have Ka'ahumanu continue as Queen Regent.

The royal party arrived at Portsmouth, England, on May 18, 1824. Fifty-seven days later, as arrangements were being readied for their audience with King George IV, Liholiho and his beloved Kamamalu, the victims of measles, both died. Before the day had ended, England's foresighted Secretary for Foreign Affairs, George Canning, counseled George IV, "Mr. Canning humbly presumes that your Majesty will not disapprove of a Ship of War being allowed to carry back the Suite of the deceased Chief, with the remains of himself and his wife to the Sandwich Islands; an Attention perhaps the more advisable as the Governments of both Russia and of the United States of America are known to have their Eyes upon those Islands: which may ere long become a very important Station in the trade between the N.W. Coast of America and the China Seas."[8]

Not all "civilized" Englishmen viewed the event as a tragedy. Gentleman poet Thomas Cook published a couplet to celebrate the occasion, "Waiter! Two sandwiches! cried Death; And their wild Majesties resigned their breath."

King George approved Canning's request and the Right Honorable Lord Byron, cousin to another more sympathetic poet, and captain of the 46-gun frigate *H.M.S. Blonde*, was given command of the return voyage to Hawai'i. He was also given secret instructions which in part read, "... you will be apprised of the position in which these islands stood with regard to the Crown of Great Britain; and that his Majesty might claim over them a right of sovereignty not only by discovery, but by direct and formal cession by the Natives, and by the virtual acknowledgement of the Offices of Foreign Powers. This right his Majesty does not think it necessary to advance directly in opposition to, or in control of, any native Authority;— with such the question should not be raised, and, if proposed had better be evaded ... but if any Foreign power or its Agent should attempt, or have attempted, to establish any—Sovereignty or possession ... you are then to assert the prior rights of His Majesty, but in such a manner as may leave untouched the actual relations between His Majesty and the Government of the Sandwich Islands; and if by circumstance you should be obliged to come to a specific declaration, you are to take the Islands under his Majesty's protection and to deny the rights of any other Power to assume any Sovereignty, or to make any exclusive settlement in any of that group."[9]

Lord Byron was ordered further to maintain a strict neutrality in internal affairs and, when possible, to cultivate an understanding subjects in Hawai'i. He was to "pay the greatest Regard to the Comfort, and the Feelings, and even the Prejudices of the Natives."

The British encouraged the hardening of the status quo in Hawai'i and apparently had no wish to interfere with the authority of the king or his chiefs. Lord Byron had detailed suggestions from London that might better define the system which already existed. Briefly, "that the King be the head of the people, that all the chiefs swear allegiance to the King, that all lands now held by the chiefs not be taken from them, but shall descend to their legitimate children, except in cases of rebellion, and then all their property shall be forfeited to the King, that a tax be regularly paid to the King to keep up his dignity and establishment, that no man's life be taken except by the consent of the King, or the Regent, for the time being, and that the King, or Regent, can grant pardons at all times, that all people shall be free and not bound to any chief, that a port duty be laid on all foreign vessels."

When Bingham, whose idea of law was not the Bill of Rights of his native America, but rather the strict and rigid enforcement of the Ten Commandments, asked Byron what his feelings were regarding missionaries, his Lordship replied "... that he had heard that the Missionaries had an intention of drawing up a code of laws for the people, and to this he decidedly objected; but, so long as these gentlemen did not interfere with the laws or commerce of the Country, he could not object to their instructing the natives in reading, and in the Christian religions."[10] Bingham responded that "the missionaries had no wish to change Hawaiian laws or to interfere in their commerce."[11]

Bingham's answer to Byron regarding his intentions toward Hawaiian law was deceptive. He had already become the chief legislative moralist of the islands and, with the support of the Regent, succeeded in having the Ten Commandments adopted as Hawai'i's code of laws. Not only did she proclaim the Commandments as the law of the land, but she actively evangelized before huge audiences. Bingham added a drab touch in making it a crime for any Hawaiian to wear a flowered lei because, in his words, "the way they are worn could have a vicious meaning."[12] He viewed the Hawaiians as having "the appearance of destitution, degradation and barbarism," and characterized them as "almost naked savages, whose head and feet and much of their sunburnt swarthy skins are bare and appalling." He called them stupid because they listened to "abominable priests." He described Hawai'i as "a rude, dark, vile part of the world."

When the explosive voice of Ka'ahumanu began to quiver with evangelistic excitement and she spoke thunderously of crushing the wickedness around her, Hawai'i was on the road to becoming "civilized," missionary-style.

In 1831 an eager, young medical missionary reported "natural affairs appear now to be in a very prosperous state as it respects the native population; good order, peace and faithful obedience to the laws are observed. But the foreigners cause the chiefs no little trouble by withstanding and throwing obstacles in the way of the execution of the laws among them, and some individuals have added personal insult and threats to their opposition, they use every art to entangle the chiefs in foolish bargains, and get away with their land, they eagerly catch at everything which will afford a pretext however futile in which to ground a complaint to the English or American governments. It appears to us that unless counter influence is exerted the country will soon come under the government of a foreign power."[13] Gerrit P. Judd was portending the time when a partnership of American missionaries and their defrocked brethren, American businessmen, would govern all of Hawai'i.

During that time perhaps the cruelest of all the changes which came about for all Hawaiians was the rigid super-imposition of Christian sexual beliefs and practices. They previously felt no sin surrounding sexual activity. They did not believe in chastity before marriage, nor monogamy, nor did they look down on homosexuality. From ancient times they had employed a game called *'ume,* wherein they sat by a roaring bonfire in a circle laughing and shouting, awaiting the magic touch of the feathered *'ume* wand.[15] When a man who sang a lascivious song and played the role of *mau* selected a woman and a man touched each with his feathered *maile*, they were free to enjoy a new partner for a night of pleasure without being challenged to a duel, punched in the nose, or impaled on a spear in the dark of night. Order prevailed throughout the proceedings. Ancient Hawaiian chants describe the activities of such evenings in vivid detail. Many Hawaiians, bewildered by the new philosophy of their King and Regent, accepted their decrees. But Governor Boki of Oʻahu, who had already accommodated himself to American business ways, owned several flourishing grog shops which he refused to close. The white traders and whalers simmered, awaiting violent confrontations. Bingham succeeded in having Kaʻahumanu enact a law forbidding Hawaiian women from going aboard foreign ships. Lt. John Percival, Master of the *U.S.S. Dolphin*, threatened to shoot Bingham on sight and told Boki that, "... missionaries are liars and I want that law lifted or I will fire upon your houses."

Sailors from the *Dolphin* cornered Bingham one day near his house and tore off his clothes, while waving whalebone knives under his chin. The embattled missionary defended himself with his rolled umbrella and screamed for help. Several Hawaiians rushed to his rescue, stacking the sailors like cordwood. Bingham recalled, "I instantly felt the bowels of tenderness more, and entreated the natives not to kill the foreigners." But Percival, Boki and others with commercial interests prevailed. The law was overturned.[16]

Many of his white contemporaries were not kind in their evaluation of "King Bingham!" Honolulu merchant Stephen Reynolds labeled him as leading missionaries who were "... blood sucking, cash sucking ... a lazy, lying wretch."[17] His brother missionary, Richard Armstrong, saw him as "a compound of vanity, self-importance, forwardness, obstinacy, self-complacency, and at the same time, filled with kindness, moderation, conscientiousness, firmness and piety."[18] But John Young was more sanguine. "Good morals are superseding the reign of crime ... a code of these things are what I have longed for, but have never seen till now."[19]

When Bingham wrote that Hawaiians were "... too stupid and ignorant to farm lands and become self-providing," he overlooked the fact that 300,000 Hawaiians were successfully supporting themselves when Cook came ashore in 1778. When asked to participate in an anniversary celebrating Cook's arrival, Bingham exploded in anger, "How vain, rebellious and at the same time contemptible for a worm to receive homage and sacrifices from the stupid and polluted worshippers of demons and of the vilest objects of creation ..."[20]

Logic and a sense of history didn't seem to be among the strongest attributes of Hawaiʻi's Protestant cross-bearers. John Young would shock the Reverend Lorenzo Lyons in 1835 by telling him that he had witnessed the sacrifice of 13 people at Kamehameha's

Puʻukoholā temple in 1791. Less than a century earlier, 23 creatures of the devil were burned at the stake and many more were tortured before the frenzy died down in Salem, Massachusetts. More than a hundred women had been found guilty of witchcraft by a puritanical tribunal made up of Lyon's forefathers.

When King Kamehameha III was 19, Kaʻahumanu died. Within a year he abolished all the puritanic laws in his kingdom except those dealing with theft and murder. Overnight he became a liberated hedonist, outshining his late brother Liholiho in horse racing, card playing, woman chasing and rum drinking. He revived the ancient sports of surfing, canoe racing, spear throwing and that "depraved native dance," the *hula*. Laura Fish Judd, wife of Gerrit, reported: "Vile heathen songs and shameless dances ruin and wretchedness becomes rampant."21

The young king sternly admonished the white man to keep his place. "Ye men of foreign lands, let not the laws be by you put under your feet. When you are in your own countries, there you will observe your own laws."22 However, the entrenchment of the missionaries was too formidable to undo. Another student of Hawaiian history, John Dominis Holt, offers his assessment of this critical period. "In its pious attempts to bring the civilization of the west to the Hawaiian people in their hour of need, the Protestant American Mission achieved little to stay the awful spread of death. Launching illogical and indefatigable attacks on almost the whole of native institutions the mission destroyed the chance they might have had to help Hawaiians bridge the revolutionary gap that existed between the past and the present. With more humane understanding of the true needs of the Hawaiians, the mission could have been more help to the native people. Instead, Hawaiians were subjected to thunderous denunciations of their traditional beliefs. They were told quite bluntly that they could not be themselves because their way of life was full of evil. They must denounce all aspects of their heritage and become overnight something of an American—New England variant ... the Hawaiian began to disappear from the face of the earth. They willingly gave up their souls and died, or as it was said among themselves, *'Na kanaka ōkuʻu wale aku no i kau uhane,'* that is, 'The people dismissed freely their souls and died.'"23

•

On the other hand, the Reverend Abraham Akaka, a native Hawaiian and longtime pastor of the Bingham-founded Kawaiahaʻo Church, expressed a contrary view in 1951. "Rather than bringing extinction and extermination, the missionaries were a people who,

like the grapes of Canaan long ago ... brought joy of heart and glad-
ness of soul to my people."[24]

•

The old system had broken and Hawai'i was without the
industry needed to sustain itself. In the 1830's it took a ship sailing
from the islands 20 days to reach San Francisco, 146 days to New
York, and 169 days to England. These sailings were irregular at best,
depending on tide, wind and the availability of space. With whaling
yet to become a thriving industry, Hawai'i's economy languished in
the tropical sun.

Hiram Bingham, whose religious convictions had been astrin-
gent enough to intimidate an entire kingdom, left Hawai'i on August
3, 1840. He died in New Haven, Connecticut, on November 11, 1869.

Bingham, the son of a man who fought as a foot soldier in a
bitter war to preserve a constitution which derived its uniqueness and
much of its strength from its separation of church and state, wrote,
"The state deriving all its power from God, both rulers and subjects
being bound to do God's will, and its chief magistrate being God's
minister ought to be, and is in an important sense, a religious institu-
tion."[25]

Chapter Five

JOHN PALMER PARKER
1830

The animals were taken to the plain of Waimea which was very rich and productive, occupying a space of several miles in extent, and winding at the foot of...lofty mountains far into the country. In this valley is a great tract of luxuriant, natural pasturage, whither all the cattle and sheep...were to be driven, there to roam unrestrained, to "increase and multiply" far from the sight of strangers.

— Captain George Vancouver
March 2, 1794

JOHN PALMER PARKER

In 1830 Hiram Bingham paid a visit to the Big Island home of his earliest benefactor, John Young ... "About as desolate a place as I have ever seen, nothing but barrenness, with here and there a native hut. Kawaihae is scorched, withered and desolate yet its evenings are pleasant, and the ocean as the sun sets, indescribably beautiful."[1] Bingham, there to celebrate the tenth anniversary of his arrival in Hawai'i, wrote, "It does one's liver good to look out from my study window upon the snows of Mauna Loa and Mauna Kea and to feel the New England air while the mercury stands at 60."[2]

Governor Young's home at Kawaihae on the Island of Hawai'i was the hub of a compound which reflected both European and Hawaiian styles of architecture. The main house was stone and held together with coral reef mortar. It had a thatched roof made of *pili* grass and, except for its roof, looked like a typical English country house. Coral was mixed with *taro* roots and hair to give it the cohesiveness of mortar. Standing on a bluff with a panoramic view of the Pacific, it was the first western-style house built in Hawai'i. His other houses, where his Hawaiian wife and children lived, were in the native style.

After two days of reminiscing with Young, Bingham saddled a stallion and rode the rolling knobs of Kohala Mountain foothills to nearby Waimea town, where he eyed "several striking exhibitions of seizing wild cattle, chasing them on horseback, and throwing the lasso over their horns ... and subduing or killing these mountain-fed animals."[3] Amid bellowing calves, choking clouds of dust and the pungent odor of branded cow flesh, Bingham renewed the acquaintance of sturdy John Palmer Parker, Hawai'i's first cowboy. Parker was shouting out commands in pidgin Spanish to cowboys who yahooed reluctant heifers into the corral run.

Parker, born in Newton, Massachusetts, on May 1, 1790, had already been riding Waimea's meadows for 16 years. Earlier, in 1803, an American sea captain, Richard J. Cleveland, wrote, "We left Kealakekua Bay on June 23rd and the next morning anchored in Kawaihae Bay, for the purpose of landing the mare with foal, for which Young was very urgent, professing to take all possible care of the animal. In the expectation, that the chance of increase would be better secured by placing the horse in the care of different persons, we accorded to his request, and landed the mare in safety near his place. This is the first horse that ever trod the soil of Owhyhee (Hawai'i) and caused among the natives incessant exclamations of astonishments."[4]

When Parker first arrived in Hawai'i aboard a sandalwood trader in 1809, he had promptly jumped ship at Kealakekua Bay and found employment tending the royal fishponds at Honaunau. Soon he became fluent in Hawaiian; but, after two years, he was too restless to stay and signed aboard a sandalwood vessel owned by Winship and Davis for a voyage to China. The British, then at war with the United States, blockaded that ship in the harbor at Canton for almost two years. Parker returned to Hawai'i in 1815, after having sailed to the Northwest coast of America and up the Columbia River. Having already made the acquaintance of Kamehameha during his stay at the fishponds, he approached the king with a business proposition. Kamehameha accepted, granting him permission to settle at Kawaihae and to hunt the wild herds of cattle that roamed the soaring slopes of Mauna Kea. Before the year was up, Parker had moved his headquarters to Waimea and had begun in earnest to thin out those roving packs, which had multiplied a thousandfold during the 22 years since their arrival. These wary-eyed longhorns trampled at will throughout the unfenced countryside, decimating *koa* forests, munching farm crops, flattening new forest growth and spreading fear among the people.

Parker was told to solve the problem either by killing them

off or by taming them. His decision to domesticate them, despite the fact that Polynesians had no taste for beef, was the first step toward building a cattle empire. As a partial solution to having few customers for the fresh meat of the cattle he was weeding out, Parker began preserving it in salt taken from the nearby ponds. This salted beef was not only used for barter with passing ships, but also tended as payment for debts owed by Hawaiian chiefs to American sandalwood traders. Those Hawaiians who had survived the rigors of carrying sandalwood down Mauna Kea's slopes a year or two before were strapped into harnesses again to lug sides of beef to the waterfront. Parker also cured the hides and set up a crude tannery to process leather for boots, saddles, trappings and trade. More significantly, he laid solid foundations for what would become the largest ranch in America under single ownership, with 600 miles of fenced grazing land encompassed in over 250,000 acres of royal ranch land. Soon these lands would support 51,000 head of Herefords, 1,000 quality horses, 132 ranch hands, 213 paddocks, 50 corrals and water reservoirs capable of servicing a small city. In 1816 Parker consolidated his business agreement with the king by marrying Kipikane, the granddaughter of Kanekapolei, who was among the 22 wives of Kamehameha I.

Peruvian cowboys were brought to Waimea to teach the Hawaiians their art. The hard-working Hawaiians soon became master cowboys, driving cattle down the long hill to Kawaihae Landing, where they grouped the animals into foursomes, their horns tied to tow lines, and floated them through the gentle surf to ships anchored outside the surfline. There, the *paniolo* and their Polynesian pupils urged their horses near the reluctant cattle, coaxing them into sailcloth slings and making them ready to hoist aboard the ships.

As business improved, cattle shipment became the prime industry of Kawaihae and cattle raising the principal occupation of Waimea. John Young oversaw trade with the increasing number of vessels anchored offshore, supplying them with salt, sweet potatoes and exotic tropical food, including coconuts, breadfruit, *taro*, bananas, melons and sugar cane. Ships bartered tools, gunpowder, furniture, firearms, paper and other needed commodities for Young's goods and for hogs, *tapa* cloth and fowl from other islanders.

When Bingham and his fellow missionaries arrived in 1820, Parker boarded the *Thaddeus* at Kawaihae as part of the welcoming party. Later, Bingham wrote to Parker explaining, "Six American gentlemen and their wives have arrived in Hawai'i to diffuse the blessings of science, of civilization and Christianity in these isles of the sea."[5] Bingham wrote of the anguish and embarrassment his companions had suffered when bare-bosomed women and naked men swam out to the *Thaddeus* to greet them. That particular attire was precisely what Parker and his rotund wife chose to wear while vocalizing Hawaiian chants during the construction of their new house. That house, which still stands, reflects Parker's character: strong, practical, austere and enduring. "The *koa* forest of Hanaipoe became the great center for cutting down of trees, selecting the best to be milled into lumber, the piling of koa lumber on hilly ground so that the air could get between the boards and season the wood ... two underground cisterns were dug and plastered around for water, their roofs were of slate. Next the cornerstone was laid for a story-and-a-half dwelling house for Parker and family.

"Under the cornerstone was laid a Bible, a loaf of bread, an ear of corn, money and newspaper of the time. The house was called *Mana Hale*. The ground floor had four bedrooms, a large hall, dining room, kitchen, pantry and a closed-in porch, while the upper story had three rooms. Everything in and out of this house, even to the nails, was of *koa* grown on Parker lands, and sawn in his saw pits."[6]

Cast in a conservative mold, Parker gambled more than 30 years of his life, doing the toughest imaginable kind of physical labor against the possibility of one day owning some of the range land he had worked. On January 14, 1847, he became one of the first whites to receive a Royal Land Grant. Parker's Land Commission award bore the number seven and the signature of Kamehameha III. It deeded him two acres at *Mana Hale*.

"By energetic work Parker made a considerable fortune. Some of the land purchased from the king was paid for in butter. He possessed a fund of curious details about the customs and manners of the natives. His stories were told without any pretensions and were interspersed with fragments of native chants, phrases and proverbs. He could chant very well."[7]

An eloquent Frenchman, Charles de Varigny, who served Kamehameha V as Minister of Foreign Affairs, paid a social call on John Parker in 1858. "Riding up the east coast and visiting Waipio, we at length came to Waimea, and at *Mana* were the guests of John Parker. We were in the midst of patriarchal life. On our arrival ten natives ran out to hold the bridles of our horses. Several young girls attracted by the noise, also came out. Some went to the dairy and the kitchen. The cattle were bellowing, the sheep bleating, and a sweet odor of dinner greeted our olfactory nerves. We were lodged in a box or, if you like it better, in a house of compartments all of varnished *koa*, a wood of the country which looks like mahogany. Roof, doors, partitions, ceilings, floors, the interior as well as the exterior, all made of *koa*: all very like one might say a gigantic toy. Mr. Parker often spoke of Kamehameha I. We spent the evening with him and he had a peculiar charm as a narrator. I have spent few evenings so agreeable."[8]

Success polished roughhewn John Palmer Parker. His bright blue eyes squinted beneath a silver hedge of brows. Snow white mutton-chop whiskers rode down his thin, aging face to a junction with his jowls. His nose, sharp and crooked, cast a shadow that softened the hard lines of his thin lips that sometimes belied the sense of humor hidden therein. At age 77 Parker remarked, "Death is an incurable disease that men and women are born with; it gets them sooner or later."[9]

He died on March 25, 1868, leaving the foundation of what would become a large fortune to his grandson Samuel Parker.

•

In 1991, 188 years after Vancouver brought the first cattle to Hawaii, the Parker Ranch occupies 250,000 acres, has 50,000 head of cattle and 117 employees, including 40 *paniolo*.

Chapter Six

HERMAN MELVILLE
1841

"... the first and greatest writer to touch the South Seas with any genius."

— Robert Louis Stevenson

HERMAN MELVILLE

In January of 1841, an obscure 21-year-old wearing a worry-etched face, sailed from Fairhaven, Massachusetts, on a voyage which would affect almost all literature from that time on. Later Herman Melville would be given credit for writing "the best tragic epic of modern times and one of the finest poetic works of all times ..."[1]

Melville tells why he embarked on that voyage: "Some years ago—never mind precisely—having little or no money in my purse and nothing particularly to interest me on shore, I thought I would sail about a little and see the watery part of the world. It is a way I have of driving off the spleen and regulating the circulation. Whenever I find myself growing grim about the mouth; whenever it is a damp drizzly November in my soul; when I find myself pausing before the coffin warehouses and bringing up the rear of every funeral I meet; and especially whenever my hypos get such an upper hand of me, that it requires a strong moral principle to prevent me from deliberately stepping into the street and methodically knocking people's hats off—then I account it high time to get to sea as soon as I can."[2]

The second of four sons in a family of eight children, Melville was born in New York City on August 1, 1819. His mother, Maria Gansevoort Melville, was an Albany socialite, her father having been a general in George Washington's army. His father, Allan, was a handsome American aristocrat of Scottish descent who imported finery for the carriage trade of New York. The family entourage included a cook, nurse and governess, and the Melvilles cherished the values of duty, sobriety and regularity. Herman, who displayed a contrariness of mood in his early years, was both blessed and cursed with the qualities he had inherited from his parents. His mother gave him his sternness and gentility. His father gave him buoyancy, excitability, a capacity for compassion and the facility for dreaming.

In 1830, because of the scarcity of foreign exchange, the family business collapsed. The Melvilles moved to Albany, where Maria's health broke and Allan began to show signs of deep depression. Two years later, when death mercifully silenced the gibberish of his father, Herman was not yet thirteen. He left school to clerk in a bank. A poor mathematician, he soon lost that position and, shortly after, another as a clerk in his brother's import shop. He moved to his uncle's farm in Pittsfield, Massachusetts, but found chores to be drudgery and gave up farming to teach in an academy. When the semester ended, his employers were unable to pay him. In the image of Benjamin Franklin, he began to educate himself by joining a literary and debating society and by writing for a newspaper.

In 1840, a year after he had made a voyage to Liverpool as a merchant sailor, Herman and a friend began exploring inner America along the Erie Canal. They followed that meandering ribbon by steamer from the Hudson to Lake Erie and then on to Detroit, Chicago, Cairo, Illinois, chugging on to Wheeling, West Virginia, and then by horseback, over the green hills to the beaches of the Virginia coast. They then headed northward toward Philadelphia, finally completing the circle at New York. This trip, taken during another severe economic depression, left Herman hungry for more adventure but penniless and discouraged on the eve of his 22nd birthday. He was a stocky five foot ten, with pale blue eyes that sometimes twinkled with humor, long straggly brown hair, and a curly beard that covered most of his homely face and softened a grim mouth.

Some critics prefer the view that going to sea for Melville was a last resort; that emotional despair drove him; that of the five times he went to sea, the first four were out of desperation. Others feel that Melville was lured to the sea when his imagination was stoked by tales told by seafaring uncles and cousins who had ventured across the South Pacific in the 1820's. As the 104-foot whaler *Acushnet* sailed out of Buzzard's Bay in January of 1841, Melville was launched on a major adventure that was to take him down the east coast of South America, making port at Rio de Janeiro, around Cape Horn, and on to the little-known islands of the Pacific, and finally to Hawai'i.

On July 9, 1842, after 552 days at sea, Melville landed at Nuku Hiva, capital of the eleven volcanic islands named in 1595 for the Viceroy of Peru, the Marquess de Mendoza. Although whalers occasionally made port at the Marquesas when they were short of stores, few whites dared to mix with the natives, who were reputed to be the most savage headhunters in the Pacific. When Melville stepped ashore at Nuku Hiva, the Polynesians who lived in the interior were isolated by towering mountains and crashing surf.

Although Melville's first published works, *Typee* and *Omoo,* are fictional, he took extraordinary care to state those assertions regarding missionary behavior toward native islanders were eye witness accounts of what he personally observed, not fictionalized accounts. "There are few passages in the ensuing chapters which may be thought to bear rather hard upon a revered order of men... Such passages will be found, however, to be based upon facts admitting of no contradictions, and which have come immediately under the writer's cognizance."[3]

Upon alighting at the Marquesas, Melville and his friend Richard Tobias hastened to desert the *Acushnet.* Fearing harsh punishment should they be caught, they set out to climb a mountain and slip into the safety of the valley on the other side. While fleeing down the backside of that rain-slick mountain, Melville fell to a rocky slope below, severely injuring his leg. Tobias and the crippled Melville risked great physical danger as they continued their halting descent to the valley below. Later Tobias caught sight of a nearly naked young couple standing together in the dense foliage. The youngsters led Melville and his friend to a nearby village, where, fatigued from their ordeal, they lay upon the mats which covered the floor of a thatched hut already overflowing with bronze bodies, "... gleaming with wild curiosity and wonder; the naked forms and tattooed limbs of brawny warriors, with here and there the slighter figures of young girls, all engaged in a perfect storm of conversation, of which we were of course the only theme ...."[4]

They had been led to the bamboo palace of the high chief of the most warlike tribe of all Polynesia—the Typees. Because of their fierceness and almost inaccessible location, this tribe mirrored the image of ancient Polynesia. Three days later Melville, his leg still painful, persuaded his hosts to lead Tobias to civilization. Melville was destined to stay on in Typee, first as a loosely guarded and curiously regarded captive and, finally, as an adopted member of an extended Polynesian family—the *'ohana.*

Sharp of eye and probing, Melville was in an ideal situation to observe and record life as lived by unsullied Polynesians. He moved in with his new family to share their grass hut, bathe in their communal spring, eat their food, and live among a set of grandparents, and the mother and father of his 16-year-old love, slender Fayaway. There, for a few brief weeks, he lived as a Polynesian.

He discovered that to the Polynesian "... life is little else than an often interrupted luxurious nap. There were none of those thousand sources of irritations that man has created to mar his own felicity. There are no foreclosures of mortgages, no protested notes, no debts of honor ... no deeds of any descriptions; no assault and battery attorneys ... no poor relations everlastingly occupying the spare bed chamber, no destitute widows with their children starving on the cold charities of the world; no beggars, no debtors prisons; no proud and hard-hearted nabobs in Typee: to sum it all up in one word—no MONEY!"[5]

He observed and recorded that these unenlightened savages were enjoying a way of life philosophers such as Plato conjured up for their awed flocks every century or so. There was no padlock on the valley he had so painfully entered. Theft and assassination sent no quiver of fear through the Typees, since neither was within the realm of their experience. Their principles of honor and virtue were undistorted by arbitrary statutes. They believed that prolonged virginity was extremely harmful to young people and delighted in the taking and giving of sexual favors. As Melville explains, Polynesian man, although unmistakably male, was a breed unknown in civilized countries because he had somehow escaped the curse of overbearing masculinity. "A regular system of polygamy exists among the islander; but of a most extraordinary nature —a plurality of husbands, instead of wives; and the solitary fact speaks volumes for the gentle disposition of the male population. Where else, indeed, could such a practice exist, even for a single day?[6]

"I had sometimes observed a comical-looking gentleman dressed in a suit of shabby tattooing, who had the audacity to take various liberties with a lady ... in the very presence of the old warrior, her husband, who looked on, as good-naturedly as nothing was happening."[7]

Melville discovered that Polynesians, like American Indians, held the land "in fee simple from nature herself; to have and to hold, so long as grass grows and water runs; or until their French invaders, by a summary mode of conveyancing, shall appropriate them to their own benefit and behoof."[8]

Viewing the Polynesians as highly honest, Melville had a logical explanation for their behavior toward the white man: "The strict honesty which the inhabitants of nearly all the Polynesian Islands manifest toward each other, is in striking contrast with the thieving propensities some of them evince in their intercourse with foreigners. It would almost seem that, according to their peculiar code of morals, the pilfering of a hatchet or a wrought nail from a European is looked upon as a praiseworthy action. Or, rather, it may be presumed, that bearing in mind the wholesale forays made upon them by their nautical visitors, they consider the property of the latter as a fair object of reprisal."[9]

"This consideration, while it serves to reconcile an apparent contradiction in the moral character of the islanders, should in some measure alter that low opinion of it in which the reader of South Sea voyages is too apt to form."[10]

Melville fast learned the secret of the Polynesians: the extended family is as essential to paradise as is climate. "During my whole stay in the island I never witnessed a single quarrel, nor anything that in the slightest degree approached even to a dispute. The natives appeared to form one household, whose members were bound together by the ties of strong affection. The love of kindred I did not much perceive, for it seemed blended in the general love; and where all were treated as brothers and sisters, it was hard to tell who were actually related to each other by blood. Let it not be supposed that I have overdrawn this picture. I have not done so."[11]

Melville, feeling the tug of fresh adventure, eventually left aboard the Australian whaler, *Lucy Ann*. " ... how far short of our expectation is often times the fulfillment of the most ardent hopes. Safe aboard a ship—so long my earnest prayer—with home and friends once more in prospect, I nevertheless felt weighed down by the melancholy that could not be shaken off. It was the thought of never more seeing those, who had upon the whole treated me so kindly. I was leaving them forever."[12] An ailing captain, a drunken mate and a mutinous crew made conditions aboard the *Lucy Ann* worse than they had been aboard the *Acushnet*.

During the next five months, Melville endured great hardships. He went before the mast, then to prison, charged with organizing a mutiny. Finally, he became a beachcombing vagabond in Tahiti and on a nearby island he called "Eimeo." Melville would write more about the pleasure of this time, in *Omoo*, than he would of the pain. Perhaps this three-month period was, for Melville, the happiest time of his life. He satirized his personal tragedies and ridiculed his daily misfortunes, never portraying himself as a victim. Later, he philosophized "... humility became the partner of outrage, the parent of understanding."[13]

Melville wrote of a gathering in Tahiti in the midst of a syphilis plague, which had infected at least two-thirds of the commoners. The dying and terminally ill were carried before the white missionaries and laid in a field, where their spokesman cried out, "Lies, lies! You tell us of salvation, and, behold, we are dying. We want no other salvation than to live in this world. Where are there any saved through your speech? Pomaree [their king] is dead; and we are all dying with your cursed diseases. When will you give over?"

The tragedy of that time lives in a Tahitian chant: "The palm tree shall grow, The coral shall spread, But men shall cease."[14]

Melville pleaded, "Let the savage be civilized but civilize them with benefits, and not with evils; let heathenism be destroyed, but not by destroying the heathen. The Anglo-Saxon have extirpated Paganism from the greater part of the North American continent; but with it they have likewise extirpated the greater part of the Red race."[15]

After having spent more than three months living among Tahitians in their jail and in back-country villages, Melville bade *aloha* to his Polynesian friends, as the American whaler, *Charles & Henry*, eased out of the port of Papeete. "Crowding all sail, we braced the yards square; and, the breeze freshening, bowled straight away from the land. Once more the sailor's cradle rocked under me, and I found myself rolling in my gait."[16]

The *Charles & Henry* was bound for the coast of Japan, while criss-crossing the Pacific hunting whales.

WHALING

Hundreds of thousands of American dollars were at stake in the great whaling gamble. Honolulu haoles such as Samuel James Dowsett tried their luck in the whaling business, with the hopes of turning a quick fortune. Dowsett sailed the *Victoria* to the Picadoes Islands on one such expedition on June 1, 1834. A year passed and, when this Englishman had not returned, the Hawaiian government sent the brig *Waverly* to find him. But that vessel was seized by natives at Strong Island, where its captain and crew were murdered and the ship reduced to ashes. No trace was ever found of Dowsett. Other hazards, typhoons, raging Arctic gales and the frightening unknown of poorly charted areas of the Pacific awaited such voyagers.

The vessels in such enterprises were tiny but sturdy ships which could carry 2,000 barrels of oil and 15 tons of whale bone, plus the grizzled, ill-nourished sailors who manned them. These whalers, like Melville, shipped on cruises which lasted two or more years. They existed on salt pork, wormy biscuits, brackish water, courage and abuse. The hoarse cry of "Thar she blows" signaled a pell-mell dash to the open boats and then the frantic chase after the 100-foot-long monsters. The crews, armed with harpoons and oars, were fearfully aware one flip of a mighty tail could smash their boat into a thousand pieces and fling them to a watery grave.

The most dangerous hunting grounds were those in the Arctic regions, where whalers fought sea giants which could casually upend a ten-ton ice floe and then wheel about to bash in a ship's bulkhead with consummate ease.

Many superstitious white crew men cowered before such wonders. One observer thought that the Hawaiians fared better "These Kanakas are large and well built men, as active as monkeys and make the best seamen. It is almost impossible to drown them. In time of a storm they will sport in the surf where a white man could not live for a minute. They will even attack and kill sharks in the water. The mate pointed out one ... who was cast overboard one dark, stormy night. When they found him an hour afterward he was swimming straight for the nearest land, twenty miles away, and did not seem to be afraid."[17]

After five months of whaling aboard the *Charles & Henry*, Melville stepped ashore at Lahaina, Maui. Twenty-three years earlier two whaleships, the vanguard of a vast fleet, sailed into Hawaiian waters and quickly established bases in the port cities of Lahaina and Honolulu, where white merchants supplied their needs and welcomed their gold. Fertile sperm whaling grounds had recently been discovered in the Arctic regions off the coast of Japan. Japanese feudal lords, who bristled at the thought of trading with the white man, attacked foreign whaling ships and drove them away from their ports whenever these vessels approached. Thus, the Sandwich Islands, little more than an outpost, became port for the huge whaling fleet.

Lahaina was near the peak of its whaling prosperity when Melville arrived. With nearly 400 whalers flying Old Glory anchored offshore that year, sailors, angry with the missionary curfews, rioted on Front Street. Shore boats lined the beach and disorderly drunks overflowed jail doors spilling out on the sidewalk, impeding the progress of early churchgoers.

The Polynesians of Lahaina were drowning in the backwash of whaling commerce, while sailors who had swept the Pacific from Sydney to Hong Kong, from Ponape to the northern ice barriers in search of the precious booty of oil, whalebone and blubber, were off on a spree. Many ships remained during the off-season, making great demands upon limited Hawaiian resources. The port cities became rough, bawdy liberty towns. Those same chiefs who had been sandalwood brokers for the white man stepped in again to make a profit on the common Hawaiian man. Food, firewood, sailing gear, water and recreation were provided as business prospered.

Lusty crewmen released from months at sea spent their wages and their liberty on women and rum. Debauchery and brawls shattered the tropical calm. Circus entertainers and acting companies from San Francisco appeared. Desertions were prevalent, as was manslaughter. Hawaiian youths were shanghaied to replace white deserters. Local haoles protested these kidnappings because their prime source of cheap labor was disappearing over the horizon. Whaling worked a tremendous hardship upon the Polynesian. Malo wrote of the fate of Hawaiians who joined the whaling fleet "Some become sailors by profession and do not return, some dwell permanently in the countries to which they go and some upon other islands in the Pacific ... Some, however, return and are married to young girls who become attached to them and ... quickly spend without economy, the prosperity they may have acquired and when it is gone, they go ... and leave behind the women they have married. Thus the wives live without their husbands for many years and when some of them return, it appears that in some foreign port they have become diseased, and returning infect their own wives ... and when they perceive their own wives' disease they forsake them again and go to foreign countries."[18]

Those creatures who had greeted their first white lovers with open arms and affection were diseased and deserted by their own. Idyllic Polynesian love had vanished. Hawaiian women were rendered barren by the white man's diseases and their bodies bartered for cash.

Prostitution became such a flourishing industry that an act was introduced in the House of Nobles to "prevent females from collecting in ports during the times great numbers of ships are at anchor." A few ship captains were glad to have missionaries pass laws prohibiting the sale of liquor and females. Some devout New England mariners even upheld the law that imposed a fine for sabbath-breaking. Most, however, scoffed at a government whose constitution provided sweepingly that "no law shall be enacted which is at variance with the word of the Lord Jehovah and whose criminal code was a translation of the ten commandments."

One captain, livid with anger, threatened to hang Hiram Bingham from the yardarm. A ship swung its cannons broadside and bombarded Lahaina. A mob, led by sailors, attacked the house of the Reverend William Richards and when it was driven away by Hawaiians, Richards was brought to trial for interfering with U.S. commerce by an officer of the United States Navy. The editor of the *Sandwich Island Gazette*, Stephen Mackintosh, promoted the cause of the "foreign element" in Hawai'i and voiced strong editorial opposition to the American missionaries. Despite the hubbub going on around them, they could still dwell on their "achievements." One, writing to New England during this period, reported: "...27 prominent chapels, schools and government buildings have been completed with... fifty-five houses ... being a town five-sixth of a mile long and two-thirds wide ... few towns of its size in the world are under better police and municipal regulations. Riots and brawls ... rarely if ever known, while Sabbaths are proverbial for the quiet and order which reign."[19]

Despite this supposed progress, an alarmed Hawaiian spokesman for the people of Lahaina pleaded with Kamehameha III

"The Hawaiian people will be trodden under foot by the foreigners. Perhaps not now, or perhaps it will not be long before we shall see it. Another thing, the dollar is becoming the government for the commoner and for the destitute. It will become a dish of relish and the foreign agents will suck it up. With so many foreign agents, the dollar will be lost to the government ... and instead of good coming to the Hawaiian people, strangers will get the benefit from the wealth."[20]

The king responded, "Kindly greetings to you ... I desire all the good things of the past to remain ... and to unite with them what is good under these new conditions in which we live. That is why I have appointed foreign officials, not out of contempt for the ancient wisdom of the land, but because my native helpers do not understand the laws of the great countries who are working with us."[21]

The Lahainans persisted "The laws of those governments will not do for our government. Those are good laws for them. Our laws are for us and are good for us, which we have made for ourselves. We are not slaves to serve them. When they talk in their clever way we know very well what is right and what is wrong ... We don't believe that Kamehameha would put faith in the skill and cunning of strangers ... It was never heard that he followed completely the advice of foreigners, and he never made them members of his secret council to discuss good government."[22]

In 1843, 64 years after the death of Captain Cook, the American missionaries took a census. They counted 100,273 Polynesians in Hawaii.

IN HONOLULU

Melville made his way to bustling Honolulu town, where he roamed its dusty lanes looking for work. He found it in a bowling alley as a pin setter and discovered new friends who performed at the court of Kamehameha III.

One was a jolly little black called Billy Loon "... tricked out in a soiled blue jacket, studded all over with rusty bell buttons and garnished with shabby gold lace, is the royal drummer and pounder of the tambourin." While Joe, a peglegged Portuguese "... who lost his leg to a whale," played the violin "meanwhile a villainous-looking scamp ... Mordecai juggled."[23]

Other matters in Honolulu were less laughable. "Not until I visited Honolulu was I aware ... that ... natives had been civilized into draught horses. I saw a robust, red-faced missionary's spouse who took her regular airings in a little go-cart drawn by two of the islanders ... both being, with the exception of the fig-leaf, as naked as when they were born. Rattling along ... the streets the lady looks

about her as magnificently as any queen .... A sudden elevation soon
disturbs her serenity ... to be sure, she used to think nothing of driving cows to pasture on the old farm in New England .... She ...
bawls out 'Hookee, Hookee!' (Pull, pull) and rap goes the heavy han-
dle of her huge fan over the naked skull of the old savage: while the
young one shies on one side and keeps beyond its range." [24]

•

In December 1842, ex-missionary William Richards met with
Secretary of State Daniel Webster in Washington, D.C., to discuss the
future of Hawai'i. He returned home with a document signed by
President Tyler, which stated the Sandwich Islands should retain their
independence. Gerrit P. Judd replaced Richards as advisor to the king
and the local battle between the Americans and the British for control
of the islands almost erupted into warfare. British Consul Alexander
Simpson charged that His Majesty's subjects were being discrimi-
nated against and called for armed assistance. The British frigate
Carysfort under the command of Lord George Paulet answered his
call. When Paulet attempted to intervene, Kamehameha III refused to
grant him an audience; instead he referred him to Judd. Paulet
refused to speak with Judd and threatened to shell Honolulu unless
his demands were met. Judd hastily urged the king to acquiesce. That
action prompted Paulet and Simpson to go further than they had
intended by demanding the unconditional and complete cession of
Hawai'i to the United Kingdom. The Hawai'i flag was ceremoniously
lowered, and the Union Jack was run up to the accompaniment of a
thunderous twenty-one gun salute from the *Carysfort*. Judd, scrib-
bling by flickering candlelight in the Royal Tomb, using Ka'ahumanu's coffin as his desk, penned urgent dispatches and arranged for
them to be smuggled to Washington and London. Five months later
the British foreign office revoked Paulet's action and restored
Hawai'i's independence. Kamehameha III elevated Judd to Secretary
for Foreign Affairs "... because they know more than we ..."

Now in the employ of Isaac Montgomery, an English merchant, Melville protested Judd's version of that incident. "No transaction has ever been more grossly misrepresented than the events that
occurred upon the arrival of Lord George Paulet at Oahu .... High in
the favour of the imbecile king at this time was one Dr. Judd, a sanc-
timonious apothecary adventurer, who was animated by an inveterate
dislike to England. The ascendancy of a junta of ignorant and designing Methodist elders in the council of a half civilized king, ruling
with absolute sway over a nation just poised between barbarism and
civilization, and exposed by the peculiarities of its relations with foreign states to unusual difficulties, was not precisely calculated to

impart a healthy tone to the policy of the government ... the British Cabinet never had any idea of appropriating the islands! And it furnishes a sufficient vindication of the acts of Lord George Paulet, that he not only received the unqualified approbation of his own Government but that to this hour the great body of the Hawaiian people invoke blessings on his head, and look back with gratitude to the time when his liberal and paternal sway diffused peace and happiness among them."[25]

A Quaker minister joined with Melville: "The government is inefficient, partly from the character of the King, who is very much influenced by the whites and half-castes whose interest leads them to encourage his dissipated, thoughtless course of life, and partly because his native simplicity and inexperience are ill-adapted to cope with designing adventurers, who are ready to take every advantage."[26]

Melville questioned the idea that a Christian God could allow such inhumanity to flourish and at the same time permit the perpetrators to congratulate themselves for being so virtuous. Hawai'i's missionary/businessmen operated under a belief system which turned amassing of wealth into a religious exercise. It made sympathy for the poor and unfortunate almost a sacrilege under the rule that everyone got what they deserved under Providence. Hawai'i's missionaries were not alone in their belief. Episcopal Bishop William Lawrence, who counted financier J. Pierpont Morgan among his New York flock, declared, "The rich man is the moral man. Godliness is in league with riches."

Melville knew and respected Polynesians throughout the Pacific. He railed against the activities of the foreigners who lived well in Hawai'i, had the means of eliminating poverty, disease, starvation and death, and yet did little to help those conditions. He actively agitated for the betterment of the Hawaiian. Later, literary reviewers admonished readers not to read his works. In person he was shy and unsure of himself, mysterious, a loner, a disenchanted idealist and a man who frequently walked the tightrope between sanity and insanity, while dealing with the terrifying paradoxes at the center of man's nature—love and hate, justice and injustice, compassion and greed.

Melville spent four months in Hawai'i. However, he spent almost five years in the Pacific, with two of those years in intimate contact with Polynesians in a variety of environments. On August 14, 1843, barely avoiding a confrontation with the ship he had deserted, Melville signed aboard the frigate *United States* and sailed for the port of New York.

•

During the next 12 years Herman Melville wrote and published nine novels; eight were flawed, but one, *Moby Dick*, became a ranking work of American literature. That novel charted his personal development, which ended ultimately in a denial of his art and a prolonged studied silence. Melville's fiction mirrors his tormented genius.

The notices of his death on September 28, 1891 were scarce. *The New York Press* summed up his passing with the observation "Probably, if the truth were known, even his own generation had long thought him dead, so quiet have been the late years of his life."

Chapter Seven

SAMUEL CHENERY DAMON
1842

Father, you spoiled a first class businessman to make a second class preacher.

— Samuel Mills Damon

SAMUEL CHENERY DAMON

Dr. Jonathan Spaulding of the Seaman's Friend Society gave the following instructions to neophyte minister Samuel Chenery Damon on the eve of Damon's departure for Hawai'i: "The special objects of our solicitude, prayers, and efforts will be the sons of the ocean ... you are to stand erect as a minister of Jesus Christ. At Honolulu you will be a citizen still of the land that gave you birth, and entitled to its civil protection. The honor of your country, therefore, as well as Christian and professional considerations will cause you to abstain from all interference with the local and political interests of the people. Never let the preacher of Christ become the partisan of the world."[1]

Writers attest that Samuel Chenery Damon was a man of restless intellect, a man of the cloth who related to Polynesians as equals rather than as inferior beings; a man who led a lost cause for Hawai'i's common man, one who proclaimed he was "a friend of the friendless," and that America was the "emancipator of the enslaved, and the genuine apostle of human freedom." In the mind of Hawai'i's Caucasian establishment and in the mind of many of those who wrote its history, Damon approached impeccability.

On October 6, 1842, pleasant-faced, warm-eyed Samuel Chenery Damon and his pale, hollow-cheeked wife, Julia, brought their goblets together with one extended by Captain Jonathan Spring. Acknowledging his toast to their first wedding anniversary, they appeared weary, having spent more than five sea-tossed months out of

New York. Spring reassured them, "God, tides and trades willing, we will land in Honolulu in less than a fortnight."

Thirteen days later Damon, towering above his fellow passengers at the rail, eyed Honolulu Harbor, where sturdy New England whalers elbowed each other for space. On shore more than 100 of Honolulu's 8,000 residents waved *aloha*. Nearly 600 whites were already established in Honolulu. They controlled 11 wholesale outlets, two auction houses, two hospitals, five hotels, six boarding houses, two pool halls, seven bowling alleys, 12 grog shops, 14 retail stores, and other enterprises such as butcher shops, blacksmiths and tinkers.

Damon recalled the words of his mentor, Hiram Bingham, regarding the salvation of the lowly American sailor, of which more than a thousand would take liberty in Honolulu that year. "Once on shore after a cruise of three or four years, these strangers in a strange land find themselves beset on every hand by brothels and grog shops."[2]

It was in 1842 that President John Tyler, speaking before a joint session of Congress, brought America's interest in Hawai'i into sharper focus. He extended the Monroe Doctrine to include the Sandwich Islands, proclaiming, "They lie in the Pacific Ocean much nearer to this continent than to any other." A newspaper editor in San Francisco labeled Hawai'i as "a luscious pear" and admonished Congress "to pick it before it falls out of reach!" Across the continent in Albany, New York, they celebrated Franklin Pierce's election as President with the expansionist toast, "Cuba and the Sandwich Islands: May they soon be added to the galaxy of states."

When Damon began publishing *The Temperance Advocate and Seaman's Friend* in 1843, it became a clearinghouse for news concerning the Pacific whaling industry and a mail drop for seamen. At that same time, the Reverend Henry T. Cheever, disavowed the need to mourn the passing of the Hawaiians. "... none need be sorry for the occasion that has called forth so convincing a success, which will be none the less real and true though, in the mysterious providence of God, the whole native race expire as it is Christianized."[3]

The Reverend Titus Coan, an impassioned evangelist who set up an assembly line to baptize thousands of Hawaiians in a single day, reported from Hilo that "whale ships are now in, and our streets are alive with sailors ... No man staggers, no man fights, none are noisy and boisterous. We have nothing here to inflame the blood, nothing to madden the brain. Our verdant landscapes, our peaceful streets, our pure cold water, and the absence of those inebriating vials of wrath which consume all good, induce wise commanders to visit this port in order to refresh and give liberty to their crews."[4]

Not so in Honolulu town, where a night seldom passed without a brawl between the missionary-controlled "*kānaka* police" and the rambunctious "blubber heads" of the whaling fleet. Damon implored, "Let not the friends of the cause falter, but lend a hand. Come ye, whalemen, get ready your harpoons and lances, spades and cutting knives, show what you can do! Oh, see well to it, that the old monster does not give you a blow with the flap of his tail, or drag you out of sight of the good temperance ship, at whose main there flies a pennant with the inscription: Death to the Monster Intemperance."[5]

A week later, with 147 square riggers tugging at their anchors in Honolulu Harbor, a Hawaiian jailer clubbed to death a sailor in a prison cell at the fort. Within 48 hours, hundreds of outraged whalers joined ranks in a solemn torchlit funeral procession. Their volatile mood exploded into a riot that left a charred swath through downtown Honolulu. The mariners looted, fought their way to the police station, where, freeing all prisoners, they burned that building to its coral foundation. Terror-stricken missionaries hid in their cellars, praying for deliverance, while other sailors, who preferred life ashore, put the torch to ships of the whaling fleet. Damon never mentioned those same optimistic feelings about his charges again.

CHARLES REED BISHOP

Dapper William Little Lee, a Harvard law graduate, and his handsome friend, Charles Reed Bishop, arrived in Honolulu in the fall of 1846. Both were destined to have enormous influence in shaping the future of the kingdom. Lee, who had given up his law practice in Troy, New York, because of tuberculosis was enroute to Oregon hoping for a more salubrious climate. Bishop, born in Glen Falls, New York, was a descendant of sturdy New England stock, his grandfather having fought for American independence in the Revolution. He came without special educational qualifications and without cash. He was tagging along with his friend Lee, who was headed for the Northwest Territory seeking adventure and fortune. Their ship, the *Henry*, having been severely battered during the longest passage ever recorded around the Horn—231 days—needed major repairs. Damon, who often rowed out into the harbor to hand-deliver copies of *The Friend* to men aboard ship, met the impatient twosome on one such expedition. Upon learning that Lee was a lawyer, he took them to the vestry of his Bethel Church, where Hawai'i's only court of law was in session. Damon quickly introduced Lee to Hawai'i's Minister of Interior, Gerrit P. Judd, who immediately arranged for the appointment of Lee to the Hawaiian bench, where he was to share with Judge Lorrin Andrews jurisdiction over all civil, criminal, admiralty, probate and legal cases coming to trial on the island. Thus, only seven weeks after arriving and at the age of 27, Lee became one of the most powerful men in the kingdom. He would soon "control almost every important action of the government."[6] He was appointed Chief Justice of the newly created Superior Court, selected to serve on the Privy Council, was given the Chairmanship of the Land Commission by Judd, drafted a set of civil and criminal codes for the Legislature, and was elected to a seat in the House of Representatives. In 1852 he did much of the preparation for the drafting of Hawai'i's new Constitution and wrote Article 12, which states "Slavery shall under no circumstances whatever be tolerated in the Hawaiian Islands; whenever a slave shall enter Hawaiian territory, he shall be free." When the document was adopted, he became Chief Justice of the reconstituted Supreme Court and Chancellor of the kingdom.

He also became the highly paid President of the Royal Agriculture Society and, as such, organized and administered a program of contract workers with China and Japan that amounted to little more than rounding up slave labor for his employers, the sugar planters. He regarded the Hawaiian as "Living without exertion, and contented with enough to eat and drink, they give themselves no care for the future, and mope away life, without spirit, ambition or hope."[7]

Meanwhile, Bishop, whose success in Hawai'i was to be even more spectacular than Lee's, took a dollar-a-day job posting books for the financial department of the government. Damon had made yet another fateful introduction possible by arranging, through Judd and Amos Starr Cooke, a meeting between handsome, 25-year-old Bishop and Chiefess Bernice Pauahi Paki, who one day would become heir to the Royal Lands. She was barely 15 years old when she met Bishop at a party at the Cooke home.[8] Those introductions, arranged by Damon, would enhance the financial security of Samuel Chenery Damon and his heirs.

On June 4, 1850, Bishop married 18-year-old Bernice Pauahi in a quiet ceremony at the Royal School. Her parents, whose objections to the mating were loud and well publicized, did not attend.

Within 90 days of the discovery of gold in California, Hawai'i lost more than half of its foreign population to that territory and a severe economic depression engulfed the islands. Two major ports, Monterey and San Francisco, dropped their moorage fees for Pacific whalers and lured many of them away from Honolulu and Lahaina. Damon left for San Francisco in April, 1849, and wrote "It is our intention to embark today ... on board the *U.S. Propeller Massachusetts*, Captain Wood having kindly and generously proffered us a free passage to San Francisco via Oregon ... During our absence the recollections of the many acts of kindness we have received from the residents of Honolulu during a sojourn of six years at the Islands, will serve to hasten our return home."[9]

He traveled to Astoria, Oregon, where he wrote of the transition of the Hudson's Bay Company, "As steam and tide bore us down the stream and I gazed up the hills and forest of Oregon, I endeavored to fix a panoramic view of nature's handiwork upon the tablet of my mind ... I found pleasant reminiscences ... I had witnessed intelligent citizens busy laying the foundations of civil, religious, political and literary institutions which were to bless posterity ... May Oregon become the New England of the Pacific."[10]

A trip up the San Joaquin River led him to Stockton and to Fort Sutter, where California's gold rush had begun earlier that year. There, at a tent camp called "Kanaka Diggings," he found Polynesian 49'ers. "It was ... pleasant to be welcomed by many whom I had known in the Islands. They gathered around us ... as there had been much difficulty between Americans and foreigners in other places, I was desirous of cautioning them to be on their guard and not give offense. I invited all to assemble and about seventy-five made their appearance near a beautiful spring under some excellent shade trees. I endeavored to explain ... the causes of the difficulties. They had sensible inquiries to make."[11]

When General Winfield Scott withdrew his victorious "gringo" troopers from Mexico in 1848 and that war was concluded with the Treaty of Guadalupe Hidalgo, which ceded all of Texas and California to the United States, many teenage American troopers headed west. Damon asked readers of *The Friend* to believe that God was on the side of the American economy. "It is feared that vast multitudes of young men will sadly degenerate in morals by coming to this country. I witness scenes almost every day that are sad. Yet, God reigns. It is no fortuitous circumstance that He has allowed these mines to be opened at just the moment when the American flag was hoisted."[12]

On the return voyage to Honolulu, Damon wrote, using what he called his "double eye," one story version for the readers of *The Friend* and another for his family circle. He confided "One thing is certain, quite certain, I was glad to once more return to this Christian land. Be not surprised that the Sandwich Islands are a Christian land, in comparison with California. This is the profession of even the profane as they land upon our shores. We are glad once more to see a Christian land. Many who arrive remark, 'if we are to die, we are glad to get away from California and to die in a Christian land.'"[13]

•

Early in 1851, the Chaplain, who was fast becoming a partisan of Hawai'i's business and political world, publicized his intention to visit the east coast of the United States. He took the precaution of informing readers of *The Friend* his expenses were to be paid through the "liberality of private friends," not by the Seaman's Friend Society. Although he failed to give his readership a list of those "private friends," the roster of his prosperous flock at Bethel Union Church included Charles and Bernice Bishop, William and Catherine Lee, Doctor and Mrs. Gerrit P. Judd, Theophilus Davies, Samuel Northrup Castle, and Amos Starr Cooke. On the eve of departure, in a nostalgic mood, he took stock of the progress of Honolulu during the eight years of his residency: "We have a new market, new reservoir and aqueduct, new town clock, new stores, new wharves, new fences, new names to our streets, new people and new Athenaeum. Before the year shall end we hope to be able to report that many other new and desirable improvements and changes have been made. The word has gone forth, 'let there be light,' and darkness flies apace. I trust to run with increasing alacrity the Christian race and pursue with higher views and holier aims the calling of a Gospel minister laboring among seamen."[14]

All evidence points to the fact that foreigners were winning the race in Hawai'i. Assuredly, the Hawaiians weren't. Their numbers were diminishing at an alarming rate. In 1853, there were barely 70,000 of them left to be counted.

The Sailor's Home, providing lodging for 75 men in 1856, lent an air of respectability to the whaler in hostile Honolulu town. Because of the communications network established through the "Home," laws protecting the sailors were enacted. Damon elaborated in *The Friend:* "In some respects our laws, regulating ... the discharging and shipping of foreign seamen, might well be copied by other nations ... the disgraceful scenes attending the shipping of seamen elsewhere, are not to be witnessed in Honolulu. It is exceedingly rare for a sailor to be shipped in a state of intoxication. He knows who he is going with, and what money is advanced. He can make his own bargain. I feel proud to make these statements. If a sailor is harshly dealt by, in Honolulu, the fault is his own. Here he may call himself a man, if he chooses. The sailor here has the 'Bethel,' his 'Home,' his 'Hospital,' and his true friends."

Damon continued, "The labors of a seaman's chaplain are such as to require the constant exercise of a strong and vigorous faith. Seamen are the links of that great chain holding the inhabitants of the world together. I have been trying to seek these wandering, impulsive and thoughtless men. I have always found them accessible. I cannot now recall an unkind word from any of them. I love them, and I love the labor for their welfare, temporal and eternal."[16]

Autocratic-appearing Reverend Richard Armstrong, who arrived with the Fifth Missionary Company and became minister of public restoration for Kamehameha III, wrote of the takeover of the government by the American whites in 1844: "Since the restoration, the government has been going more and more into the hands of *natu-*

ralized foreigners ... we have pilots, harbor masters, collector of imports, sheriff and constables, *all* naturalized foreigners. But such is the native character, so deficient in point of intelligence, faithfulness and enterprise in business, that more important affairs, indeed I may say all the important affairs of government are now being administered by these *adopted* foreigners. I must confess that my hopes for the existence and prosperity of the nation, do not rise of late, but rather sink. Foreigners may flock in and take the oath of allegiance and be very zealous for the king and country and all that and still be *foreigners* pursuing their own end and at last break the native to bits, by their squabbles and contentions."[17]

There were fewer than 60,000 Polynesians left when Damon wrote of racial harmony with peace and tranquility, "We shall continue to do so, in our confident belief, if we continue to treat *man as man*, unrespective of color or race; but a war will come when the wicked doctrines of the London Times are allowed to prevail, and the *Anglo-Saxon is allowed to displace an inferior race in the interests of trade* ... under the ameliorating influence of evangelistic effort we rejoice to witness a blending of races ... Now away with all these race antagonisms, convert all to Christ!"[18]

MARK TWAIN
1866

On a certain bright morning the Island hove into sight, lying low in the lonely sea, and everybody climbed to the upper deck to look. After two thousand miles of watery solitude the vision was a welcome one. As we approached, the imposing promontory of Diamond Head rose up out of the ocean, its rugged front softened by the hazy distance, and presently the details of the land began to make themselves manifest first the line of the beach; then the plumed coconut tiles of the tropics; then cabins of the natives; then the white town of Honolulu, said to contain between twelve and fifteen thousand inhabitants, spread over a dead level; with streets from twenty to thirty feet wide, solid and level as a floor, most of them straight as a line and few as crooked as a corkscrew. [19]

— Mark Twain

Mark Twain took his lodgings at the corner of Fort Street and Chaplain Lane in Honolulu, where Samuel and Julia Damon were his closest neighbors. They met the man who would soon become America's most popular writer when he returned from an outer island trip and was, as Twain phrased it, "bedded with boils." The Damons supervised the changing of soothing, steam towels.

Already a seasoned journalist, Twain, with flaming red hair and a drooping mustache, was on his first assignment as a foreign correspondent for the *Sacramento Union*. His intention to visit Hawai'i for a month was soon forgotten. He became enchanted and lingered four months longer. "I look on a multitude of people, some white in white coats, vests, pantaloons, even white cloth shoes, made snowy with chalk duly laid on every morning; but the majority of the people almost are as dark as Negro—women with comely features, fine black eyes, rounded forms, inclined to be voluptuous, clad in single bright red or white garments that fall free and unconfined from shoulder to heel, long black hair falling loose, gypsy hats encircled with wreaths of natural flowers of a brilliant carmine tint; plenty of dark men in various costumes, and some with nothing on but a tattered stove-pipe hat tilted on the nose, and a very scant breech-clout; certain smoke-dried children were clothed in nothing but sunshine—a very neat fitting and picturesque apparel indeed."[20]

An open boat with 15 sailors dying of exposure washed ashore at O'ahu on June 21, 1866. These men from the sunken clipper ship *Hornet* had been adrift at sea for 43 days and had somehow survived the ordeal with rations for less than ten days. Twain, still bedridden, heard the news from Damon and, although in extreme pain, ordered that his cot be carried to the hospital corridor, where he interviewed the castaways, staying awake until morning writing their story which was rushed aboard ship for San Francisco that morning giving Twain the greatest news beat of his life.

Twain left Hawai'i that July and, though he never returned, he reminisced "No alien land in all the world has any deep, strong charm for me but that one, no other land could so lovingly and so beseechingly haunt me, sleeping and waking, through half a lifetime, as that one has done. Other things leave me, but it abides; other things change, but it always remains the same. For its balmy air is always blowing, its summer seas flashing in the sun, the pulsing of its surf-beat in my ear; I can see its garlanded crags, its leaping cascades, its plumey palms drowsing by the shore, its remote summits floating like islands above the cloud rack; I can feel the spirit of its woodland solitudes; I can hear the splash of its brooks; in my nostrils still lives the breath of flowers that perished twenty years ago."[21]

But Twain, whose flowery snippets were to be cribbed by Honolulu hucksters for use in Visitor Bureau ads, whiffed more than blossoms. "The traders brought labor and fancy diseases ... in other words, long, deliberate, infallible destruction, and the missionaries brought the means of grace and got them ready. So the two forces are working harmoniously, and anybody who knows anything about figures can tell you exactly when the last Kanaka will be in Abraham's bosom and his islands in the hands of the whites. No doubt, in fifty years a Kanaka will be a curiosity in his own land . . . "[22]

•

The Damons, with four sons comfortably gathered about them in their rambling house on Chaplain Lane, sat down at a well-laid table to celebrate their silver wedding anniversary. It was October 6, 1866. In less than three years their eldest, Samuel Mills Damon, now 24, would be launched on a financial and political career sponsored by his obliging mentor, Charles Reed Bishop.

Damon, his wife Julia and his 17-year-old son, Frank, arrived at Sacramento in 1869, again, with the "liberality of private friends," to celebrate the driving of the last spike in the ties of America's first transcontinental railroad. Damon, too busy to compose, borrowed a report from the *California Journal* for publication in *The Friend* "The signal which announced to all the laying down of the last rail and the driving of the last spike at Promontory Point was given a shot from the 'Union Boy' and simultaneous blasts from twenty-three locomotives on the levee and the ringing of all the bells in town. This deafening clamor lasted fifteen minutes."

Soon after, the Damons joined a throng of affluent Honolulu friends to experience the first west-to-east trip across the U.S. by rail. They rolled across the Great Plains of America; Omaha, Cedar Rapids, Des Moines, Milwaukee, slicing southward through Illinois to kneel and utter a silent prayer at Lincoln's grave near Springfield and on eastward to Pittsburg ". . . where iron is king, coal is queen, and coal oil is prime minister."[23]

Damon arrived in Boston and found himself in a social melange of America's most celebrated artists and scientists as he attended a gathering to honor Baron Alexander von Humboldt, German naturalist and explorer best known for his work in charting oceanic currents. He spent the afternoon mingling with Ralph Waldo Emerson, poets Longfellow and Lowell, abolitionist Garrison, naturalist Holmes, and orators Wilson and Sumner. Later that evening, and in a more sober mood, he participated in a temperance meeting at Framingham, Massachusetts.

Continuing his travels, Damon crossed the Atlantic and headed for a small village outside London to speak with William Ellis, a retired missionary who was the first white to preach to Hawaiians in their own tongue. Then he boarded a ferry for a quick channel crossing to begin the grand tour of Europe's capital cities, circling the Mediterranean, and finally to the Holy Land for a pilgrimage. "During all of our journeying by land and sea, we experienced no accident or disaster, having traveled by steam from Honolulu to Jerusalem and back, except 35 miles from Jaffa to Jerusalem, which part of our journey we made on horseback."24

Upon his return to Honolulu, Damon remained until May 10, 1876, when he was off again to join nine million Americans on their way to Philadelphia to celebrate the U.S. Centennial. "America has never stood a child among old and storied nations. She has cherished hopes rather than memories; has entrenched herself in forests, not in crumbling feudal castles; has gloried in the birth of the new and honored names, rather than in the luster of a far-off past. But the time of her coronation has come, and from this terraced height all hearts turn back with loyal love to the grand and glorious picture which gleams luminously through the mists of a hundred years. From all lands have come those to do her homage and to lay gifts at her feet, and her children glory in her name."25

Part of that gleaming picture that Damon omitted included the news that the presidency of Ulysses S. Grant was tottering on the edge of a great disaster, barely surviving the corruption-ridden resignations of his Secretaries of War and Treasury. The House of Representatives had already opened a probe into layers of irregularities reeking of reconstruction graft. As Phineas Taylor Barnum put it, "American people like to be humbugged." Damon fell in with fellow Americans swarming over 200 exhibits all powered by a 700-ton Corliss engine. He eyed a Liberty Bell sculptured from tobacco plugs, gazed upon a likeness of George Washington sporting a wig made from the hair of Simon Bolivar, ran his hand across the keyboard of a newly invented typewriter, squinted before the glare of a lamp powered by electricity, and heard six voices carried over a wire. He lined up, paid a nickel fare, boarded a narrow gauge railroad car and rode through 400 acres of exhibits breezing along at eight miles per hour.

There were daily parades, with marching bands and torchlight processions flickering through the county-fair atmosphere. Damon turned away, shocked by the nudity on display in the Main Building Art Gallery, and listened, sitting on the steps, to a scathing sermon against immorality delivered by a fellow minister.

He failed to record his reaction to the Indian exhibit in the U.S. Government Building, where "official policies" regarding aboriginal Americans were rationalized and a pair of handstitched moccasins made out of the tanned hide of a real Indian were pointed out amid giggles. A reporter for *Atlantic Magazine* exclaimed, "The Red Man was a hideous demon whose traits could inspire no emotion but abhorrence."

The strains of "Yankee Doodle," "The Battle Hymn of the Republic," and the exhortations of the Generals Sherman and Sheridan were still echoing along Philadelphia's cobblestones when the news of Little Big Horn rocked the exhibition. Lieutenant Colonel George

Custer, known to the Sioux as Yellow Hair and to his own men as Iron Butt, and 213 of his men were dead as the result of a succession of lethal charges by the Sioux and Cheyenne. Later, historian Thomas B. Marquis would blame the demise of so many soldiers on the prevailing misconceptions of the red man which infected Custer's troopers, "... generated by various selfish interests to create racial hatred that would excuse the greedy encroachments of the white men and would justify the killing of an Indian. Indians were diabolical." Marquis concludes that the popular frontier slogan, "when fighting the Indians, keep the last bullet for yourself," became the basis of a suicidal panic among Custer's men. "That panic," wrote Marquis, "triggered by the stampede of their horses spooked by the fearsome whoops of Sitting Bull's painted warriors, conjured up the horrors of excruciating torture, causing some frightened soldiers to turn Enfield and Colt barrels to their own temples."*

When Damon returned to Honolulu, he headlined the fact that the Centennial was a force for good because its directors had closed its gates on the Sabbath.

Four years later, Damon and Julia boarded the *City of Sydney* on February 16, 1880, bound for San Francisco and points east. After enjoying a whirl among friends atop Nob Hill, they entrained for New York. Upon arrival, they scurried off to New England, where they were especially delighted by a sleigh ride over a spring blanket of crusty snow. Back in New York they mounted the gangplank of the *City of Berlin*—destination Liverpool. They rested for a month in England, while enjoying the countryside. Renewing their journey, they sailed across the North Sea to Holland, there boarding a train and then a riverboat to explore the roots of their protestant ancestors in Dresden, Halle, Wittenberg, Gotha, Leipzig, Prague, Vienna, Salzburg and Munich. By November they were back in San Francisco, rushing to board a Honolulu-bound ship.

In 1884, Damon set out on what was to be his final journey. Arriving in Canton, China, on May 1 to witness the marriage of his son Frank to the daughter of an American missionary, he combined business with pleasure by negotiating with Chinese warlords on the price of coolie labor for Hawai'i's canefields. He then boarded a ship at Hong Kong and steamed through the East China Sea enroute to the port of Yokohama. While ashore there, he tied up the ends of a contract labor agreement between Japanese officials and the friends he represented among Hawai'i's sugar planters. He returned to Honolulu late that same year, and on his heels came Hawai'i's first Japanese indentured laborers.

---

*Marquis, *Keep The Last Bullet For Yourself*, 1976.

Samuel Chenery Damon was described by his granddaughter and principal biographer—who destroyed his diary after reading it—as a "godly person above the influence of materialistic considerations." Perhaps he should also be remembered as the man who brought together the whites who successfully contrived to wrest control of the land from the Hawaiians.

He was laid to rest on February 7, 1885.

CHAPTER EIGHT

KAMEHAMEHA III

We do not wish that foreigners be allowed to take the oath of allegiance and become Hawaiians...if the Kingdom is to be ours, what is the good of filling the land with foreigners?

— David Malo

THE LITTLE KING

By 1837, Kamehameha III and his royal advisors found themselves as sitting ducks for itinerant warships. The narrowness of missionary views regarding the spread of Christianity in the islands was a contributing factor.

The French, with a few priests converting Hawaiians to the Roman Catholic faith, became an irritant to Hiram Bingham and Gerrit P. Judd, who, as royal advisors, drafted and persuaded Kamehameha III to issue an ordinance rejecting Roman Catholicism. "Therefore, I with my chiefs, forbid ... that anyone should teach the peculiarities of the Pope's religion, nor shall it be allowed to anyone who teaches those doctrines or those peculiarities to reside in this Kingdom; nor shall the ceremonies be exhibited in our Kingdom, nor shall anyone teaching its peculiarities or its faith be permitted to land on these shores; for it is not proper that two religions be found in this small Kingdom. Therefore, we utterly refuse to allow anyone to teach those peculiarities in any manner whatsoever. We moreover prohibit all vessels whatsoever from bringing any teacher of that religion into this Kingdom."[1]

The French ordered their frigate *L'artemise,* under the command of Captain C.P.T. Laplace, to Honolulu. Laplace arrived on July 9, 1839, with orders to "... apply yourself to destroy the malevolent impression which you find established to the detriment of the French name; to rectify the erroneous opinion which has been created as to the power of France; and to make it well understood that it will be altogether to the advantage of the chiefs of those islands of the Ocean to conduct themselves in such a manner as not to incur the wrath of France."[2]

Laplace demanded, under the threat of war, that Catholic worship be declared free; that a site for a Catholic church in Honolulu be given to the priests by the king; that all imprisoned Catholics be set free; that the king put up $20,000 as a guarantee of future conduct toward France; that the king sign the treaty with the batteries of Honolulu saluting the Tricolor with twenty-one guns. With the assistance of some Honolulu merchants who supplied the cash, Kamehameha III, heeding the advice of the white ministers, quickly complied with all French demands.

At that same time, David Malo, a native Hawaiian historian who is regarded as the great authority and repository of Hawaiian lore, wrote to his king from Maui, "I have been thinking that you ought to hold frequent meetings with all the chiefs ... to seek for that which will be of the greatest benefit to this country ... This is the reason. If a big wave comes in, large fishes will come from the dark Ocean which you never saw before, and when they see the small fishes they will eat them up. The ships of the white men have come, and smart people have arrived from the great countries which you have never seen before, they know our people are few in number and living in a small country; they will eat us up, such has always been the case with large countries, the small ones have been gobbled up ... Therefore get your servant ready who will help when you need him."[3]

Since Kamehameha III was the first Hawaiian king educated by the missionaries from the beginning of his childhood, he constantly faced the problem of living in two worlds: In his native Hawaiian world he would have been permitted, even encouraged, to marry his sister Nohi'ena'ena, and the other Western Christian world forbade such unions, as well as drinking alcoholic beverages, dancing the *hula* or surfing on the waves. Caught between the two, he became a vacillator and was miserable.

Because of the fear of a takeover by a power other than America and the knowledge that a legal document was necessary for the maintenance of a Yankee business community, Hawai'i gave birth to a constitution. The document conceived by Judd and Reverend William Richards was eased from the passive Hawaiian womb by frock-coated midwives. On October 8, 1840, Kamehameha III signed a 64-page Constitution into law. It gave Hawai'i a plan for its government and defined the authority and responsibility of its various officials. It stated that no law could be enacted which was at variance with the word of God and that there should be complete freedom in the matter of religion. The French, it seemed, had made their point.

The Constitution also declared that every innocent person injured by another should have redress and all who were convicted of a crime should be punished after a lawful trial. It included a foreign interpretation of Hawai'i's land ownership through "the principles on which the present dynasty is founded." It elaborated, "The origin of the present government is as follows: Kamehameha was the founder of the Kingdom, and to him belonged all the land from one end of the Islands to the other, though it was not his own private property. It belonged to the chiefs and people in common, of whom Kamehameha I was the head, and had the management of the landed property. Wherefore, there was not formerly, and is not now any person who could or can convey away the smallest portion of the land without the consent of the one who had, or has, the direction of the Kingdom. These are the persons who have had the direction of it from that time down, Kamehameha II, Ka'ahumanu I, and at the present time, Kamehameha III. These persons have had the direction of the kingdom down to the present time, and all documents written by them, and no others, are the documents." The king's white advisors had drafted a constitution that assigned all land ownership directly to him. Since these Hawaiian-speaking advisors were in position to manipulate the king, their efforts represented the first legal step to gain control of Hawaiian land.[4]

By 1845 there were ugly rumblings among the Hawaiians regarding the king's policy of filling all important high offices with white men. A missionary-physician at Lahaina, Maui, Dr. Dwight Baldwin, became alarmed and asked the king's principal land advisor, The Reverend William Richards, about the situation. "But what strange doings have you had at O'ahu? Something seems to have stirred the natives to the bottom ... there has been a meeting here and is to be another today to draw up a petition to the National Council. I know not what was done at the meeting—nor what is to be done today—but I am told the object is to bring about 'no *haole* rulers.' The natives requested me to attend the meeting—but I excused myself, saying it was a political meeting, very proper for them to engage in—but our work is more exclusively with the gospel."[5]

The Lahaina group, with David Malo as their spokesman, pressed their case with the king, who, in turn, played billiards with the traders in the afternoon, sang hymns with the missionaries in the evening and, through it all, stayed tipsy on cognac. "We do not wish that foreigners be allowed to take the oath of allegiance and become Hawaiians ... if the Kingdom is to be ours, what is the good of filling the land with foreigners? ... what will be the end of these numerous cases of the oath of allegiance being taken by foreigners? This is our opinion; to give up this Kingdom to them and to give it up quickly too. Foreigners come here with their properties in dollars; they are prepared to buy the land; but we have no property; a people unprepared are we; the native man is palsied like a man long ailing in the back. We have lived under the rulers, expecting to do according to their wish, and not often our own notions; and for this cause, we are not ready to be set adrift to strive with the foreigners ... If a good thing, let the coming of foreigners into this country be delayed for ten more years perhaps, and let there be given to us lands with the understanding that they are to be cultivated and have cattle raised upon them, and so perhaps we shall lose our present palsy, and it will be good perhaps to encourage foreigners to enter the country."[6]

No moratorium on land ownership by foreigners was declared by Kamehameha III. Instead, he appointed a committee, whose chairman and most persuasive members were whites. "Our opinion is that it is by no means proper to sell any piece of land to aliens, or to give them lands ... but we think that land should not be sold to the subjects of His Majesty lest they should wander away .... It is right to sell some land to nations, it is also right to sell some to naturalized foreigners in order that they may cultivate together and the skillful ones teach him who is less skillful."[7]

In April, 1846, Kamehameha III gave his answer to Malo's Lahaina militants by announcing his new cabinet appointments. They included Robert C. Wyllie as Minister of Foreign Affairs, Gerrit P. Judd as Minister of Finance, William Richards as Minister of Public Instruction, and John Ricord as Attorney General. All "naturalized foreigners," these gentlemen, holding the advantage over a king who was more often drunk than sober, were already into the second phase of negotiating landownership for whites. From that day forward, David Malo, and the Hawaiians he spoke for, referred to Kamehameha III as "The Little King."

Soon the whites on Oʻahu would package their "land reform" product and put it on the market, with a label reading *The Great Mahele.*[8]

CHAPTER NINE

GERRIT PARMELE JUDD
1845

How can you buy or sell the sky, the warmth of the land?

The idea is strange to us. We do not own the freshness of the air or the sparkle of the water. How can you buy them from us? Every part of the earth is sacred to my people. Every shiny pine needle, every sandy shore, every mist in the dark woods, every clearing and humming insect is holy in the memory and experience of my people.

We know that the white man does not understand our ways. One portion of the land is the same to him as the next, for he is a stranger who comes in the night and takes from the land whatever he needs. The earth is not his brother, but his enemy, and when he has conquered it, he moves on. He leaves his fathers' graves, and his children's birthright is forgotten.

There is no quiet place in the white man's cities. No place to hear the leaves of spring or the rustle of insect wings. But, perhaps, because I am a savage and do not understand, your clatter only seems to insult the ears. And what is there to life if a man cannot hear the lovely cry of the whippoorwill or the arguments of the frog around the pond at night?

— Authorship disputed*

GERRIT PARMELE JUDD

Dr. Gerrit P. Judd chose a frontal approach to the issue of land for whites in 1845, when, as Minister of Interior, he recommended the appointment of a Commission to Quiet Land Titles. This Commission, under its President, the Reverend William Richards, met to study all claims to lands and to reverse its opinion, which per-

---

* Best evidence available found in *Uncommon Controversy*, report: University of Washington Press, 1970, p. 29.

mitted all Hawaiian subjects, both native and foreign born, to purchase land "as freehold property forever."

Judd, the individual most responsible for Hawai'i's "Land
Reform," was born on April 23, 1803, at Paris Hills, New York. His
father, Elnathan Judd, was a country doctor and a deacon in his
church. Elnathan and his 19-year-old bride, Betsy Hastings, the
daughter of a Connecticut physician, were among the first pioneers to
trek westward into the green-carpeted, black-soiled Hudson and
Mohawk valleys, where he soon became the leading medical practi-
tioner in a frontier community, setting broken limbs amid shrieks of
pain, doubling in dentistry and delivering babies for a fee of three
dollars. Established, respected, confident and bursting with pride,
Elnathan reached his forty-ninth year, when he was publicly accused
of sexual misconduct with three young women. Two were medical
patients and the third, a 13-year-old servant girl who helped Betsy
with household chores. He was brought to trial and, although the
church committee which heard the case acquitted him, they admonished him from the pulpit. "We do think facts proved which amount
to imprudent and unguarded conduct and that brother Judd be, and is
hereby admonished to be, more on his guard in similar
circumstance."* Gerrit was 20 years old at the time.

The censure sent Elnathan into a fit of rage. He and Betsy
packed necessities and fled that disgraceful episode in the mist of
prairie schooner dust, finding refuge in Troy, Michigan. Three years
later Elnathan died.

Gerrit, who remained in New York became a member of his
debating team and on one occasion he chose to uphold the negative
on the question, "Ought imprisonment for debt be abolished?" His
righteous eloquence on shipping defaulting debtors off to jail helped
his side to victory. His rhetoric was not deterred by his knowledge
that his grandfather had spent three miserable years in a colonial
debtor's cell.

Bruised by his father's conduct, Gerrit struggled to regain his
composure as he joined the Young Republicans of Paris Hills. Later
that same year, the College of Physicians & Surgeons at Fairfield,
New York, awarded him a medical degree. Soon he experienced the
full fervor of an evangelistic exposure and took his place in line with
500 other sheet-shrouded souls to be plunged into the chill waters of the
Housatonic River. "I came to the determination," he explained 20 years later,
"to devote myself to the works of a missionary among the heathen."**

Although doctors were in scarce supply and Judd longed to be
a full-time disciple of Christ, the American Board of Commissioners
for Foreign Missions received his application and promptly "mis-

* See Henry Adams, *History of...*, I-3. Also, Daniel Wager, *Our Country...*, pp. 90, 144.
** G.P. Judd, Journal, May 13, 1843.

placed" it. After waiting six months for a reply, Judd confided to his journal, "I am so wicked that it seems impossible that I can ever be of any use in the works of the Lord."[1]

When he pursued his objective by pleading his case in person, he was finally accepted as a probationary candidate and enthused: "If God be for us, who be against us?"[2] Upon the order of his superiors to change his marital status, Judd began a lightning courtship of Laura Fish and exchanged wedding vows with her on September 20, 1827, at Clinton, New York. She would bear him nine children.

Two weeks later, the Third Missionary Company, including the Judds, five other missionary couples, four missionary maidens, and four young Hawaiians returning home, sailed from Boston on the *Parthian*. The Missionary Board made advance payment of $100 a head for the passage of the missionaries, with the Hawaiians being carried at $50 a head. Precut material for two frame houses, a printing press, type, paper and 40,000 copies of an elementary Bible tract in Hawaiian language were also shipped for an additional $700 fee.

Early in January a severe storm hit the east coast of Argentina, near the port of Santa Cruz. Laura reported, "Yesterday about noon, the wind shifted. The sky darkened and there was every appearance of a tremendous gale. I was on deck. Capt. Blinn says, 'Boys not a moment to lose.' Things on deck were lashed with double caution; sails taken in or reefed closely. Orders were given and obeyed with the greatest alacrity, and many a fearful and anxious glance was cast to that part of the horizon where the storm was gathering. I remained on deck as long as my sensitive nerves could endure it. About 3 o'clock, I went below and the hatchways were closed, the dead light put on and the cabin converted into a perfect prison.

"The timbers creaked and groaned like human beings in dying agonies. Three thunder showers followed each other in rapid succession, accompanied with lightning ... that ... almost blinded me. Once between the gusts of wind I could distinguish the Captain's voice giving orders. About midnight the little green boat that we left the wharf in, was carried away and the railing on the side of the ship to which it was lashed with sixteen of our chairs in it; ... it seems as if the ship must rock to pieces. Never before did I feel so much the exceeding weakness and impotency of human will and human skin."[3] As a result of being hurled across the deck and slammed against a bulkhead during that storm, Laura lost the baby she was carrying. According to Gerrit, the crew then formed a raucous chorus and "...amused themselves in ridiculing us in the most vociferous tones, the most profane, obscene and vulgar songs."*

Near the end of that harrowing voyage, Judd and his brethren

---

* Judd, Gerrit, P., Diary 1827 - 28 *Fragments III.*

went over the line of patience and reportedly became a menace to the captain and the crew. American commercial agent John Coffin Jones, Jr., wrote to *Parthian* owner Josiah Marshall: "A more unwelcome cargo was never brought .... Captain Blinn was apprehensive at one time that they would take command of the ship from him and got his arms in readiness to protect himself." He continued, "I believe it is a fact ... that the natives are fifty percent worse off in every vice since the missionaries began their hypocritical labour here; these blood-suckers of the community had much better be in their native country gaining their living by their brow, than living like lords in this luxuri-ous land, distracting the minds of these children of nature with the idea that they are to be eternally damned unless they think and act as they do; and would that Providence put a whip in every honest hand to lash such rascals naked through the world."[4]

When the cloud-brushed mountains of Oʻahu poked into view on Sunday, March 30, 1828, the *Parthian's* passengers and crew crowded the rail. They heard the tolling of the church bell across Honolulu Harbor as Christians ashore were being called to worship. "... some rushed below to their staterooms to pour out their hearts in gratitude and thanksgiving, others fear to turn away lest the scene fade or prove a delusion, like our dreams of homeland, some exhaust their vocabulary in the exclamations of delight—others sit alone in tears and silence."[5]

Laura saw "Honolulu ... a mass of brown huts, looking pre-cisely like so many haystacks in the country; not one white cottage, no church spire, not a garden, nor a tree to be seen save the grove of coconuts ... the thatched church was browsed all the way around, as high up as wandering goats and cows could reach, giving it a ragged look." Eyeing the huts, Gerrit remarked that "they looked like pig styes rather than houses."[6]

Hiram Bingham, who was being rowed to the *Parthian*, looked "careworn and feeble." As to the city, nothing could be less attractive. James Jackson Jarves described it: "Conceive a thousand or more thatched huts, looking like geometrical haystacks, most of them low and filthy in the extreme, scattered higgledy-piggledy over a plain, and along the banks of a scanty river, surrounded in general with dilapidated mud walls, and inhabited by a mixed population of curs, pigs ... poultry, and unwashed natives ... a most disagreeable, filthy place where you are subjected to sights, which would make any city lady blush fifty times a day."[7]

The Judds waited out the Sabbath aboard ship. Coming ashore the next morning, they followed near-naked Hawaiians bearing their meager possessions to the already-crowded house of Hiram and Sybil Bingham. They would reside there for the next seven years.

Upon the death of Kaʻahumanu in 1832, Kamehameha III

became sole ruler. He was 17 years old and enthusiastic. "The young king threw off the restraint of his elders," Laura noted, "and abandoned himself to intemperance and debauchery ... vile, heathen songs, games and shameless dance, which had gone out of use, were revived. Rum and wretchedness became rampant; and the quiet of our lovely dells and valleys was disturbed with bacchanalian shouts and the orgies of drunken revelry."[8]

With the death of their benefactor, Ka'ahumanu, and the return to Hawaiian ways by the young king, the takeover of Hawai'i by the American missionaries faltered. They realized the need for a powerful new sponsor who could be persuaded to share their aspirations and objectives. Without such a person, their mission would fail. But Judd, ashore barely a month, had already found such a potential patron in the course of performing his services as a physician. Her name was Kīna'u. She had been one of the wives of Kamehameha II and was a half sister of the reigning monarch. When Judd first explored the feasibility of using her to further the missionary cause, he was discouraged to discover that she held neither title nor power. He outlined a plan for her to follow in order to obtain both. "Our arguments convinced her. By our advice, she presented herself to the king and claimed her rights, which were acknowledged, and she was in due time proclaimed as *Kuhina*."[9]

Three years later, through his skillful manipulation of Kīna'u, Judd became principal advisor to the king. The missionaries were welcomed back to the royal court because the king "... trusts Kīna'u his half sister with the reins, she is entirely governed by the American missionaries who through her govern the Islands with unlimited sway."[10]

Not only did Kīna'u favor the American missionaries, but she did her utmost to enhance their position under Judd's guidance by making it almost impossible for any other religion to gain a foothold in Hawai'i. She bickered with her half brother, Kamehameha III, who was pulling in the direction of the past, trying to return to the customs of his ancestors, while she wanted the penal laws, introduced by the whites, strictly enforced and also demanded the *hula* be banned again. Kamehameha III wanted power returned to the monarchy and bitterly regretted having acknowledged her claim to the regency. At the same time, she aggressively sought more power for herself, which would further the aims of the missionaries.

For the second time in the short period of Hawai'i's western history, a bible-thumping missionary had strengthened his political position by bringing state and church closer together through the manipulation of a naive royal female. Even though they were violating a cardinal principle of their homeland by merging state and church, these American missionaries supported the United States whenever it suited their purpose. Events would soon change their allegiance to the U.S. The role of the American missionary in Hawai'i would have been impotent had it not been for the zealous support of such royal women as Ka'ahumanu and Kīna'u.

Soon after their arrival and with Bingham's tutelage, Gerrit and Laura Judd became proficient in the Hawaiian language. Judd became the Royal Physician and Official Interpreter of the Kingdom. This gave him easy access to those who dispensed power. Laura noted, "As Dr. Judd was not a clergyman, and had been the medical attendant and personal friend of the royal family, it was natural that they should often apply to him."11

In 1841, the High Chiefess Kapi'olani,who defied the volcano goddess *Pele,* causing tens of thousands of Big Islanders to convert, submitted to surgery that Judd termed severe. He removed her right breast without anesthesia. According to one among the assembled crowd of onlookers, she "uttered neither cries or groans." Judd reported, "Almost six weeks after the operation, deeming my attendance no longer necessary, I gave her permission to visit Maui ... In preparation for leaving, she took a long walk in the heat of day, which brought on a pain in her side. The next day she visited each of the missionaries at their houses ... Erysipelas now made its appearance, which after two or three days affected the brain by matastosis [sic] and she sunk away into palsy and death."12

In a moment of compassion, the physician continued, "The state of the natives, too, cries for help. They are fast decreasing in numbers. Go where we may we find the poor improvident creatures left to suffer on a sick and perhaps dying bed. The native doctors are a miserable set of quacks who often shorten the lives of their patients by their remedies."13

Hawai'i's first Polynesian language book on anatomy was published that same year by Judd. The somber doctor frequently gave free medical aid, even to those among the foreigners whom he considered to be enemies of the faith. Three sailors fell from the rigging of a ship. "We found one just where he fell—his thigh fractured, the bone driven through the flesh, his chin injured and several of his teeth knocked out. Another with a fracture of the ribs, and the third much bruised but no bones broken. We dressed them as well as we could and brought one of them ashore. He is lying in a grog shop ... somewhat deranged and in a very critical state."14

James Jackson Jarves, a close personal friend of the Judd family and editor of the government organ, *The Polynesian,* whose salary and budget were controlled by Finance Minister Judd, praised his superior, "I have seen the same individual perform skillful surgical operations, practice medicine extensively, plough and direct natives in the culture of their farms, build the stone walls, and raise the massive roof of a church, a tinker and a carpenter at home, a music teacher and a school master, an interpreter for government, a translator for foreigners in drawing up deeds, in fact, an adept in every good and useful work, whether medical or manual."[15] Jarves, along with William Little Lee, would be among the select few who survived the entire reign of Judd.

•

The visit in 1842 of Sir George Simpson, Governor of Hudson's Bay Company, opened the way for Judd to become the most powerful white in the islands. Judd introduced Simpson to Kamehameha III and then joined with Sir George in urging the king to make treaties with the United States, Britain and France, guaranteeing Hawai'i's sovereignty. The king agreed and commissioned High Chief Ha'alilio and the Reverend William Richards to carry out this diplomatic mission. Before he sailed for London, Simpson, in return, persuaded the king to appoint Judd as political advisor to the throne. His elevation caused rumblings among his clerical brethren, who were all officially barred from governmental activities by their Boston headquarters "You are to abstain from all interference with the local and political interests of the people. The Kingdom of Christ is not of this world, and it especially behooves a missionary to stand aloof from the private and transient interests of chiefs and rulers." Judd resigned from the mission, explaining "It is impossible for me to express to you the deep anxiety I feel for the young government of these Islands. I have unaware been drawn into the deepest assimilation of all my interests with theirs, and ready to sacrifice everything for the welfare of the nation."[16]

Aside from his "concern over the young government of these Islands," there is another highly probable reason why Judd withdrew from the mission. Earlier he had accepted a cash payment of $700 from U.S. Naval Commander Allen Wilkes for medical services rendered. Since Judd had sworn a sacred oath to engage in a nonprofit religious endeavor and had used mission medical supplies in earning the fee, his fellow missionaries objected when he pocketed that cash and claimed it was not church property, but his own.[17] His new appointment provoked stinging criticism. Stephen Reynolds, an American trader, dubbed him, "King Judd, who rides us down to the dust. We have not mercy to expect of him. The King is nothing—nobody. Judd orders him as you would a boy."[18]

British Consul Alexander Simpson became so irate with Judd that he challenged him to a duel, which Judd declined. Simpson labeled him as "narrow and illiberal" and added that Judd "rode roughshod over residents, chiefs and people. Thus did individuals who came out for the avowed purpose of teaching the religion of the meek and lowly Jesus use the influence which they had acquired for the furtherance of their own ambitious purposes."19

Fellow missionaries registered their disapproval of the "underhanded" method Judd had used to attain his new position. Barely a week before his new appointment, Judd, who had already organized a company to establish a sugar plantation and mill near Honolulu for private profit, wrote to the American Missions Board in Boston, masking his intentions of becoming prime minister "I'm plodding on in my new and strange course much better than I had feared I would. Our troubles are not yet over with either England or France, but I think the day is dawning, and trust my watch will soon be over. Astonishing changes seem to be at hand in these Islands, for good no doubt in the end."20

Astonishing changes in the ownership of Hawaiian land were indeed at hand, and Judd would play a stellar role in bringing them about.

THE MAHELE
1848

On March 9, 1844, Judd mounted a platform at Hawai'i's Supreme Court, along with Chief Justice Lee and Charles Reed Bishop, where they each took a solemn oath renouncing their United States citizenship and then another "swearing everlasting allegiance to the Kingdom of Hawai'i." Lee administered the vow to his benefactor Judd and then to Bishop. Changing places with Judd on the platform, Lee then raised his own right hand over the Bible, as Judd somberly administered the oath to him. They were anticipating a law which would make whites eligible to acquire land in Hawai'i. They would soon complete the drafting of that law and carefully lobby it through the Judd-controlled Legislature and then persuade the Little King into declaring it the law of the land.

As the heretofore man of quiet tastes, somber moods and drab shades settled comfortably into his newly won prime ministership, Judd took on the accoutrements of royalty.* He ordered his own coat of arms designed in Paris. When it arrived, he set up a ceremony wherein Kamehameha III presented it to him amid the blare of a dozen court trumpets and ringing applause. When Judd appeared at official functions attired in a vivid blue coat with gold insignia, white vest and trousers and the plumed hat of a field marshall, he regularly received 17-gun salutes as he alighted from his gilt-encrusted, plush brocade coach, which once carried Queen Victoria. Within a year of

---

Hawaii: An Informal History, G. P. Judd IV, p. 70.

assuming government control, Judd appointed 14 cooperating whites and two Hawaiians to his cabinet. In his eleven year "reign", 48 whites held cabinet-level positions. The Hawaiian became all but invisible.

When his missionary friends criticized him for renouncing his U.S. citizenship and leaving the church, he withdrew all financial support by the Hawaiian government from their projects until they, too, renounced their U.S. citizenship.[21] This brought admonishment from Judd's senior, Reverend Artemas Bishop, "Keep humble, Brother Judd, cultivate a spirit of prayer and meekness and be diffident of self esteem, and I will not doubt of your eminent usefulness in the midst of the temptations that surround you."[22]

When the news of Judd's bill, which made clear that land ownership would be reserved for citizens of Hawai'i only, leaked out three days before its passage in the Legislature, it caused a stampede of missionaries, including the Reverend Artemas Bishop, who suddenly decided to renounce their "much treasured" U.S. citizenship.

Judd began to suffer physical ailments, thought to be "contradictions within his mind." He heard bells when none were ringing and experienced loud uncontrollable giggling during solemn occasions of state. He wrote, "The transactions of government are becoming daily more complicated and intricate. Those affecting foreigners are quite sufficient to engage the individual attention of one man, and those affecting the interior administration of the Kingdom another; yet much of both devolve upon me, and thus I am overborne with mental and physical labor and anxiety."[23]

One can almost hear the bells pealing in Judd's head when his presence was required at Hawai'i's lusty royal court. Kamehameha III was renowned among his subjects and notorious among the missionaries for his merry-go-round sex life. His promiscuousness extended from close relatives to lesser subjects to foreigners and, it was rumored, even to a fallen missionary wife.

Judd vowed to change the flow of Hawai'i's sexual river. Robert C. Wyllie, a Scot who was about to become Hawai'i's new Minister of Foreign Relations, noted Judd's hidden reason for wanting to change that court: "From the numerical predominance of Americans in this community, Mr. Judd fears a growing tendency toward Republicanism, which he believes to be incompatible with the welfare of the islands, and which he considers it his duty to the King to resist. Hence arises his wish to establish some sort of Royal Etiquette, and that the King's administratives should be made respectable in the eyes of both foreigners and natives."[24]

Judd lost the sight of his left eye to a cataract in 1845 and, by spring of that year, he had relinquished his Foreign Relations chair to Wyllie while remaining Minister of Interior. He had by now created enemies among all levels of society and all ethnic groups. He insulted the French, English, Scots, Polynesians, Germans and the Russians, and did not spare his own countrymen. Each, in turn, savaged him when given the opportunity. Charles Brewer, an American trader, branded Judd and his cabinet favorites as being "arrogant and oppressive in the extreme toward all foreigners, and should they not be checked soon, it will be intolerable to reside here." Brewer called Judd a "damned rascal, who is extremely unpopular with the residents in general." He questioned Judd's competence, saying "government offices never were in more confusion."[25]

A French-born Irishman, Guillaume Patrice Dillon, who became French Consul to Hawai'i in 1843, viewed Judd as "... a narrow-minded little American from whom no Frenchman could ever obtain justice." The dashing young English lord, George Paulet, to the king, "I have to state that I shall hold not communications whatever with Dr. G. P. Judd, who it has been satisfactorily proved to me has been the punic mover in the unlawful proceedings of your government against British subjects." On New Year's Day, 1845, Judd reached the height of self-congratulation, when he proclaimed to a friend in Boston, "You must know that I am at present the King Bingham of the Sandwich Islands."[26]

When the Legislature convened later that year, Judd stood on the podium at the right hand of Kamehameha III, as the king haltingly read the speech propped up before him. When he faltered and moved his eyes toward Judd, the evangelistic politician prompted the monarch without referring to the text of the speech. U.S. Commissioner Anthony Ten Eyck commented, "The King and his native chiefs are mere automatons in the hands of his ministers ... I think of Dr. Judd as a man of ordinary talents, ambitious, fond of power, self willed and one that allows his personal feelings to control his public acts."[27]

Judd was ready to launch land reform. He read his first report as Minister of the Interior to the Legislature in May, 1845, urging "Commissioners be appointed to inquire into and determine the validity of all titles to lands and houses." He also pleaded for a review of the entire land tenure system. The Legislature followed his recommendation by passing the laws that Judd wanted. Also established was the Board of Commissioners to Quiet Land Titles, with Judd hand-picking its chairman, Chief Justice Lee; its president, the Reverend William Richards; and its directors, Attorney General John Ricord and Hawaiians James Young Kanehoa, John 'I'i and Z. Ka'auwai. Lee described the setting: "The Commission met in an old grass house, floored with mats, without benches, seats or comforts of any kind, with one corner partitioned off with calico, for judges office, clerks office, police court and jury room. On many occasions, Dr. Judd acted sole judge in land disputes."[28] In that setting,

Judd's Commission, which was to divide Hawai'i's land equitably among royalty, chiefs, commoners and whites, was ready to begin its work. Judd exclaimed, "There was no one but myself who had the knowledge and if I may say the resolution, to act efficiently. I therefore volunteered my services to the King, and on the condition of his appointing as my fellow-laborers those whom I named, pledged myself to make the division."

The first reported results of the Commissioner's labors surfaced at the end of 1847. Within 41 days there were recorded the initial divisions of lands between the king and 251 chiefs, including six persons with non-Hawaiian surnames. Each chief set aside land parcels for his or her exclusive ownership and signed a statement giving up any right formerly held in other parcels. The king did likewise with a list of land under his name. As recorded in the *Mahele Book*, the lists of lands named for each chief became the basis for awards made later by the Board of Commissioners to Quiet Land Titles, the King's Lands and the land later called Crown Lands.

The *Mahele Book* is a record of the division of land between the king and 251 chiefs. These are not strictly Land Commission awards. In order to obtain Land Commission awards claimed in the *Mahele Book*, the chiefs had yet to go to the Land Commission, present their claims and turn over to the government a portion of their land in return for fee simple ownership.

One of these awards, curiously dated 10 months before anyone was eligible to acquire land, gave Dr. G. P. Judd fee simple title to a Nu'uanu Valley tract of 7.61 acres. Judd paid $50 for his first parcel of choice land.

Judd's great land grab had begun in earnest. Certainly no other event in the history of the kingdom had such shattering political, social and economic effect upon Hawai'i's few surviving Polynesians. In one sense, it plunged Hawai'i's commoners back to feudalism, since the white man was soon to have control over their lands and their lives. There is no record of a missionary speaking out regarding the hypocrisy of preaching moral values to the Hawaiians on Sunday and then acquiring their land during the rest of the week. In less than four years, after having created the laws that made it possible for certain whites to own Hawaiian land, 16 prominent members of the Congregational Mission had acquired title to 7,888 prime acres on O'ahu. The average acreage privately owned in fee simple by these leading disciples of Christ was 493 acres each.

Judd spoke before the Legislature: "It is the wish of His Majesty ... so to improve the tenure and leasing of land as may facilitate its acquisition by the poorer classes, secure a proper reward for their industry, and encourage population by enabling them to provide for and derive profit for their children.[29] He demonstrated his con-

cern for the common class of Hawaiians by slicing up Hawai'i's land
as follows: From a total land mass of 6,415 square miles, or more
than four million acres, the Crown Lands received somewhat less
than 1,000,000 acres; Government Land, nearly 1,500,000 acres;
Chief's Lands, a little more than 1,500,000 acres; the common people's land less than 30,000 acres."[30] Approximately 8,750 Hawaiian
commoners were to receive title to about 28,600 acres, or an average
of 3.5 acres each.* Judd received personal fee simple title to 22 prime
acres in Waikiki, 2,184 rolling acres at Hana, Maui, and 3,081 ranch
acres bordering the beach on windward O'ahu at Kualoa. A total of
5,295 acres are listed in Judd's name in the yellowed pages of
Hawai'i's land title record book. There were charges that Judd used
another name to buy an additional 17,000 acres for a total purchase
price of fifty cents.[31] Other missionaries, fast becoming businessmen,
hung out Hawai'i's first realtor shingles, buying and selling land
between sermons. Ten members of the missionary clan averaged better than 22 sales each, per year.

The *Mahele* destroyed Hawaiians economically because the
vast majority of them were still living on a hand-to-mouth subsis-
tence level. They were kept out of the market economy by the
Mahele. Without common land, they were unable to grow food to
feed themselves and were forced to become dependent upon those
who now held the land in fee: the chiefs, the whites, lesser chiefs,
and others. Because of the sky-rocketing market in Northern
California created by the gold rush, whites came to Hawai'i and
began speculating in sugar, wheat, rice, potatoes, cotton, and cattle
for export to San Francisco. In exchange for the profit to be had from
this California market, whites became anxious to relieve
Kamehameha III of his authority and the kingdom of its independence. From 1850 on, the economic pulse of the islands accelerated,
but to the distinct disadvantage of the Hawaiian; it was clear the
Mahele, as created and implemented by Judd and Lee, had sparked
that process. "While the Hawaiian cares but little for home or property, the civilized and Christian man must have both, or be all the
more miserable. Then is it not more cruel than charitable to send missionaries to convert the heathen, and by the time they are advanced
enough to appreciate homes and lands and all the blessings of civilization, to have them cheated out of their lands, and set them adrift
...? I have spoken before of how the white men get their lands, but
this is not all. They have monopolized the waters that sweep their
shores. There is hardly a mile of coast where a poor native can fish
without paying rent to a white landlord. We are robbing the heathen
nations of their country faster than we are converting them."[32]

*For a detailed breakdown of how one scholar who specializes in the *Mahele* assesses
how the Hawaiians fared in the division of land, see page 191.

•

The 1987 State of Hawai'i Data Book depicts how four million acres of Hawaiian land have been maneuvered into ownership blocks. A million and a half acres are owned by the State, almost two million acres are the property of 70 corporate owners, and the U.S. government has approximately 400,000 acres. Less than 30,000 acres are the property of all other smaller land holders. What happened to the two and a half million acres that Judd's *Mahele* stated would be "held in trust for the people?" Almost half of all Hawai'i's lands—1.8 million acres—was taken over by the U.S. Government at the time of annexation, without any compensation to the Hawaiian people. After Statehood in 1959, the Federal government returned all but 432,000 acres to the State— keeping 175,000 acres for the Defense Department and 218,000 acres for National Parks. The State of Hawai'i leases many thousands of acres back to the Department of Defense, including the 28,000 acres at Kaho'olawe, an island of historical significance to the Hawaiians. The Navy has been using Kaho'olawe for bombing and artillery practice since World War II. Kaho'olawe's 28,000 shell-shocked acres represent less than .9 percent of Hawai'i's total of four million acres. That's the same percentage of land that was awarded to Hawaiian commoners as a result of Judd's *Mahele*.

•

In 1848 George M. Robertson, a commissioner to Quiet Land Titles, filed 16 impeachment charges against Judd. The specifications which included embezzlement and other specific violations of Hawaiian law, totaled 175 in number. The king, at Judd's urging, appointed Chief Justice Lee to hear the evidence on those charges. Lee, who owed his entire judicial career to Judd was both embarrassed and frightened by the order and begged to be allowed to withdraw from the case. He also pleaded with the king not to appoint any other member of the Commission to hear the evidence because they were all in debt to Judd.

At that same time a series of unsigned articles criticizing Judd's alleged criminal activities appeared in the *Sandwich Island News*. Judd, furious at this unattributed exposure, "borrowed" $300 in government funds and used it to bribe an informer who told him Anthony Ten Eyck, United States Commissioner to Hawai'i, had authored the articles. *Sandwich Island News* publisher Elija A. Rockwell, charging a violation of the freedom of the press, tried to bring suit against Judd. When the case went to the Supreme Court for an opinion, Chief Justice Lee dodged the issue by assigning the case to the newly appointed government attorney, Asher B. Bates. Married to Judd's sister, Bates informed Rockwell that, because of his high office, Judd was above prosecution. Rockwell, without recourse, dropped his case. Judd promptly demonstrated the degree of his control over the government by submitting a voucher to recover the $300

he had "borrowed" for the bribe. He entered the item on the kingdom's financial books as an "official expenditure" and transferred the
sum to his personal account.

Meanwhile, at the impeachment hearing, Chief Justice Lee,
whose plea to withdraw had fallen on deaf royal ears, held that only
six of the 16 charges filed against Judd were impeachable offenses.
The Judd-appointed Land Commission met 45 times before arriving
at a sham acquittal. Robertson resigned.

Judd had reached his peak. He was a wealthy landowner, the
king's closest advisor and translator, a royal treasury board member,
royal Minister of Finance and constitutional architect. He held one
other influential position which has been ignored by his biographers
and Hawai'i historians. Judd held an iron-fisted grip on the office
that advanced the legend of his career at the expense of the facts. He
was, for the length of his political life, the keeper of the records
which were to become Hawai'i's archives. The State Archives of
Hawai'i were established in 1905, after the overthrow of the monarchy. Judd and his descendants, as documented later in this text,
tainted historical truth by willfully destroying accounts and omitting
documents would have thwarted their political ambitions or portrayed
them unfavorably. They simply stacked the deck of Hawai'i's history
to favor themselves and to further their aspirations. *The Polynesian,* a
government propaganda organ, and other state records, were manipu-
lated by Gerrit P. Judd, his son Albert F. Judd, and other family
members and their in-laws. Moreover, much of what passes as
authentic Hawai'i history for the period that Judd held office was
authored by his wife, Laura Fish Judd.

•

In August, 1849, Rear Admiral Legoarant de Tromelin,
Commander of the French Navy Pacific, led his marines ashore at
Honolulu to protect French Catholic interests, which were again
being sorely abused by American Protestant missionaries. An eyewit-
ness reported that the French pillaged the fort. "All the guns were
thrown from the wall ... and spiked. The magazine was opened and
the powder poured into the sea. All the old muskets, swords, and bayonets ... were broken to pieces, and every article on the premise [sic]
destroyed, not sparing the old clock on the wall of the governor's
house ... even the calabashes were smashed and thrown into the well.
The ground is covered with broken muskets, cartridge boxes, bayonets, and swords. Every window and door of the governor's house is
broken and battered, and the walls are covered with charcoal
sketches. Every box, barrel, and calabash is crushed to atoms."[33]

Father Yzendoorn, a Roman Catholic mission historian, told

of a dozen Hawaiian Catholics who were tried in 1837 in a court of law and sentenced to hard labor. Although the offenders included five women, a blind man, a six-year-old girl and three men over 50, they were each required to build a "wall 50 feet long by 6 feet high and 3 to 4 feet wide," to atone for their sins.

With Judd at the helm, Hawai'i was sailing on a dangerous diplomatic course with both England and France, when de Tromelin detained all vessels flying the Hawaiian flag and took possession of all government offices, including the customs house. Kamehameha III appointed two commissioners to confer with the French Admiral. When his appointees, Judd and Lee, failed to come to an agreement, it angered the Admiral to the extent that he confiscated the king's personal yacht. A solemn protest, appealing to America and England to intervene with the French on behalf of Hawai'i, was dispatched.

Judd succeeded in urging the king to appoint him as Special Commissioner and Plenipotentiary Extraordinary to the three major powers. High on his list of priorities for discussion in Paris was a demand for an indemnity of $100,000 for confiscation of the royal yacht. Judd also carried a secret document, signed by the king, authorizing him to place Hawai'i under the protection and rule of a foreign government, should an emergency arise. Additional secret instructions gave Judd the power to sell all private lands of the king and his chiefs. Judd persuaded the king to allow two Princes, Alexander Liholiho, 15, and Lot Kamehameha, 18, to accompany him. All of these arrangements concerning Hawai'i's foreign relations were made between Judd and the king without Robert Wyllie, Hawai'i's new Foreign Secretar,y being consulted.

The Plenipotentiary Extraordinary and his two royal charges sailed into San Francisco Bay on the first day in November, 1849, where they shared narrow board sidewalks with overall-clad gold seekers and met with President Polk's newly appointed Commissioner to Hawai'i, Charles Eames. Leaving San Francisco, they journeyed south to California's adobe capitol at Monterey, boarded a ship and sailed down the coast, with pauses at San Diego's mission, Acapulco, Mazatlan and then by land in a stagecoach across the Isthmus of Panama, on to Kingston, Jamaica, arriving at New York City on a cold, dreary December 7. Whirling through a crowded five-day social calendar, they sailed from Jersey City, making port at Halifax, Nova Scotia, and on to Liverpool, where they entrained for London, arriving there in time to celebrate Christmas. Having spent an enjoyable month in England, they were presented at the court of Louis Napoleon, president of the Second Republic of France, on January 26, 1850, where Prince Alexander reported, "... General LaHitte piloted us through the immense crowd that was pressing from all sides, and finally we made our way up to the President ... Mr.

Judd was the first one taken notice of, and both of them made slight bows to each other. Lot and myself then bowed, to which he returned with a slight bend of the vertebrae. He then advanced and said, 'This is your first visit to Paris,' to which we replied in the affirmative. He asked if we liked Paris to which we replied very much indeed. He then said, 'I am very gratified to see you, you have come from so far a country,' then he turned towards the doctor and said, 'I hope our little quarrel will be settled.' To which the Doctor replied, 'We put much confidence in the magnanimity and justice of France."'[34]

The two handsome young princes and Judd wore full Royal Hawaiian military uniforms, heavy with decorations and bright sashes. Lot and Alexander studied French and took up the foil to learn fencing. They excelled in both, while Judd sought the indemnities of his mission. Near the end of March, as negotiations with the French were about to close, the Doctor broke his silence, with Wyllie telling him after four months without results he was discouraged.

They left Paris on April 8, returning to London to seek help from the English and were immediately granted an interview with Prince Albert at Buckingham Palace. "When we entered, the Prince was standing a little aside of the door, and bowed to each of us as we came in. He was a fine man, about as tall as I am, and had a fine bust, and straight legs. We kept standing. Palmerston on my right and the Doctor on my left, and then Lot. The Prince began the conversation by asking if we intended to make a long stay to which I answered by saying that we expected to leave in about a week and then Dr. Judd made a few remarks on his business. [35]

"The King of the Sandwich Islands sent me to endeavor to obtain justice of France for the injuries he has suffered from French officers and directed these young princes to accompany me in order that they may profit by what they would see in foreign countries. I have applied in vain to France and now have addressed myself to the greatest diplomatist in Europe."[36]

Albert was gracious but impervious to the flattery and offered no assistance in the matter. Judd, Lot and Alexander disembarked at Boston, where the Mayor John P. Bigelow hosted a reception in their honor; and Hiram Bingham, now living in Connecticut in his sixtieth year, eyed the princely figures, exclaiming "... among the first and most beautiful fruits of the plantings of missionary labors in Polynesian regions." [37]

Judd was more successful when he met with President Zachary Taylor's Secretary of State, John Middleton Clayton, in June. "Mr. Clayton said that he should notify France and England that his government will not look with indifference upon any act of oppression committed or any attempt to take the Islands but will not permit any other nation to have them. I asked if the U.S. would go to war on our account. He replied yes—that is they would send a force and retake the Islands for the King and if that made a war they would carry it out."38

Judd squired the princes on a gala round of Capitol Hill parties, where such sonorous luminaries as Daniel Webster, Henry Clay and Sam Houston raised crystal goblets to candlelit chandeliers, extending their heartiest welcomes to the dusky young men. They were escorted into the White House amid fanfare for a fifteen minute chat with President Taylor, who, according to Alexander's account, greeted them with a cough, saying "Gentlemen, I am at your service." But the Prince noted, "the old fellow's mind seemed to be on other subjects." The Prince was perceptive. Taylor, a slave-holding Southerner surrounded by militant abolitionists, had much to occupy his mind. Judd explained to the President that it was a very real possibility the Islands would seek annexation should a crisis arise and that he, Gerrit P. Judd, had the secret power in his pocket to effect it.39

Sir Henry Buliver, the British Ambassador in Washington, met with Judd and reported to Foreign Secretary Palmerston ,"I understand that if France persists in her claims, there is an intention on the part of the King of the Sandwich Islands to endeavor to place himself under the protection of the U.S. government."40

Judd's secret was common gossip among Washington's diplomatic corps. The issue was precarious. Perhaps Judd would have succeeded in bringing about the union of Hawai'i and the United States had it not been for an ugly incident. While Judd was supervising the loading of the royal luggage at the Baltimore train depot, the 16-year-old who would become Hawai'i's sovereign in four years walked into the parlor car of the waiting train, sat down in the seat assigned and was unceremoniously ordered to leave by a conductor. Alexander wrote angrily, "... probably taken me for somebody's servant just because I had a darker skin than he had. I must be treated as a dog to go and come at an American's bidding. I must state that I am disappointed at the Americans. They have no manners, no politeness, not even common civilities to strangers. In England an African can pay his fare and sit alongside Queen Victoria. The Americans talk and think a great deal about their liberty, and strangers often find that too many liberties are taken of their comfort just because his hosts are a free people."41

Years later, Frederick W. Seward, writing in *Reminiscences of a Wartime Diplomat*, recalled Alexander and Lot: "They were educated, erect, graceful and were Royal Princes. Washington society was disposed to adore their rank, but balked at their complexion. It was feared they might be black."

When they landed in Panama late in July, Judd was shaken to

hear that the French Foreign Minister had made an open threat to invade Hawai'i. Later events proved that the Frenchman was bluffing, but Judd, taking the man at his word, panicked in the presence of his charges. His glamorous adventure into the realm of foreign affairs now a virtual fiasco, Judd reached Honolulu on September 9, 1850, withdrawn, vindictive and convinced his pawn was to be taken by the French knight.

Secretary of Foreign Affairs Wyllie, still smarting from Judd's usurpation, scolded the Plenipotentiary Extraordinary before the royal cabinet. "Mr. Judd recommended himself for the mission, attached Princes of the Kingdom to it ... was ordered to begin negotiations in Washington and end them in Paris, but began them in Paris and ended them in Washington, received abundant supplies of money and expended it just as it pleased himself ... bolted right from Paris just as he had commenced negotiations in due form ... bolted off from London without waiting to give facts .... My report applauds his zeal in understanding the mission and places in a prominent point of view the sacrifices that he made in abandoning his family to undertake it, but I have yet to learn that he deserves praise for anything else."[42]

Judd lashed back, but even his protege, Chief Justice Lee, began to abandon him. "Unfortunately there exists a break in our cabinet. The slumbering files of the old discontent broke out afresh on Judd's return .... While aboard he got the foolish notion into his head, that he could displace Wyllie and get the king to call on him to form a new cabinet ... I told him ... that any step of that kind would be wrong and end in his own ruin ... he gave my advice no heed, and told the cabinet he or Mr. Wyllie must resign. The result is, that he has put himself in a fix. He will not resign, and can hardly stay where he is with honor. Judd is decidedly in the wrong, and I have told him so, but cannot make him see his error."[43]

The French pressed harder for the protection of their island interests, while Honolulu trembled in anticipation of cannon fire from warships flying the Tricolor. At the king's behest, Wyllie prepared an official statement of cession to the United States. But Secretary of State Daniel Webster, whom Judd depicted as "... more formal, cold and stiff than any lord in Europe," was opposed to annexation and summarily rejected Wyllie's proposal. Judd, who still held the royal puppet strings in his grasp, adamantly opposed doing anything to appease the French, even as combat seemed imminent and the breach between him and his last close friend widened. "Judd has a great advantage in his knowledge of the native language, and is bold and cunning, but in mind and heart, in all that is generous, liberal and manly, Wyllie is far his superior...Ever since Judd came home he has been uneasy and dissatisfied. His arbitrary temper, his wounded pride, his hate of all rivals, his solicitude to promote his relatives, and his ambition to preside over the department of the interior, all conspire to render his position grievous to himself and his friends."[44]

As Judd sank deeper into trouble, Wyllie added a paragraph to Lee's new constitution that forbade missionaries to hold seats in the House of Representatives. Judd's anger at that news boiled over into public fury. As that simmered, Judd was publicly accused of nepotism, when it came to light he had urged the Privy Council to grant Aaron B. Howe, who was courting his daughter, an interest free loan of $3,000. Judd countered that thrust by accusing his clerk, William Jarrett, of embezzling over $200 in royal funds. When the court acquitted Jarrett, Judd fired him and proposed that his son, Charles Judd, replace him.

"The land commission (which Judd founded in 1849) recommended in 1851 that every missionary who had served eight years in Hawaii and did not own 500 acres of land be allowed to purchase that amount at a reduced rate. This became law, and several individuals including Charles Reed Bishop—the originator of the Island-wide Bishop Trust—purchased large tracts of land for $1.45 an acre. The list of missionary purchasers includes such names as Alexander, Baldwin, Dole and, Gulick."*

In June of 1852, the House of Representatives ran an audit on Judd's Department of Finance. They discovered a second set of books, with $2,930 in public funds missing, and held him responsible. Additionally, Judd, in his role of public official, purposely had set a low price on a number of government-owned houses, had bought them dirt cheap, and then had his son Charles auction them off, turning a neat, but illegal profit of more than $3,000.

On October 22, 1851, a group of Hawaiian prisoners broke out of the fort jail. They were recaptured in the act of turning a cannon around in order to fire upon Judd's home. A month later, when a sailor was clubbed to death by a policeman during a riot, Judd gave his official sanction to that act. Subsequently, a mob led by a whaler twirling a coarse rope marched up Nuʻuanu Valley to get him. A club swinging squad of *kānaka* police saved his neck.

A parsimonious attitude and unyielding stubbornness led to fatal consequences and to the removal from government service of Dr. Judd. On February 14, 1853, the ship *Charles Mallory* arrived at Honolulu Harbor carrying a passenger riddled with smallpox. Wyllie, who had a medical education, immediately proposed a mass inoculation of the entire population with a virus taken from the smallpox victim. Judd fought Wyllie, advocating instead a vaccination with cowpox. Honolulu's physicians banded together, agreeing to inoculate all Hawaiians on Oʻahu with the smallpox virus *from victims and*

---

* Joyce Chapman Lebra. *Women's Voices In Hawaii*, p. 77.

from cows for a token fee of ten cents apiece. They asked that the dimes be paid out of Judd's royal coffers. Judd appointed himself as Commissioner of Health and caused an impasse, refusing to release the funds unless the Hawaiians were vaccinated exclusively with cowpox. Meanwhile, the disease was spreading. The Honolulu doctors were still squabbling with the adamant Judd three months later, when the scourge hit the especially vulnerable Hawaiians with full impact. More than 11,000 cases were reported; there were 5,947 death notices, almost all carrying Hawaiian names. According to a census taken in 1853, there were fewer than 60,000 Hawaiians left. [45]

Elizabeth Judd wrote of her father's heroics during the epidemic that his obstinacy had helped to create: "My father worked day and night, until he became a mere shadow. The Hawaiians were just superstitious and ignorant enough to be unmanageable. Hundreds of them lost their lives because they bathed in the sea or sat in the wind to cool their fever."[46]

Doctors Wesly Newcomb and George A. Lathrop, who had organized Honolulu's physicians in a desperate effort to check the epidemic, publicly attacked Judd for "most wickedly" refusing to authorize the immunization of the Polynesians who were dying in wholesale lots.[47] It would have cost the Judd-controlled Royal Treasury 600 ten cent pieces, or $60, to perhaps save the lives of 6,000 Hawaiians. A rumor was prevalent that Judd had pocketed a bribe from Honolulu business interests to let the epidemic run its course among the Hawaiians. There were vicious rumblings of a plot to cast the political doctor adrift in the Pacific without food, water or oars. Protest marches turned into rowdy demonstrations demanding Judd's resignation.

The internal situation became so inflammatory that "respectable residents," especially those who had benefited most from *Judd's Mahele* and those who had supposedly offered the bribe, led by Charles Reed Bishop—now president of Hawai'i's only bank—petitioned the king for immediate and peaceful annexation to the United States, "in order to preserve prosperity and political quiet in the Islands." Other signatures in that petition included Samuel N. Castle, William H. Rice, and Amos Starr Cooke, all missionaries who had given up their U. S. citizenship and their offices in the mission to become powerful landowners in Hawai'i. Had the petition of the missionaries-turned-businessmen succeeded, they would have preserved their ownership of land, regained their U. S. citizenship, and saved the political career of Judd, who had made their prosperity possible.

When that petition failed, Judd approached the king with yet another scheme to sell the entire Kingdom of Hawai'i to New York shipping magnate Alfred G. Benson, who had already agreed to let the whites retain title to their lands upon completion of the sale. In return for "valuable services rendered," Benson secretly appointed Judd as silent partner and president of the Sandwich Island Steamship Company.

Prince Alexander, still smoldering from the racial ugliness in Baltimore, opposed Judd's every move. Prince Lot added his weight to his brother's opposition and finally the king, who thought "the Dr.'s annexation" schemes had excited suspicion, crowned the insult to Judd by sending Alexander, heir to the throne, to demand the Doctor's resignation.

Chief Justice Lee was bewildered by Judd's frantic annexation schemes, all of which contradicted his previous position on the subject of Hawaiian independence. Lee raised his voice, calling for Judd's resignation.

A "Committee of Thirteen," formed to hasten annexation and the departure of Judd from political office, invited the Hawaiian people to attend an open meeting, where a proclamation citing "relief of a people from bondage and a malignant tyranny" was celebrated with "a torchlight procession with music and banners paraded through the town and called at the house of former U.S. Consul Elisha H. Allen, the new incumbent, with speeches and hurrahs."[48]

After submitting his resignation, Judd lived out the remainder of his life in Honolulu, where, setting aside the practice of medicine, he opened a drugstore and paid forty dollars for a permit to become one of Hawai'i's first opium dealers. He became Hawai'i's first locally based insurance agent and, in partnership with son-in-law Samuel Gardner Wilder, became the principal agent for the American Guano Company. He acquired more acres of prime land and retired a $3,000 unrecorded mortgage with Charles Reed Bishop without payment except perhaps in the guise of past favors.

Nearing the end, he wrote, "... The native population are fast fading away. Of the vast numbers one hundred years ago, only 58,765 remain ... for a group of Islands capable of sustaining from 3,000,000 to 5,000,000. The Islands are now ruled by a King (Lot Kamehameha) whose health is not good, and by a number of persons of foreign birth who are the real rulers, not one of whom is American at heart. The chiefs or true aristocracy are almost extinct, and were the King suddenly to decease, there is reason to fear there would follow a period of anarchy and confusion, perhaps bloodshed."[49]

Gerrit Parmele Judd died of a massive stroke on Saturday, July 12, 1873. His pallbearers included Minister of Foreign Affairs Charles Reed Bishop and Samuel N. Castle, missionary member of the House of Nobles and founding partner of Castle and Cooke, Ltd.

Chapter Ten

LAST OF THE KAMEHAMEHA MONARCHS
1854 - 1874

The decrease of our population is a subject in comparison with which all others sink into insignificance. Our first and great duty is self-preservation. Our acts are in vain, unless we can stay the wasting hand that is destroying our people.

— Kamehameha IV
Address to the Legislature, 1855

ALEXANDER LIHOLIHO
1854 - 1863

"The age of Kamehameha III was that of progress and liberty, of schools and civilization and fixed laws; he secured the people title to their lands, and removed the last chain of oppression. He gave them a voice in his councils and in the making of the laws by which they are governed. He was a great national benefactor, and has left the impress of his mild and amiable disposition of the age for which he was born."[1] Thus did Alexander Liholiho eulogize his late uncle Kauikeaouli in December, 1854. Kamehameha III had been in ill health for more than a year and was in the thirtieth year of his reign when he died. Since he had no heir he had adopted Alexander as his son and his successor. The dean of Hawaiian historians, stressing the positive aspects of Kamehameha III, suggested those characteristics, "... which ought to be remembered are ... mildness of character, amiability of disposition and soundness of judgment."[2]

A more widely read writer who chronicled that era stated that "The Little King" had been a "sot and a vacillator."[3] A year before his death, Kamehameha III, who had spent the better part of a decade in an alcoholic haze,[4] had indeed vacillated on the question of

118

annexation to the U.S. and on the decision to remove Judd from office. Alexander implored his uncle not to sell out Hawai'i's independence to racist America and urged him to get rid of Judd. Had Alexander failed to sway his uncle, there would have been, in all probability, no kingdom left for him to inherit. When he ascended the throne on December 15, 1854 at the age of 20, it was clear to those around him that Alexander Liholiho was gifted with a brilliant mind, an active ambition and an esoteric manner. Although brooding, the dispossessed Judd described the new king as "... handsome, with a well-formed head, tall and slender, a fair linguist, intelligent, and more European than Hawaiian in his ideas and tastes."[5] Since he was the last ruler in a position to save some remnant of the population and culture of Hawai'i from the whites, it was a bittersweet catastrophe to the Hawaiian that Alexander had been cast with tragic flaws.

Kamehameha IV, son of *Kuhina Nui* Kīna'u and grandson of Kamehameha I, was born in 1834. As chronicled earlier, he had traveled widely in Europe, the United States and in South America. During the second year of his reign, he married Emma Rooke Naea, granddaughter of John Young, the companion, philosopher, and general of the conquering army of his patron, Kamehameha I. Emma, the great-granddaughter of Keali'imaika'i, who was the younger brother of Kamehameha I, was adopted, *hanai* style and reared by her maternal aunt and her British uncle, Dr. T. C. Rooke. More English than Hawaiian in her interests and presence, Emma seemed the perfect match to Alexander, who was anti-American and fearful of the very real encroachment of the United States upon his island kingdom. Their court was a graceful blend of Polynesian simplicity and European elegance. Dinners were formal. Alexander became an outstanding cricket player, and the *hula*, which had again been suppressed under "King Judd," was revived.

The royal couple was not afraid to show affection openly and was compassionate toward their people, who were dying at an appalling rate. They worked to establish a hospital to treat their disease-ridden race.

Alexander's critics among the American missionary enclave labeled him as despotic, haughty, arbitrary, dissolute, passionate, quick-tempered and pro-British. His quick temperedness and immoderate drinking were to trigger two events hastening his death. Upon hearing a rumor that his beloved Emma and his trusted American secretary, Henry A. Neilson, had become lovers, Alexander banged on the door of Neilson's cottage with the barrel of a pearl handled dueling pistol. As Neilson, rubbing sleep from his eyes, cautiously eased the door open, Alexander poked the barrel into the narrow opening and shot him through the right anterior chest. Neilson lingered between life and death for more than two years before dying.

During that period Alexander withdrew, engulfed by terrible guilt and self-incrimination. His depression was so deep that he came to the brink of abdication. He had barely emerged from his self-imposed confinement when his four-year-old son, Prince Albert, threw a temper tantrum; the king became angry and punished the boy by holding him under cold running water for 20 minutes. Albert went into nervous shock, and four days later he died. Fifteen months of seclusion passed before Alexander joined his son in death. He was 29 years old.

Lili'uokalani, a bosom friend, penned his epitaph, "Alexander Liholiho, known to history as Kamehameha IV, had all the characteristics of his race; and the strong passionate nature of a Kamehameha is shown in his benevolence as in his less commendable acts. To him was due the introduction of the Anglican Mission. He personally translated the English Prayer-Book into our language. He also founded the Queens Hospital ... and both foreign and domestic affairs; of his government were ably administered."6

LOT KAMEHAMEHA
1863 - 1872

Inferior to his late brother in refinement, grace of manner, and general culture, he is I think his superior in energy, perseverance, and strength of will .5

Kamehameha V (Lot), the last of the Kamehameha bloodline, became King on November 30, 1863. His first act was to refuse to take an oath to support the Constitution which had been conceived by Judd and Lee. That Constitution, revised by Lee in Judd's absence during 1852, gave each branch of the government a check upon the other and gave the vote to all men over 20 years of age. The idea that all men were born free and equal was distasteful to Lot, and he discredited the idea of universal suffrage, remarking that he, the king, knew the nature of his people far better than the whites who had written the Constitution. He acted swiftly by calling for a constitutional convention.

Mark Twain sketched his portrait after a dinner party: "The King is thirty-four years of age, it is said, but looks all of fifty. He has an observant inquiring eye, a heavy massive face, a lighter complexion than is common with his race, tolerably short, stiff hair, a moderate mustache, and imperial large stature inclining somewhat to corpulence ... has fleshy hands, but a small foot for his size, is about six feet high, is thoughtful and slow of movement, has a large head, firmly set upon broad shoulders, and is a better man and a better looking one than he is represented to be in those villainous popular photographs of him, for none of them are good. The King was dressed entirely in black—dress coat and silk hat—and looked rather democratic in the midst of the showy uniforms about him . On his breast he wore a large gold star ...."[8]

Lot's constitutional convention was called to order on a sizzling summer day in 1864 and he gave its delegates one, and only one, chance to agree with his philosophy. When they had orated themselves into a deadlock, Lot regally waved them off and made known his intentions in a remarkable speech: "I am sorry we do not agree. It is clear to me, that if universal suffrage is permitted, this government will lose its monarchical character. As we do not agree, it is useless to prolong the session, and as at the time His Majesty Kamehameha III gave the Constitution of the year 1852, he reserved to himself the power of taking it away if it was not for the interest of his Government and people, and it is clear that the King left the revision of the Constitution to my predecessor and myself, therefore, as I sit in His seat, on the part of the Sovereignty of the Hawaiian Islands, I make it known today that the Constitution of 1852 is abrogated. I will give you a Constitution."[9]

Lot dissolved the Judd-Lee Constitution and, within the week, introduced his own, which provided "the Kingdom is the King's." That constitution was to remain as the basic law of Hawai'i until 1887.

•

At this juncture, events 5,000 miles away intervened to stimulate prospects for Hawai'i's infant sugar industry. General Sheridan's scorched earth policy had left a terrible path of destruction from which the sugar plantations of the South would never recover. Since Hawai'i's supply of sugar fell far short of the stepped up demand, more field hands were needed immediately. "... the Hawaiian who has simple food and shelter is not eager to work for anything more. His ancestors did not trouble themselves about cultivating sugar, rice, or cotton, and he sees no reason why he should toil in the sun on plantations, nor has he energy to do so successfully, even if he had the disposition."[10]

In desperation, several hundred Chinese "Coolies" were imported, causing a rash of complaints from whites who feared the "yellow peril," but to no avail, because sugar was to become the crop that saved the kingdom. Soon 1,700 Chinese cane workers were imported, having been hired in China under indenture-like contracts. The immigrants were signed up for three to five years of hard labor at wages of $3 per month. If they defaulted, they could be flogged and forced to serve double time in the fields or be sent to prison. The United States government officially opposed this type of contract labor, but American planters in Hawai'i who profited from such a cheap work source had made such methods legal. Sanford Dole, a descendant of missionaries who later became President of the Hawaiian Republic, said of the practice, "The prosperity of the country, the demands of society, the future of the Hawaiian race only comes in secondarily, if at all on the part of supporters of the system. Is this not so? The burden of your cry is labor, we must have labor, and the plan which promises that cheap, and immediate, you favor without asking many questions .... Tried in the balance of the free and equal rights principle, the contract system is found wanting."[11]

In 1865 King Lot appointed Dr. William Hillebrand as commissioner "to procure, contract and import to this kingdom laborers from such countries in Asia, as can best supply them." The Board of the Planter's Society instructed him to proceed to China and there secure "About 500 coolies of the most respectable and best class of persons who go by that name and arrange for their transportation to Hawai'i. It is very desirable that your best exertions should be given to induce some proportions of the coolies to engage with their wives, or wives and families ... proceed to the East Indies and such other places as your own judgment shall dictate to ascertain where, if anywhere, and how, other descriptions of laborers can be obtained and to satisfy yourself of their value relative to the coolies of China." Hillebrand later noted, "The difference between a coolie and a slave is only one of degree, not of essence."[12]

In remarking on the quality of imported laborers, the President of the Royal Hawaiian Agricultural Society said, "... though they were first found useful, and still are to some extent, yet as they become more familiar with our customs and regulations, they become unmanageable, and on most plantations where they were at first employed they have been discharged."[13] White tradesmen and mechanics petitioned Lot, stating that, "a great number of Chinese coolies, who are out of employment, and have no honest means of earning a livelihood, are now congregated in and around Honolulu, where they are to be seen, prowling about, at all hours of the night, without limit or restraint."[14]

Since almost all phases of economic life in Hawai'i soon became dependent upon sugar, the stream of immigration needed for sugar production increased. Before long it would include Japanese, Scotsmen, Portuguese, Koreans and Filipinos. By July 7, 1898, when President McKinley signed the Annexation Resolution, fewer than one-fifth of the population of 154,000 were white, two-fifths were Japanese, one-sixth Chinese and one-eighth were Portuguese.[15]*

*See Arrival Dates beginning on Page 193.

During the reign of Lot, Hawaiian-American relations were not cordial. Hawaiians in and out of the government were wary of what Charles de Varigny, then France's Minister to Hawai'i, wrote about later: "I consider ... that the only danger which Hawaiian independence could run into would come from the United States, and that the agent of France ought to unite himself closely with the agent of England in order to ward off that danger. That is what I did and with such success as to attract to myself the violent animosity of the annexation party."[16]

United States Secretary of State Seward remarked in 1864, "when our civil war is over we will take good care of our interests in the Sandwich Islands." In 1867, with jeers of "Seward's folly" ringing in his ears, he signed the U. S. treaty which purchased Alaska, causing great unrest in Hawai'i. France and England did not trust the United States, and the U. S. was suspicious of French and English motives in Hawai'i. Lot feared sugar planters would bring in large numbers of foreign laborers and eventually the native Hawaiians would be outvoted. This, coupled with Seward's expansionist policies, he felt would lead to annexation by the United States. The Hawaiians backed their monarch and often repeated a legend to illustrate how kingly attitudes had changed since the sandalwood days. While surveying his kingdom, Lot, so the tale goes, spent the night in the crude shack of one of his subjects. He gave the man a twenty dollar gold piece to pay for his lodging. When the man returned it, saying, "You are my king and everything belongs to you," Lot handed it back, allegedly saying, "I am not the king to get everything I can out of my people. I receive a salary to pay for what I need."

HONOLULU AFTERNOON
1872

"The parliament of paradise meets in Honolulu on the last day of April in each alternate year. Its meeting is an event which astonishes the natives, and gives the white people an opportunity to air their well-preserved fashions in the splendor of a royal court.

"A stranger can see that something unusual is at hand ... flags are flying from the hundred flagstaffs which adorn the city. Natives ... hair sleek with coconut oil ... are shuffling along the sidewalks and mounted on shying ponies, and loping through the streets. Sauntering along the street I meet white women in black silks, and yellow women in white muslins, wending their way to the courthouse, a large square, coral building in Fort Street. Its second story is the legislative hall ... its northern windows, admitting the trade wind, and its southern windows, looking off upon the sea make a place for cool reflections.

"Spectators ... occupy seats in the center of the hall, the whites in front, the natives in rear. In this throng I recognize the oldest missionary, and the latest invalid from the states; and between these extremes, I see represented all the gossip and fashion of Honolulu. In front are seated the nobles and representatives comprising the legislature—a curious mixture of Hawaiian and Anglo-Saxon men, of which the Hawaiians are decidedly the best looking. On the right of the rostrum are seated the 'ladies of the court,' most of them Yankee girls once. On the left sits the black-clothed minister of the United States, the British and French Commissioners, the officers of the British frigate *Scout*, now in port, and the consular corps, all in gold lace, gilt buttons, swords, and whatever else adds pomp and circumstance to the occasion. There is an apothecary, Consul for Austria, a whaleman's agent, Consul for Italy, an auctioneer, Consul for Chile, who, although a Protestant Yankee, shuts his shop and sets his consular flag at halfmast, on Good Friday.

"At twelve o'clock exactly, the King leaves the 'Iolani Palace on King Street; and a salute is commenced at the battery on Punchbowl Hill. In company with his Chamberlain—a white man—he enters a barouche drawn by four horses, and is escorted by his staff on horseback, and by the Hawaiian army, which consists of two companies of natives with a company of whites sandwiched between them.

"... in the hall we can hear the band playing its favorite air, — *'Ten Thousand Miles Away,'* —which has aroused the town from sleep many a morning lately. Soon we hear the strains of 'God Save the King' expressed with an extra quantity of base drum, and we know that the King is alighting from his carriage in front of the court house.

"The marshall of the kingdom enters, and throws over the Chair of State the royal mantle, or *momo* [*mamo*]. It was the war-cloak of Kamehameha I, made of bright yellow feathers taken from a bird called the *momo*, which was found only in the mountains. As each bird furnished but two feathers for it, one from under each wing, the birds required to supply the material were unnumerable. It is four feet long, and spreads eleven and a half feet at the bottom. Nine generations of chiefs were occupied in making it ... enter four native men in dark broadcloth overcoats, and capes and black silk hats of stovepipe style, bearing the royal presence. There are long staffs, called kahilis, whose upper parts are covered with brilliant bird feathers of various colors fixed at right angles. They look like a gay chimneysweep's brush, or a costly swab for a large spout. These four men, hats on, kahilis erect, stand at the four corners of the rostrum; when now enters the chancellor, head of the Supreme Court of the kingdom (a New England born gentleman); then the King, Kamehameha V; then, at a respectful interval, the ministers and staff officers—all white men in brilliant uniforms.

"I cannot repress a smile at the appearance of these civilized men, caparisoned with barbaric glory! There is our American-born banker, a scarlet ribbon around his neck, from which hangs the sparkling insignia of Hawaiian Knighthood. There is the little minister of finance, an excellent American-born dentist. There is the tall, scheming minister of foreign affairs, also minister of the Navy that is yet to be, and of war not yet declared, once an American lawyer. There is the dignified minister of the interior, general manager and police supervisor of the kingdom, once a crusty Scotch physician. There is the attorney general of the crown, who recently went to New England, and married a wife. All these are in cocked hats and blue broadcloth, brilliant with gilt bands, laces, and decorations; their rapiers buckled at their sides, and they themselves appearing to be very uncomfortable!

"When the King enters ... the audience rises, and every eye is turned upon him. He looks like a King; large, tall broad-shouldered, dignified, portly, self-possessed. He is faultlessly attired in a blue-coat with gilt buttons, black trousers, white vest, and white kid gloves. He walks deliberately to the chair, like a man who understands what is expected of him. After a prayer in Hawaiian, by the archdeacon of the Episcopal Church, the assembly rises to its feet while the King stands up, and reads from a page, in a velvet folio, his speech to the legislature, in the Hawaiian tongue. Then he turns the page and reads the same in English. When he opens his mouth and speaks, my illusion of royalty vanishes. So it is often with a stranger, who, before speaking has made a favorable impression. The first word uttered reveals something that either confirms or dispels the favorable opinion. The King's voice is small, scanty, indistinct, not at all the voice of the King he appears to be.

"He congratulates the ... establishment of steam communication between the islands, California and the Australian colonies ... says that agriculture is the life of the nation, and has repaid those who have pursued it during the past two years; that since their adjournment he has signed a treaty of amity and commerce with the Emperor of Japan, that the proposed treaty of reciprocity with the United States has now been ratified ... with the customary generalities about education, Justice, peace, and prosperity, he concludes with the words, 'We do now declare the legislature of the kingdom opened.'

"Then he retires to an adjoining room where he receives the congratulations of those who have the right to give them. Entering his carriage, he is driven at full speed to the palace; the natives crowding

along the sidewalk after him, saying to each other, '*Ka moi! Ka moi!*'
— The King! The King! and his four *kahili*-bearers running by the
side of his carriage, each one trying to keep his place by the wheel.
The staff-officers gallop pell-mell after him; the immense army
marches leisurely back to its quarters, following the noisy band; and
the legislature adjourns until the morrow."17

That was Lot's finale before the Legislature. He died seven
months later, on December 11, 1872, childless and without a blood
relative who would accept the crown. He refused to name a
successor. When his body was placed in state at the palace, the area
suddenly filled with thousands of Hawaiian chanters, wailers,
contortionists, minstrels, *kahuna* and sorcerers. Shielded from the
whites by royal guards with bayonets at the ready, they proceeded to
give Lot the licentious send-off he reputedly deserved. One witness
wrote with broad strokes, perhaps, bordering on bigotry, "Half-naked
women swung rattling calabashes, while they swayed their bodies in
lascivious dances; sorcerers screamed their incantations; men rushed
at each other in feigned contests; professional wailers rocked and
wailed for the dead King; and minstrels recited the physical power
and licentious exploits with endless repetition. It was like the funeral
saturnalia of the first Kamehameha fifty-three years before."18

WILLIAM LUNALILO
1873 - 1874

Queen Emma I do not trust; Lunalilo
is a drunkard and Kalākaua is a fool.

— Lot Kamehameha from his death bed

The grandson of a half brother of Kamehameha I, William
Charles Lunalilo ascended the throne on January 8, 1873. The first
Hawaiian monarch to be elected, Lunalilo shunned the royal coach
and its trappings to march bareheaded in the official procession to
Kawaiahao Church, where he took the solemn oath of office. Then
his first act as sovereign ruler of Hawai'i was to fulfill a childhood
fantasy. He commanded the Royal Hawaiian Band to the palace
grounds; after they had assembled, he took the bass drum from the
astonished drummer, strapped it to his chest, marched to the head of
the band and proudly led the group on a triumphal march around the
square, thumping vigorously all the while. He topped off this whimsy
by ordering up square faces of gin for all hands and hoisting the royal
goblet in toast after toast.

In six months he became seriously ill and his newly

appointed Minister of Foreign Affairs, banker Charles Reed Bishop, declared, "He was imprudent and took a severe cold which affected the right lung." The royal physician was quoted in a dispatch to the U. S. Department of State as saying Lunalilo "cannot live very much longer unless he totally abstains from the use of intoxicating drinks." With the king on his death bed and the power of white sugar planters burgeoning, the issue of annexation to America was drawn.

The Advertiser announced, "There is unquestionably a large party, respectable in the point of wealth and position, that is now openly and earnestly advocating ... the annexation of these islands to the United States of America." That paper went on to editorialize about the best natural still-water harbor in the entire Pacific being dangled before Washington's military leaders. "We can, in brief, offer to the United States a position for a harbor and coaling station ... We refer, of course, to the Pearl River ...."[19]

At a meeting of the Honolulu Chamber of Commerce on February 12, S. N. Castle asked that a committee be sent "to confer with the Government and ascertain if any measure can be devised to induce the Government of the United States to enter into a Treaty of Reciprocity with the Hawaiian Islands."[20] That committee, made up of Honolulu's business elite, met with Lunalilo's cabinet, Charles Reed Bishop, Edwin O. Hall, Albert Francis Judd, Robert Stirling, a Scotsman, and Chief Justice Elisha H. Allen. All of them, except for the Scot, urged the king to cede Pearl Harbor in return for the treaty favoring Hawaiian sugar. They pleaded that reciprocity was the last hope Hawai'i had of escaping its economic depression and that the only way to obtain reciprocity was to hand over Pearl Harbor to the United States.

In a confidential memo to his associates in London, another member of Honolulu's Chamber of Commerce, Englishman Theo H. Davies, confided, "I am confident that none of the ministers would knowingly sacrifice principle—but I cannot absolve them of the charge of almost criminal weakness in allowing the interests of the Chamber of Commerce—to dictate the sacrifice of territorial integrity for the promotion of commercial success."[21]

Lunalilo, gravely ill, agreed Bishop should pursue the reciprocity treaty, based on the exchange of Pearl Harbor with the United States, subject to his final approval. When word of this plan spread, its opponents organized and Davies, continuing his correspondence to London, wrote, "Every week strengthens the opposition of the Hawaiians to the idea of any alienation of soil; and a most bitter feeling is being aroused in the native mind against the party, chiefly Americans, who have urged this cession." In disgust, Queen Emma replied, "There is a feeling of bitterness against these rude people who dwell on our land and have high handed ideas of giving away somebody else's property as if it were theirs."22

Sobered by the avalanche of protest, the king reluctantly ordered the offer be withdrawn. His popularity plummeted even further when he signed a bill which called for strict segregation of Hawaiian lepers. His royal guards, agreeing with other Hawaiians that such a measure was unnecessary and cruel, organized a mutiny which resulted in an assault upon Adjutant General Charles Hasting Judd.

William Lunalilo, the last Hawaiian king to *claim* a blood relationship with the Kamehameha family, died at Waikiki on February 3, 1874, at the age of 39.

CHAPTER ELEVEN

A CURIOSITY IN HIS OWN LAND

But what of the fate of the native islanders over whom this surf of civilization is rolling? Are they to be swept away, like the American Indians, and give place to another race? They have been dying fast since first they saw the white man. In 1823, the population of all the islands was estimated at 172,000. In 1832, a census was taken, and the number found to be 130,000; in 1836 a census gave 108,500; in 1850 only 82,400; in 1853 the number had fallen to 73,100; in 1860 to 69,700; in 1866 to 57,125; in 1872 the entire population does not exceed 50,000. During the six years preceding the census of 1866, the number of deaths exceeded the births by 1,123 annually.

In 1867, 1868 and 1869, the annual excess of deaths over births was 1,155; in 1870 and 1871 it was 1,175. The flood of death rises higher every year, threatening the race with annihilation. A large business that thrives in one of the back streets of Honolulu is the manufacture of plain coffins.

Marriages between the natives are not prolific, even when the married are in comfortable circumstances and of industrious habits. Offsprings are regarded as a calamity.[1]

A CURIOSITY IN HIS OWN LAND

By 1872 the Hawaiian found himself fulfilling Twain's prophecy of becoming "A curiosity in his own land." In June of that year the Reverend Sereno E. Bishop urged his American flock to keep children of Hawaiian parentage out of their all-white schools. "None know or can conceive, without personal observation, that nameless taint that pervades the whole garrulous talk and gregarious life of all heathen people, and above which our poor Hawaiian friends have not yet risen."[2]

During that same period David Kalākaua, an ambitious member of the Legislature, pleaded for the repeal of a law that prohibited the sale of liquor to Hawaiians. "The restrictions imposed by this law do the people no good, but rather harm; for instead of inculcating the principles of honor, they teach them to steal behind the bar, the stable and the closet, where they may be sheltered from the eyes of the law. The heavy license imposed upon the liquor-dealers, and the prohibition against selling to natives are an infringement upon our civil rights, binding not only the purchasers but the dealer, against acquiring and possessing property. Then, Mr. President, I ask, where lies virtue? Where lies justice? Not in those that bind liberty of his people by refusing them the privilege they now crave—of drinking spirituous liquors without restriction. Will you, by persisting that this law remain in force, make a nation of hypocrites? Or will you repeal it, that honor and virtue may for once be yours, O'Hawai'i?"[3] The Legislature declined to repeal it.

Hawaiians searched for someone to champion their cause. Hopes rose and were dashed again when, after a lively election campaign, their candidate, the dowager Queen Emma, lost the crown to David Kalākaua. When the official announcement of Kalākaua's victory was made on the steps of Honolulu's courthouse, a club-swinging riot broke out. Emma's disgruntled followers killed one legislator who had voted against her by hurling him out of a second-story window and sent several other Kalākaua backers to the hospital with broken limbs.

Kalākaua, who had been outspokenly anti-American as a member of the Legislature, had put the interests and rights of his fellow Hawaiians in limbo in order to gain the throne. In a secret arrangement with sugar interests, he had agreed to help them obtain price advantages for sugar on the American market by ceding Pearl Harbor to the United States. In return for his promise to help them get their reciprocity treaty, the sugar planters agreed to support him in his election bid. Following his inauguration in 1874, which was played down for security reasons, Kalākaua paid off the first installment of his debt to the planters by leading a mission to Washington, D.C., where he proceeded to persuade President Grant into helping sway the U. S. Senate into approving the treaty favoring Hawaiian sugar. When the Reciprocity Treaty went into effect on September 9, 1876, it helped to weld the bond between Hawai'i's land-holding sugar planters and the United States government. When word of Kalākaua's sellout to the whites became common gossip in Hawai'i, Hawaiian resentment toward him grew to such proportions that he pleaded with the United States Commissioner to provide him with a detachment of marines to act as the royal bodyguard. The United States obliged him by landing 150 marines at Honolulu. These troops were also to be made available to protect the newly acquired U.S. interests at Pearl Harbor and to enforce provisions of the treaty which prohibited the Hawaiian government from assigning any commercial, political or territorial advantage to other foreign powers.

Reciprocity caused a boom among the sugar planters. In 1875 there were fewer than 20 sugar plantations. By 1880 their number had grown to 63, and cheap labor was urgently needed to chop and mill thousands of acres of ripe cane. The whites who owned sugar colluded to fix prices and to recruit labor from the Orient.

As more American housewives sweetened their apple pies with Hawaiian sugar, the islands began to experience unprecedented prosperity. Sugar became such big business that five factoring agencies established their operations to take care of it. Two of these agencies, Alexander & Baldwin, and Castle & Cooke, were named for the missionaries-turned-businessmen who founded them. Theo H. Davies, Hackfeld & Company, and C. Brewer and Company, founded by other businessmen, completed the entity known as the Big Five. Later, a sugar executive explained. "When the firm of Castle & Cooke began, its primary activity was the importing of merchandise and its sale .... Development of sugar plantations was an expensive and risky business. Most early sugar companies had to obtain financial assistance, and bank terms were most drastic. Wholesale houses such as Castle & Cooke stepped into the breach and permitted certain plantations to issue drafts on them and to run accounts for the merchandise they required. Soon Castle & Cooke broadened the scope of its activities to permit it to manage, act as agents, factors or trustees for estates, plantations, factories, persons and companies."[4]

An enterprising white need not have trusted his entire success in the islands to his business skills. There were short cuts to power and wealth and, according to one witness, some ambitious men, less inhibited by scruples than others, took that route: "When a white man marries the right kind of a native woman, he is a candidate for public honors and perquisites, and becomes one of the photographic celebrities of the Kingdom—sold to strangers at twenty-five cents each."[5] A shining example was Charles Reed Bishop, who, after marrying Chiefess Bernice Pauahi, climbed his way up the ladder of island finance to become Hawai'i's first bank owner. As such, he enjoyed a 26-year monopoly on banking in Hawai'i while "bank terms were most drastic." Later, he became administrator of his wife's land holdings, the largest privately owned estate in Hawai'i, and finally he rose to the position of cabinet rank advisor to kings. Having a virtual monopoly on banking in Hawai'i, Bishop's fortunes soared after reciprocity. Displaying enlightened self-interest, he was the driving force behind the white group which had helped to elect Kalākaua. But, during the 17 years of Kalākaua's reign, Bishop, involved with a variety of financial interests, changed political horses several times.

Robert Meredith, a literate member of America's working class, gave his view: "In 1874 the Islands were just beginning to realize their capacity for producing sugar. The missionaries' children and other shrewd men ... seeing this, conceived the idea of working Uncle Sam for a treaty of reciprocity. If we would admit their sugar and bananas free of duty, they would take on our grain, provisions and lumber in the same way. This seemed fair, as an honest exchange is no robbery. The parlour was arranged and the table was loaded with sugar, which was very tempting to Americans in those days, and the cunning spider sang at the door.

"Knowing that Uncle Sam was beginning to cater to men of wealth and note, and was easily dazzled ... they concluded to send over their king to make the trade. King Kalākaua ... had a wooly head, and the common talk is that he had negro blood in his veins. Although he lived in a finer palace than our President, and got as large a salary, he was nothing but a figurehead, kept there by the influence of white man, who used him for their selfish ends, and as a tool to rob and oppress his own people .... As it is so seldom this country is honored by the presence of a king, when this grand specimen of humanity was coming our government made great preparations to receive him. His royal fare across the continent cost three thousand dollars. Although there was a failure of crops in the grasshopper regions of the West and thousands of people were suffering and starving for want of bread, our Congressmen spent twenty thousand dollars in hauling this son of a cannibal around and in giving him royal banquets. But that is not the worst; they made a treaty by which sugar was admitted free into this country, thus giving them an advantage over all other countries of almost two and a half cents per pound, which amounts to the same thing as a bounty of two hundred dollars an acre on all the cane they produce .... As there is good profit in sugar without this bounty, is it any wonder that these islands have become vastly rich at our expense?

"As soon as this scheme was put through Congress . .. this gang hurried back to the islands, to cheat the poor natives out of their land before they learned that this treaty would make it worth ... what they could not buy they managed to lease for a pittance on long term. If a native was stubborn and held onto his land they would surround him with their plantations and squeeze him out, by making his land worthless to him, for a man of small means can do nothing toward making sugar. All the sugar land has long ago passed into the hands of white men and the king, and it is worth fabulous prices and there is almost no land now of any value that can be bought. This is the history of ... a hundred men who live in Honolulu and are known as sugar kings ... these fellows do not think they have done much unless they make a yearly profit of a hundred percent.

"While at work in Honolulu I used to pass by the palace of Kalākaua and see his lazy highness lounging in the veranda surrounded by his Marine guards. I always felt humbled to think our statesmen should pass by so many of our suffering people to do extravagant honors to such a man, and then sell us out for a mess of pottage."[6]

A grandson of one of the missionary founders of Castle & Cooke evaluated Kalākaua's performance: "The triumph of his reign was the securing of a treaty of commercial reciprocity by which Hawaiian sugar and a few other products were admitted free of duty into the United States. In return Hawai'i made a general remission of duties, and later gave to the United States the exclusive use of Pearl Harbor, as a coaling or naval station. This treaty assured the prosperity of the islands and marked the definite establishment of the sugar industry."[7]

Kalākaua, who up until his election had based his political career on agitation against American interests, now owed his throne to those same interests. In internal affairs the treaty accelerated the racial de-Hawaiianization of the islands because it caused a surge of immigration to meet the demand for plantation labor. Dispelling the missionary/businessman myth that Hawaiians made poor workers, more than 50 percent of the able-bodied male Hawaiians were working on Island plantations as late as 1873. On 35 plantations, there were 3,786 laborers. Of these, 2,627 were Hawaiian men and 364 were Hawaiian women. The greatest concern shown by the businessmen heirs of the missionaries regarding the enormous death toll of Hawaiians was that it decreased their supply of labor. While the Hawaiian population decline was already critical, nobody had a plan to promote the labor needed to cut the cane. Kalākaua decided to take a grand tour of the world to set up the government machinery necessary to recruit such labor. When he cried, *"ho'oulu lahui,"* to his people during his inaugural address, there were fewer than 47,000 of them on all the islands to respond to that mournful plea to "increase our race."[8]

Upon returning from Washington, Kalākaua felt his debt to the sugar interests had been paid. He sought new friends to help reverse the political tide which engulfed his Hawaiian subjects. The allies he found were industrial baron Claus Spreckels and Walter Murray Gibson, Chief President of the Island of the Sea and of the Hawai'i Islands for the Church of the Latter Day Saints. This trio—Spreckels, Gibson and Kalākaua—would upend the smug world of Hawai'i's missionary business community and prolong the life of the Hawaiian monarchy.

WALTER MURRAY GIBSON

The son of English immigrants, Walter Murray Gibson was born at sea enroute to New York. A romantic who thrived on dangerous adventures, he became a school teacher, isolated himself in a remote Indian village for almost two years, married, fathered three children and, when his wife died, traveled to Guatemala where he took his first plunge into revolutionary politics. This awakening led him to the East Indies and an intrigue with a Malayan sultan that landed him in a Jakarta jail, where he was sentenced to twelve years at hard labor by the Dutch authorities. Serving only three months, he escaped, surfacing at the side of Brigham Young in Salt Lake City, where the Mormon way of life was under vigorous attack by the United States government. Baptized a Mormon in 1860 and awarded a commission as a roving ambassador for that faith, he arrived in Hawai‘i on July 4, 1861. Gibson quickly revitalized the local Mormon mission after which contributions to the cause of Joseph Smith flowed freely. He converted this church money into land holdings on the tiny island of Lana‘i and established an elaborate Mormon settlement there. He confided restlessness in his diary: "Lanai is my calmest and healthfulest home thus far. I have been alternating from many days between plans of labor here for years and a purpose of speedy departure .... I plume for my flight in Lanai's valley, and on Lana‘i's hills. I love to go and I love to stay. Before it was always go. But now I rejoice to stay ... I say this is my haven, my shelter from the sad storms of life. My heart is full of song, of the song of the valley, of the hills, of the sea, and of my sweet child Talula more than all. Oh I do think this is something of the peace and the sweets of what is called a better world."9

Three years later, a five-man auditing team from Salt Lake City arrived on Lana‘i to appraise Gibson's erratic administration. When they discovered all deeds to the land parcels on Lāna‘i were held in his name *only,* they promptly excommunicated him. Those lands, the Mormon stronghold on Lāna‘i, became the private fiefdom of Gibson. Later he commented his "temporary connection" with the Mormon Church was for a "political objective." That objective would become clear when his overall shrewdness and his fluency in the Hawaiian language placed him at the head of Kalākaua's cabinet.

Gibson used his knowledge of Hawaiian customs, language and the slogan, "Hawai‘i for the Hawaiians," to attract Hawaiian voters. He was spectacularly successful in these efforts, becoming the only white to gain office on O‘ahu in two successive legislative elections. When he found himself at a disadvantage because of a lack of favorable publicity, which he sorely needed to advance his political career, he dipped into cash reserves and mortgaged his Lāna‘i lands to buy two Honolulu newspapers creating, overnight, his own propaganda mill. Gibson's greatest satisfaction came from wielding power. Although he was more competent, imaginative and cultured than his predecessors in high office, his fate was not better.

CLAUS SPRECKELS

A lone wolf-style businessman, Claus Spreckels fought for, and gained control over, shared enterprises. Having borrowed from an acquaintance in Bremen, Germany, to pay for steerage passage, Spreckels debarked on the shores of the land-of-opportunity at Charleston, South Carolina, in 1846. During the next decade, he worked as a clerk in New York City and then crossed the continent to become the proprietor of a grocery store in San Francisco. Seven years later he had risen to the position of chief Executive Officer of the Bay Sugar Refinery. When he became impatient to expand that operation and the Board of Directors declined to follow his lead, he resigned and immediately established the California Sugar Refinery.

A split-second entrepreneur, Spreckels arrived in Honolulu on August 20, 1876, a passenger on the steamer carrying the news that the U. S. Senate had approved the Reciprocity Treaty. Coming to acquire land for the purpose of establishing his own sugar plantation, Spreckels bought all available raw sugar and sent it on to be processed in his San Francisco refinery. Overnight he became a close and trusted advisor to Kalākaua. As his business interests in Hawai'i grew, the control Spreckels exercised over the king's cabinet sprang from his relationship with Premier Gibson. Spreckels held a mortgage in the amount of $34,000 on Gibson's Lāna'i lands.

Before the year was out, Spreckels had acquired title to, or signed, long-term leases on more than 30,000 acres of land on Maui and had petitioned the king for water rights to irrigate that soil for his sugar. Kalākaua's cabinet, still occupied by the whites who had supported his election, pondered Spreckels' request for a week. When no decision was made, the king sent a messenger to each cabinet minister's home at two o'clock in the morning to inform him of his dismissal. Kalākaua had spent the evening in a hotel room drinking champagne with Spreckels and his close friend Samuel Parker, heir to the Parker Ranch. After the California capitalist had agreed to make the king an unsecured loan of $40,000, Kalākaua had called for the messengers. As dawn broke, the king, Spreckels and Parker discussed possible candidates for the newly vacated cabinet seats.

Although the members of the "American Missionary Party" had great trepidations about having Spreckels in their midst, the editor of *Ka Nupepa Ku'oko'a*, a Hawaiian language periodical, expressed another view "... Claus Spreckels has bought extensive lands on Maui. He will bring the water from the mountains and plant the lands with sugar ... he will invest one and a half million dollars here ... his ideas concern the increase and preservation of the Hawaiian race. He will divide this land into small districts and settle whole families on them. They will plant sugar shares and get paid for their labors. The country will become prosperous and the people will multiply."

Spreckels kept his promises to the Hawaiians on Maui, and that particular group of Polynesians seemed to give the lie to the local white businessman's truism that it was impossible to find productive Hawaiian labor for the sugar industry. Hawaiians worked productively for Spreckels. Some Hawaiians, however, preferred jobs that gave them the physical challenge of danger, the opportunity for travel and other activities which allowed them freedom of movement. Hawaiians were renowned as the best sailors and horsemen in the kingdom.

In 1876, 13,000 tons of Hawaiian sugar were exported. Total sugar exports for 1898 exceeded 229,000 tons. Because of the nature of sugar production requiring large scale operations, reciprocity forced concentrations of economic power onto the ledgers of Hawai'i's factoring agencies. Sugar was king and, if any individual were to be singled out as being most responsible for its phenomenal rise and the resultant prosperity which followed, it was Spreckels.

The Advertiser, with Gibson controlling its pages, defended Spreckels when he was maligned in a sniping speech which accused him of acquiring his water rights illegally. "This is doing a gross injustice to a man who introduced more capital, employs more labor, puts more money into circulation, and stimulates trade and commerce more largely than any other man in the kingdom ... the social condition of the natives is greatly improved from what it was before that important work was commenced. The natives do not now live in abject poverty. They have frame houses, are well fed and clothed, and land formerly unproductive along the line of the ditch is now cultivated, water being furnished by seepage .... Neither have the taxpayers any cause for complaint, because the utilization of that water has turned an arid plain into the most extensive and productive sugar plantation in the kingdom, one year's taxes upon which amount to double the selling value of the property when Colonel Spreckels took it in hand."[11]

Spreckels spent $500,000 to build his first irrigation ditch on Maui. It channeled six million gallons of mountain water into his cane fields every day. He came to Hawai'i to cultivate, mill and sell sugar and, in order to accomplish those objectives, he was willing to spend a fortune and to take tremendous risks. He imported expertise from the U.S.A. and Europe to build mills, railroads, wharves, and warehouses and created Hawai'i's first steamship line to deliver his sugar to any port in the world. He was a capitalist in the Century American mold, demanding pride in workmanship, being resourceful, bold, human, decisive, shrewd and certainly ruthless when necessary. An observer called him a "staunch friend, an uncompromising enemy."

There were, however, rare occasions when an important detail escaped his attention. By 1882, after having committed a substantial fortune to his sugar holdings on Maui, he realized he did not hold perfect title to his acreage. He corrected that oversight by using his political influence to buy, in fee simple, 24,000 Maui acres for $10,000 cash. These were Crown Lands with cloudy titles which he cleared for himself by loaning High Chiefess Ruth Ke'elikolani $60,000. Spreckels then employed the legal talents of William R. Castle and persuaded the king to appoint Edward Preston as Attorney General. He, in turn, introduced a bill which passed in the House of Nobles, giving Spreckels perfect title to the acres.

The Hawaiian Gazette, a newspaper opposing Kalākaua's administration, supported the industrialist. "Claus Spreckels has certainly made out of what was worthless land a waving plain of cane .... If this is gathering wealth to the owners and projectors it is also scattering money among the Hawaiian people. We learned that during the construction of the mills the payroll of the plantation rose as high as $39,000 per month; a large portion of this must find its way into the pockets of the Maui people, native and foreign, another portion must come to Honolulu." [12] Spreckels showed a flair for public relations that left his less imaginative competitors mired in stodginess. Paving the way to a smooth relationship with Kalākaua's arch political foe, Queen Emma, he assigned his son John to squire her about Maui. The dowager queen bubbled her appreciation, "I must tell you of the very pleasant visit we are making here, everybody has been so good and kind to us. Last night John 0. Spreckels called and invited me to go and see the electric light, which they use at the mill, so this evening we started by train with a party of nearly 600 people for Puunene where his mill stands. Everything is on the most extensive scale, and the newest inventions of machinery are used, etc. Mr. Spreckels showed us the electric machines where electricity is made and conducted through wires to every part of the mill. You have seen the light no doubt, so can fancy how like unto day was the entire interior and exterior of the building. It really was wonderfully grand, he explained the various processes of sugar making ... he was awfully patient with us. There was music, vocal and instrumental, wine and cake at his house and music in the train." [13] The Spreckels mills on Maui were the first structures in the kingdom to be lighted electrically. In season these mills were worked at full capacity around the clock. 'Iolani Palace wasn't wired for electricity until 1886.

Condemned for being corrupt and reckless by the conservative local business establishment, Spreckels pumped more financial life into Honolulu's lethargic bloodstream than all of his rivals combined. Hawai'i planters and businessmen feared Spreckels. He seemed far better than they at their own game, played on their home field.

Charles Reed Bishop founded the Bank of Bishop and Company in 1858 and for the next 26 years his was the only bank in Hawai'i. Earlier, the Reverend Samuel C. Damon had given that autocratic venture his endorsement: "Upon the whole, we are glad to see the enterprise started without the usual Bank machinery of a 'charter' and 'Board of Directors.' We believe there is much in the saying that 'corporations have no souls!' ... We much prefer the personal responsibility of gentlemen whose charities are established and known."[14]

When Spreckels opened his own bank in 1884, breaking a quarter of a century banking monopoly, Bishop began for the first time to pay interest on savings accounts. The competition forced him to lower his prime interest rates from a whopping twelve percent to seven percent and he began to sell exchange on silver at par, rather than discounting it at twenty percent.

Four years earlier, Bishop had borrowed $250,000 at seven percent interest from the Royal Treasury which, having benefited from Spreckels' business activities, showed a surplus of several million dollars. Bishop's personal friends and close business associates were facing a severe financial crisis and in their hour of greatest need turned to him, still the only banker in town. His response was to loan them the surplus cash he had just acquired at seven percent for rates ranging up to 35 percent.

Then a member of the House of Nobles, Bishop was grilled on the floor of that body regarding a possible conflict of interest in borrowing that cash from the Royal Treasury. Backed into a corner, he finally confessed that he knew the government loan was illegal. Hawaiian representative A. R. Kaulukoa pursued Bishop, asking, "Then how does the Hon. Noble account for his action in assenting to anything that was not laws?" Bishop glibly replied, "Because it was a matter of great public exigency."[15]

Later that year *The Advertiser* sprang to the defense of Spreckels' bank when it became the subject of a blistering attack by Bishop and his friends. Gibson's allusion to Spreckels, and then to Bishop, was unmistakable, "... the much abused great man from San Francisco has introduced millions which the people could borrow at living rates." Spreckels had broken Hawai'i's financial shackles, freeing the people "... from the grinding tyranny of usury ... —12 percent compounded quarterly."[16]

PEARL HARBOR

Eight miles west of Honolulu, connected to the open sea by a narrow channel, lies Pearl Harbor. It has ten square miles of navigable water, with 30 miles of deep waterfront, which is calm in any weather. It is the most important harbor in Hawai'i and is as good as any on the Pacific coast of the U.S.A. When the original *Old Ironsides*, renovated and recommissioned as the *U.S.S. Constitution*, anchored off Honolulu in 1845, Lieutenant L. W. Curtis, U.S. Marine Corps, went ashore: "Allow me to call your attention to the importance of Pearl Harbor, the perfect security of the harbour, the excellence of its water, the perfect ease with which it can be made one of the finest places in the Island, all of which combine to make it a great consideration. While the harbour was being cleaned out, fortifications could be built, troops could be drilled, the forts might be garrisoned, Government storehouses built. The amount of money to be expended will be but a feather in comparison with the almost incalculable amount of wealth that will result upon the completion of these objects." 17

When Pearl Harbor officially became a coaling station for the U.S. Navy in 1886 as part of the Reciprocity Treaty, Spreckels held $700,000 in notes against the kingdom. That amount was more than half of the total public debt for Hawai'i. He treated the kingdom of Hawai'i as though it were one of his privately owned enterprises. He was rich enough and innovative enough to protect his investment in Hawai'i by expanding his operations into other avenues. In December, 1881, he founded the Oceanic Steamship Company. In addition to transporting sugar from the islands, special attention to passengers would be given, hoping, according to a press release, "thereby, to make Hawai'i a pleasure resort more frequented by San Franciscans." Before the year was out the president of Oceanic announced the signing of a million dollar contract for the building of two other steamers to service Hawai'i. "It is our intention to leave nothing undone to make these boats as complete and comfortable for this island trade as experience can suggest. We do not doubt that all such travel will tend to the material benefit of Hawai'i." 18

One year later the tug *Pele*, with the Royal Hawaiian Band on deck, chugged out to welcome the *Mariposa* on her maiden voyage. When Spreckels walked down the gangplank to enter the king's carriage, the Reformatory and Industrial School Band struck up "Hail to the Chief." The following day Gibson's *Advertiser* gushed, "Strains of music, the acclaim of a thousand voices and the booming of guns were just the proper announcements of an event which signalizes a complete revolution in our means of communications with the Coast." Behold Claus Spreckels, the founding father of Hawai'i's tourist industry!

In less than three years Oceanic was under a withering barrage from envious local businessmen who had earlier been rebuffed by Spreckels, when they had attempted to buy an interest in the venture. Gibson editorialized, "Without its breezy and invigorating influence Honolulu would be a stagnant pool of commercial inactivity today. Yet there are members of this community ... who lose no opportunity of attacking the founder of the Oceanic Company and other great enterprises for the development of the resources of the Kingdom, because he is an innovator, and tramples upon their woeful business traditions."[19]

Chapter Twelve

DAVID KALĀKAUA
1874 - 1891

Oh, what a King was he! Such a King as one reads of in nursery tales. He was all things to all men, a most companionable person. Possessed of rare refinement, he was as much at ease with a crew of "rollicking rams" as in the throne room.[1]

— Charles Warren Stoddard

DAVID KALĀKAUA

A descendant of two high chiefs who were close advisors to Kamehameha I, David Kalākaua was born in 1836. At 27, he married the other Kapiʻolani, a granddaughter of the last king of Kauaʻi. They produced no heirs.

Four days after taking the royal oath and swearing to support the Constitution, he formed a cabinet which was preselected by the monied businessmen who had made his incumbency possible. Accepting an invitation issued by these same gentlemen to travel to the United States, Kalākaua celebrated his 38th birthday on November 16, 1874, and sailed the following day for San Francisco, enroute to Washington, D.C.

Writer Charles Nordhoff described him, "Colonel Kalākaua is a man of education, of better physical stamina than the late king, of good habits, vigorous will, and a strong determination to maintain the independence of the Islands." At the same time, Henry A. Peirce, U. S. Minister to Hawaiʻi, warned his superiors that, "He is ambitious, flighty and unstable. Very energetic; but lacks prudence and good sense."[2]

As a boy, David Kalākaua attended the Chief's Children's School, where he was an adequate student with good reading habits. He traveled to the west coast of the United States on numerous occasions and later served as the foreman of a volunteer fire company, a newspaper publisher and, according to one enemy, he was a thief having resigned his office of Postmaster General under fire when he was unable to account for missing funds. Joining the House of Nobles in 1860, he took an active role in legislative proceedings for more than a dozen years. At the same time, he displayed a rather remarkable gift for poetic composition.

Soon after his inauguration, he attempted to clear the air of the bitter hangover of resentment left by Queen Emma's followers. Flanked by his U.S. Marine guard, he took to the stump, "Let us thoroughly renovate ourselves, to the end that causes of decay being removed, the nation may grow again with new life and vigor, and our government may be firmly established .... I believe that if I shall make the main object of my reign the increase of the nation, there may be secured both the stability of the Government and the national independence .... The increase of the peoples the advancement of agriculture and commerce; these are the objects which my government will mainly strive to accomplish."[3]

When rumors of a conspiracy among Hawaiians to assassinate him became prevalent two years later, the *U.S.S. Lakawanna* steamed into Honolulu Harbor with another detachment of U.S. Marines aboard. The rumors subsided and the regime proceeded with one less immediate threat to its security. When the king left Washington after having sold the idea of reciprocity to the U.S. Government, U.S. Minister to Hawai'i, Peirce, stayed behind and gave some advice to the Senate Committee on Foreign Relations: "The acquisition of the Hawaiian Islands by the United States, sooner or later, must become a national necessity to guard the approaches against hostile attempts on the Pacific States .... If reciprocity of commerce is established between the two countries, there cannot be a doubt that the effect will be to hold these islands with hooks of steel in the interests of the United States, and to result finally in their annexation to the United States ..."[4]

This treaty of reciprocity was used to further a much broader political objective. The United States became a signatory to the treaty in order to expand its influence over the islands and to keep other powers at arm's length. During the next six years no United States government representative in Hawai'i voiced significant objection to any of Kalākaua's policies. The monied interests had paid for a safe passage.

•

In an address to the Hawaiians in 1876, Walter Murray Gibson noted the "woeful condition of their race where not more than 4,000 able bodied men could be found." The census of 1890 would count 34,436 Hawaiians.

According to Dr. George L. Fitch, chief physician of the Free

Dispensary in Honolulu, "... of about 40,000 of aboriginal descent there are over 700 condemned and isolated lepers ... on Molokai and 3,000 to 5,000 undeclared lepers in the kingdom." He reported that leprosy, believed to have been brought to Hawai'i by an infected Chinese in about 1850, was everywhere; the military, the police, teachers, students, band members, men of the cloth were all infected. Fitch's official report showed 4,055 new cases of all diseases treated in the first quarter of 1882. Of these, more than 2,700 had syphilis and another 508 had leprosy. One of Honolulu's most knowledgeable doctors estimated that 80 percent of all Hawaiians were suffering from some form of venereal disease.

In what was to be a futile attempt to rejuvenate his race, Kalākaua broke with his sugar-interest partners and began to surround himself with advisors opposed to the missionary/business clique. While the three kings who preceded him to the throne had appointed a grand total of only two Hawaiians to their cabinets, Kalākaua could count 11 ministers of Hawaiian blood among the 37 cabinet appointments made during his tenure. He expressed his opinion of the local whites in a letter to his sister, Princess Lili'uokalani, "Men of conservative principles are always opposed to progress. They will not see beyond their noses ..."

Strange political bedfellows began to maneuver. Spreckels, already at Kalākaua's side, and Gibson, supporting the king with his newspapers and plunking for him at the Legislature, were joined by Celso Caesar Moreno. A well-known lobbyist in California and Washington, D.C., he arrived in Honolulu late in 1879 with an elaborate plan to establish a steamship line and an oceanic cable between Hawai'i, China, and America. Moreno, a graduate of the Italian Naval Academy at Genoa and a wounded veteran of the Crimean War, also held a degree in civil engineering. He had been decorated by both the Italian and French for pioneering commerce on their behalf in the East Indies and in China. J. M. Comly, the U.S. Minister to Hawai'i, described him as "... a subtle, crafty and extremely clever Italian of imposing and insinuating manners—a big, burly man, six feet high, with an air of some distinctions." Moreno had more than a dozen languages at his command.[5]

Although he remained in Hawai'i for less than a year, he gained the enthusiastic support and confidence of the king. He advised Kalākaua to fill his entire cabinet with Hawaiians, to float a ten million dollar loan, and to grant unlimited Chinese immigration to Hawai'i. He spoke glowingly of the untapped wealth of China and of his knowledge of how to channel that wealth to Hawai'i. In a special address to the Legislature, the king declared, "The interest of our country demands a further and more permanent establishment of our commercial intercourse direct with that of China. The opening to us of the great Emporium of Asia will add a tenfold resource of revenue and profit to our country."[6] A special legislative committee advised against appropriating a subsidy for Moreno's schemes exclaiming "Our interests are with America." Undaunted, Moreno succeeded in getting a bill passed which authorized the importation and sale of opium to the Chinese residing in Hawai'i.

A ten million dollar loan bill, which included provisions for "traveling physicians with medical stores and attendance provided free for the natives at their homes and the like," was defeated, it was said, because it included a million dollar bonus for Moreno. Gibson tried unsuccessfully to salvage Kalākaua's pride by introducing a loan bill leaving the amount blank, to be filled in later. A tragic effect of this incident involved the killing of that part of the bill which would have given medical aid to the Hawaiians, with the backing of every knowledgeable physician in the kingdom who had long since agreed "that the only means of prolonging the existence of the Hawaiians was by bringing them within the protecting reach of medical aid."[7] Amid outcries of "utter bosh" and "crazy scheme," a very real opportunity to help the disappearing Hawaiians died.

Even though Gibson's blank check bill was ruled out of order and rendered harmless, a pall of suspicion and distrust fell over Kalākaua's administration. His cabinet began a destructive debate in an attempt to clear itself and, finally, the king demanded they all resign. Later that day Kalākaua announced the appointment of a new cabinet, which was described by the American minister as "... for the most part grotesque in unfitness." Moreno, who had been naturalized as a Hawaiian citizen on that morning, became Hawai'i's Minister of Foreign Affairs that same afternoon.

Sanford Ballard Dole introduced the following resolutions: "Whereas, his majesty Kalākaua, King of the Hawaiian Islands, has arbitrarily and without cause dissolved the late ministerial cabinet while they had the confidence of the Legislative assembly and of the country at large, and his appointment in their stead a Ministry including one Celso C. Moreno, a stranger and a foreign adventurer who had identified himself with interests hostile to the prosperity of the Hawaiian Kingdom and who has neither the confidence nor respect of the community nor of the Representatives of Foreign Powers, as Minister of Foreign Affairs: Be it resolved, that His Majesty has thereby acted inconsistently with the principles of the Hawaiian Government as a Constitutional Monarchy as established and handed down by the Kamehamehas and their successor Lunalilo, and that his action therein is hostile to the permanence of Hawaiian independence, the perpetuity of the Hawaiian race and the security of life, liberty and property in the Hawaiian Islands."[8]

Contrary to that accusation, Kalākaua was exercising the

same royal prerogative Lot Kamehameha used when he abrogated the Constitution of 1852, exclaiming, "I will give you a Constitution." Lot, in fact, gave his people a new constitution, which made "the influence on the crown pervade every function of government." Kalākaua was acting under that same constitution when he dismissed his ministers and appointed new ones. His underlying mistake was to give the business interests of Honolulu sufficient reason to unite against him.

U.S. Minister J. M. Comly, who as a General represented the military might of the United States, as well as the American business community of Honolulu, agreed to intercede with the king to have Moreno's appointment voided. Having met with the king, Comly delegated Alexander J. Cartwright* to appear before a mass meeting of American, British, French and German businessmen at Damon's Bethel Union Church on April 15, 1880, where, according to *The Advertiser*, he announced, "Gentlemen, I am authorized to say to you that His Majesty, entirely of his own volition, has dismissed Mr. Moreno from the Ministry." Having tasted victory, the gathering demanded the other Kalākaua cabinet appointees also be dismissed. Comly tried to persuade against petitioning the king, but failed and wrote to the Department of State, "... a little tact would have given the King time to feel good in and then the people might have had their way. But these Old Puritans don't know, any half-way between damnation and election."

Since the British and French Commissioners to Hawai'i had both publicly "Wished to intervene with a joint or collective diplomatic representation demanding the dismissal of Moreno," Hawaiian voters who supported Moreno responded with mass meetings, protesting foreign intervention in their affairs. Posters appeared overnight proclaiming, "WAY UP—CELSO MORENO, a naturalized and true Hawaiian. His great desire is the advancement of this country in wealth, and the salvation of this people, by placing the leading positions of Government in the hands of Hawaiians for administration. The great desire of Moreno is to cast down foreigners from official positions and to put true Hawaiians in their places, because to them belongs the country .... C.C. Moreno is the heart from whence will issue life to the real Hawaiians."[9]

A Hawaiian language newspaper attacked Dole: "The King's prerogative has been encroached upon .... The Constitution does not grant the subject a right to express his opinion of censure on His Majesty the King (regarding cabinet appointments). At Mr. Moreno's resignation the critical condition of Hawaiian affairs should cease, as the foreign diplomatic difficulties have been once and for all settled.

* Cartwright is credited as the father of baseball.

Let the foreign elements in these islands beware! They might not be able to quiet the storm they have raised."[10]

Moreno remained at the palace, where Kalākaua ordered that letters be written to Washington, Paris and London, demanding the withdrawal of their ministers in Hawai'i. Minutes after Moreno had left Honolulu, at the request of the king, a committee of 13 missionary/businessmen met with Kalākaua to thank him for ridding the community of Moreno and then to demand the resignations of the remaining cabinet ministers. Claus Spreckels stepped in to admonish the king that he "... had surrounded himself with a precious set of fools; that everybody knew it except himself and that the whole thing was a laughing stock to all his enemies and the enemies of the country; the whole thing was all wrong."[11] Buckling under, Kalākaua dismissed the remaining ministers and again appointed an all-white cabinet. Kalākaua was in desperate need of a friend. Gibson editorialized, "It is folly to suppose that the native population of these islands will sit down contentedly under exclusive foreign domination, or that they will view with complacence the spectacle of their King surrounding himself with foreign advisors to the entire exclusion of their own race. Still less are they likely to let such a state of things pass without comment when they know that the sentiment of the King is wholly in accordance with their own, and feel that he must have unwillingly yielded to the clamor and agitation raised and kept up with a view of intimidating him by a party numerically small, however influential .... The King has seen fit to give way before the spirit displayed by a section of the foreign community, and he will insult his own dignity by adhering to the arrangement he has consented to ..."[12]

The Saturday Press, started by a committee of merchants to oppose Gibson-Kalākaua policies, replied, "The absence of natives ie. pure Hawaiians from the Ministry has been commented on unfavorably. We propose to deal with the question in a short and simple manner. It is best to speak plainly. The present is no time for such people to be in the cabinet. The nation cannot afford to do with less than four men who shall represent the best governing power in the country. Let us not be misunderstood. It is not a question of race, but of fitness .... Let the native qualify himself for high office and we shall rejoice to see him a real ruler in his native land. The true work of Hawai'i *nei* is to educate itself, not to lament its exclusion from office, its unfitness for which has been so abundantly proved. But at present, and we fear for some time to come, let us hear no more of native ministers."[13]

Supreme Court Justice Albert Francis Judd was not embarrassed to ask why the old-style Hawaiians should be tolerated in high office when there was a superior new breed of true homegrown Hawaiians eminently qualified and eager to serve. "A wrong impression has obtained that only those born here of the aboriginal Hawaiian stock are the true Hawaiians. A man born here of white parents who spends his talents and energies for the benefit of Hawai'i is as true a Hawaiian as if his parents were all red, or one red and the other white. Those who benefit this country by their own good character and example and life are the true Hawaiians."14

Hawai'i's white property owners felt a new surge of strength and flexed their political muscle, ready to smash anyone who stood in the way of their economic fulfillment. They discovered a method of directly attacking Kalākaua on a racial basis without offending the Hawaiians who still represented the majority at the ballot box. They whispered that Kalākaua and his sister Lili'uokalani were not true Hawaiians, but rather the children of a negro coachman, John Poppin, who had been their mother's secret lover. Hawaiians, already conditioned by their missionary teachers to look down upon blacks as inferiors, began to have serious doubts about their king's bloodlines. The Americans became even bolder and followed Kalākaua to his speaking engagements, where they held up an effigy of the coachman and jeered, "nigger," as he spoke.*15

William R. Castle, Jr., grandson of an Eighth Missionary Company businessman, forecasted, "It is a question of only a few generations, before the Hawaiians ... will be only a memory. In many ways this disappearance of the race is sad, for the Hawaiians are a people with a past that is often noble. In spite of their weaknesses and their follies they are very lovable."16

Kalākaua, avoiding confrontation, exclaimed, "Now that my troubles are over, I mean to take a trip AROUND THE WORLD."

Flanked by two portly cabinet-rank guardians and his valet, the German Baron Robert von Oehlhoffen, Kalākaua waved fond *aloha* to more than 100 gyrating hula dancers on the dock as the royal party steamed out of Honolulu Harbor on January 10, 1881. The king's new white cabinet ministers had appointed Chamberlain Charles Hastings Judd and Attorney General William N. Armstrong, whose parents were members of the Fifth Missionary Company, to accompany him on his travels. According to Armstrong, "... the useful purpose" of the globe-circling trip was "to seek over the world recruits to the depleted population of the kingdom, a depletion so steadily growing that there was imminent danger, within a few generations, of the singular case of a native monarchy without a native subject."17 Hawai'i Chief Justice Charles C. Harris objected, stating

* Letter to the editor, Honolulu Star Bulletin, April 18, 1988: "All one needs today to have a holiday declared in one's name is to be a member of a minority and to be assassinated. I refer to of course to Martin Luther King. To the many who heard him speak in the Islands some years ago, he appeared to be more Communist than American..."   — Janice Judd

that Kalākaua "... had gone for no object whatsoever, except the gratification of his own curiosity, which may be said to be object enough ... the whole thing is a mere pretext for enabling the king to travel around the world and enjoy himself."[18]

President James A. Garfield's thoughts about Kalākaua's trip ran in a more serious vein. "The King has started on a voyage around the world, and it is feared he is contemplating either the sale of the islands or some commercial treaty with European powers which would embarrass the United States. We shall probably soon have more delicate and important diplomatic work in that direction than at any previous time in our history."[19] The king and his party were under around-the-clock surveillance by agents of the U.S. Secret Service during the trip.

Word of the "incognito" king's intentions to visit Japan preceded his arrival there and, according to Armstrong's account, the greeting he received was tumultuous. When they entered Yokohama Harbor, warships flying Russian, British, French, American and Japanese flags saluted them. "The crews mounting and manning the yards cheered as we passed; the roar of two hundred and seventy-three cannon; the smoke rising in the clouds and rolling away in dense volumes toward the bay; the innumerable flags with which the warships were dressed appeared and disappeared in the smoke. The king stood impassive, lifting his hat as we passed each vessel, while our royal standard dipped in response."[20]

During the next two weeks, Kalākaua was accorded all honors befitting his rank. The Emperor Mutsuhito glorified him with the Grand Cross of the Order of the Rising Sun. He, in turn, quickly created and conferred the Grand Cross of the Order of Kamehameha upon the Emperor and proposed that the Emperor take over leadership of a "Union and Federation of the Asiatic Nations and Sovereigns."[21] Although the Emperor demurred, he later revealed that he shared a common fear with the Hawaiian. "When your Majesty was in my capital, you have in the course of conversation alluded to a union and Federation of Asiatic nations .... I highly agree with your Majesty's profound and far-seeing views. Your Majesty was also good enough to state that I might be the promoter and chief of this Federation. I cannot but be grateful for such expression of your love and confidence in me. The Oriental nations including my country have long been in a state of decline and decay: we cannot hope to be strong and powerful unless by gathering inches and treasuring roots we gradually restore to us all attributes of a nation. To do this our Eastern Nations ought to fortify themselves within the walls of such Union and Federation, and by uniting their power to endeavor to maintain their footing against these powerful nations of Europe and America, and to establish their independence and integrity in the future. To do this is a pressing necessity for the Eastern Nations, and in so-doing depend their lives."

Kalākaua's elaborate treatment at the hands of his gracious Japanese hosts and his realization that they shared a common fear of a mutual enemy, the white man, moved the king to suggest in private a marriage between the Imperial Prince of Japan and his niece and heir presumptive to the Hawaiian throne, Princess Kai'ulani. Since this Japanese Emperor had no desire to test American might, he graciously declined Kalākaua's offer to cross bloodlines and share empires. Crossing the East China Sea to Shanghai, Kalākaua was warmly welcomed and informed that General Li Hung Chang, the Viceroy of China, was in residence at Tientsin. Boarding a large steamer, the king and his party sailed up the coast to Tientsin, where they enjoyed a banquet with the Viceroy and learned it would not be possible to have an audience with the Emperor of China because he was ill. Steaming south, they were properly greeted in Hong Kong by the British Governor and left soon for Saigon and, from there, sailed up the Gulf of Siam to Bangkok, where their welcome was nothing less than spectacular. The Royal Siamese barge, manned by 24 uniformed oarsmen, escorted on the nearby riverbank by a full company of sabre-bearing cavalry, shouted their greetings to the Hawaiian monarch amid the tooting of riverboat whistles. The King of Siam appeared from within the barge accompanied by a dozen trumpeteers, and exchanged salutations with Kalākaua in English, as they drank a toast to mutual health with the "wine of the coral reef," coconut water.

Later, as the party was mounting royal elephants for a hunt in the Siamese jungle, "Our Chamberlain, with his great weight, broke the ladder as he was mounting, and dangled in the air, with a firm grip on the seat, until another ladder was brought, while the elephant grunted at the mishap of a tenderfoot."[22] After Judd was secure in his wicker seat aboard the elephant, a Siamese foreign service officer asked him, "Is it true that the civilization of Europe is due to Christianity?" Judd, testing this verbal ladder before mounting it, responded, "... this is a difficult question to answer, but that is the claim of the leaders of the churches. "Then," the Siamese purred, "if Christianity is the cause of European progress, is it also the cause of the fleets and the armies with which they are ready to destroy one another?"[23] Judd remained mute.

While sailing south to Singapore on a small charter boat, the Irish captain amused himself by entertaining his royal passenger with tall tales of the terror and brutality that Malay pirates inflicted upon their victims. Then he added, "If the pirates knew your Majesty was on board this ship, they'd like to take you and get a pretty ransom for letting you go." Armstrong commented that, "... the king did not look

upon himself as a knight seeking adventures, but as a royal bee sucking only the sweets of honours and experience in the meadows of the
earth; and now he found himself on an unarmed vessel in waters more
or less infested with freebooters. His imagination exaggerated the
danger, and he declared that a king should travel only in a warship.
He had the timidity of a man who is led by his flatterers to believe that
his life is more precious than any common lives and that unusual efforts
for its preservation should be taken."[24]

Kalākaua bubbled in the splendor of exotic oriental courts
and sent word home that a portion of his coronation funds should be
used to purchase jewels for gifts to his generous hosts.

Arriving in Calcutta, the royal travelers waved to the swarming masses that lined the alley-like streets and quickly set out across
the Indian subcontinent by train to Bombay. There they boarded a
ship, sailed west, crossing the Arabian Sea, and then into the Red Sea
and on to Suez, where they were the guests of the Khedive aboard his
private train, which sped them on to Cairo. During that stopover,
Kalākaua was awarded the title of Honorary Grand Master of the
Grand National Orient of Egypt. The king viewed the Sphinx and the
Pyramids as the guest of a sheik whose harem housed no less than
300 wives, all highly skilled in the art of the belly dance.

A wave of nostalgia washed over the party on a moonlit night
in Alexandria, where, amid streaming rockets and flickering lanterns
which shimmered on the surface of the bay, King Kalākaua raised a
golden goblet in a salute to the rotting hulk of an abandoned British
coal scow across the harbor. He said, "Let's drink a toast to that old
ship. Here's to Captain Cook's *Resolution*."[25]

On the king's arrival at Naples, Italy, Moreno, who had no
official capacity with either the Italian or Hawaiian governments,
tried to join the royal tour. When Judd and Armstrong threatened to
return to Honolulu if the king allowed Moreno to accompany them,
Kalākaua seemed resigned to a permanent split with his colorful
Italian friend. "I feel quite relieved for there has been so much fuss
and feathers made about Moreno .... I feel greatly relieved. The man
is not such a devil as he is painted."[26]

King Humberto greeted the royal party at Capo de Monte, and
two days later Kalākaua had a private audience with Pope Leo XIII.

He was presented to the Prince of Wales in London and paid
his respects to Queen Victoria at Windsor Castle, met with the
Archbishop of Canterbury, and lunched with Prime Minister
Gladstone. Although historians generally agree that Kalākaua's visit
to England was a success in that it improved relations between the
two nations, Armstrong wrote of it wryly as a "Royal circus with a
Polynesian lion in the cage. If a lion fattens on attentions, he finally
waddled out of England as fat as a poodle dog."

On July 24, 1875, Kalākaua returned to the continent to meet with King Leopold in Brussels, Prince William Krupp in Germany, the French foreign minister in Paris, Archduke Albrecht in Austria, and the Governor of Madrid in Spain. His calendar was crowded with memorable events as he toured Europe. He shared some of this excitement with his youngest sister, Princess Likelike, in a series of letters. "You ought to hear Strauss' band in Vienna. Oh! Exquisite music. The best I have ever heard. Vienna is one of the prettiest places we have visited but Paris seems to exceed all."[27]

During his short stay in Vienna, Kalākaua made a lasting impression, being compared to another royal visitor by the biographer of Emperor Franz Josef. "Let me mention in passing that the Siamese King behaved rather peculiarly. While taking a drive with Emperor Franz Josef in a gala coach drawn by four horses, he continually spat out of the carriage window. The Emperor remarked that even if the Siamese spat and did generally not behave properly, he was a good deal more decorous than Kalākaua I, the King of the Sandwich Islands. Although the latter had been received with all honors due a sovereign, and should, therefore, if for no other reason, have observed a certain dignity, he had, by howling, fearfully disturbed the variety show at a public restaurant in the prater, had taken off his uniform coat as soon as the dance began, and promiscuously kissed the women and, finally the lackeys had to take him, helplessly drunk, back to his hotel..."[28]

Kalākaua told his sister of operas he had enjoyed in London and Paris; of plumed troops which had passed before him in review in almost every country; of his visit to Waterloo's battlefields and Krupp's munitions factory in Essen. He purchased an entire battery of Austrian field artillery for $20,000. For reasons unknown in Hawai'i, it never reached its intended destination in Honolulu; instead, it ended up on a scrap heap at the U.S. Arsenal at Benecia, California. He spent another $20,000 in France for the design and creation of two jeweled crowns to be used in his belated coronation.

He met with the King of Portugal, visited in Edinburgh and Glasgow, and, upon arriving in Liverpool, boarded a ship bound for New York, where Claus Spreckels greeted him with a *lei* as he strode down the gangplank. He chatted with President Chester A. Arthur in Washington and had a serious conversation with Acting Secretary of State Robert R. Hitt, who inquired of the welfare of the Hawaiian people. Kalākaua responded, "What good do you think the Europeans and Americans have done there ... Captain Cook, and the fellows who came after him from New England, filled my people with disease and leprosy, and, besides, they forced rum on us. Where one missionary did good there were five hundred of his countrymen who debauched our women, filled them with diseases, and sold liquor to the people. The missionaries told our people to keep Sunday and stop dancing, but the countrymen of the missionaries call them bloated fools and told us not to mind them."[29]

Now the party entrained for Cincinnati and then to Lexington, Kentucky, where Kalākaua bought several thoroughbred horses from his host, General Northfield Withers. When the king arrived in San Francisco on October 11, he was taken on a round of gala parties, but took time out one evening to scan the starry heavens through the Lick Observatory telescope and to inquire of the astronomers as to the feasibility of building such an installation in Hawai'i.

Although he was the focus of a great celebration upon his return to Honolulu on October 29, Kalākaua's position on the throne was shaky. After nine months abroad, Armstrong observed, "The white subjects of King Kalākaua, though able to destroy the monarchy because they possessed the brains and the wealth of his kingdom, cordially assented though the majority of them were Americans, to its rule but insisted that it be ministerial rule. By refusing to submit to this form of government the king had already put his throne in great jeopardy and if the offense were repeated he would again be in peril."[30]

The king's Hawaiian subjects were in no position to help him. *The Advertiser* reported that, "Not one Hawaiian of pure blood in all the islands owns or exclusively operates a sugar plantation or a mercantile or manufacturing business. These enterprises are owned by Englishmen, Germans and especially by Hawai'i-born Americans Hawaiians owned little or nothing of value."

TRIUMVIRATE

Kalākaua came home to a kingdom tottering on the edge of racial upheaval. Walter Murray Gibson, vigorously campaigning for reelection to the Legislature through the columns of his newspapers, attributed this boiling unrest to the arrogant ways and extravagant expenditures of the all-white cabinet, which had been forced upon the king two years earlier. He blamed those particular whites for "the unfortunate growing feeling of antagonism of races." On January 28, 1882, *The Advertiser* publisher Gibson unveiled his "rule of action in the public service," vowing to "honor the King to promote the welfare of the Hawaiian people, maintain treaties with world powers, favor immigration, promote industrial enterprise, further education," and to "shorten legislative sessions." Gibson won in a landslide. *The Saturday Press* forecast a typhoon. "The future does not look bright. Clouds are gathering and the waves grow boisterous." Gibson coun tered, "... the election most unequivocally means a determination on the part of the Hawaiian people to stand by their independence."[31]

Gibson was one of just three foreign-born candidates elected to the Legislature in 1882 and had the distinction of being the only white elected to any office in Honolulu. The Hawaiians had spoken, and Gibson was their new champion. Twenty-seven candidates sponsored by the sugar industry had been defeated. Since their livelihoods were in great peril without the support of the Hawaiian voters, the missionary/businessmen agreed among themselves that the cabinet they had earlier selected should be reorganized. They tested Gibson's loyalty and ambition by offering him a chair in that cabinet under "certain conditions." He laughed, then refused. As one editorial written by a journalist in his employ explained, Gibson recognized "... that the game was in his own hands, for being the acknowledged leader of native inhabitants, it was natural that His Majesty, when any change of Ministry became necessary, should desire to call to his councils one who was the choice of both the natives and foreign-born populations. The new Premier, however, when sent for by His Majesty, selected his colleagues to suit the King and himself without consulting his would-be supporters who retire crestfallen, and cry out ... that the country is in danger! What? With a man of their choice at the head of affairs? If the country is in danger, which I don't believe, they have nobody but themselves to blame...

"I am aware that when Mr. Gibson declined to be made a tool in their hands the red hot Reciprocity Party subsided, and would have been glad to see even the old Ministry patched up, but it was too late, and now a new set of performers has come upon the stage and quick to take advantage of the situation, take up the cue and continue the game which the others had just thrown up."[32]

The British Commissioner characterized Gibson, "He is a very clever man, and has completely succeeded in making the too-easily led Hawaiian believe that he (Mr. Gibson) is his only real friend, and the champion of his race against the white man. Mr. Gibson's native journal has, for months past, been stirring up the natives against the whites. The idea conveyed is that foreigners are not well-disposed toward Hawaiians, and that the latter ought therefore to keep political control in their own hands. I fear that Mr. Gibson is doing a work which may lead to serious consequences. He may not be striving for disturbance or revolution but that may probably be the result."[33]

Kalākaua announced the appointment of a new cabinet on May 20, 1882. Gibson was his choice as both Premier and Minister of Foreign Affairs, the most powerful cabinet officer in the kingdom.

For the next five years Kalākaua, Gibson and, at critical times, Claus Spreckels were to exercise almost complete control over the government of Hawai'i.

Robert Louis Stevenson described an unexpected peril upon arriving at Honolulu Harbor in 1889 "... and what is far more dangerous ... being entertained by his Majesty here, who is a very fine, intelligent fellow, but O, Charles! what a crop for the drink! He carries it, too, like a mountain with a sparrow on its shoulders. We calculated five bottles of champagne and one of brandy in three hours and a half and the sovereign quite perceptibly more dignified at the end."[34]

On the ninth anniversary of his accession to the throne, Kalākaua produced a gala coronation extravaganza, where, in the style of Napoleon, he crowned himself and Queen Kapi'olani as sovereign rulers of Hawai'i. Because of the riots that followed his victory over Queen Emma in 1874 and the subsequent occupation of Honolulu by U. S. and British Marines, the original installation ceremony in 1874 had been brief and simple. Following that inauguration the royal couple had suffered the indignity of moving into the old 'Iolani Palace, described by the king as being "... filthy and in poor condition, and it is only with great effort to hide our humiliation that we live here." Before departing on his global adventure, Kalākaua had helped to lay the cornerstone for a new palace that *The Advertiser* depicted as "by far the finest and most imposing building on the Islands." The opening of the new 'Iolani Palace was highlighted by the elaborate festivities surrounding the coronation. Kalākaua, still dazzled by the brilliant courts of Europe and Asia, installed the etiquette of the Court of St. James in his new palace, reflecting what he had admired during his audience with Queen Victoria. As he dramatically placed the $10,000 crown on his own head, the strains of a hymn sung by the Kawaiaha'o choir resounded through the neck-craning throng. Then the shrill brass of the Royal Hawaiian Band burst into the Coronation March, accompanied by a fanfare from Hawai'i's shore batteries, which roared and belched smoke rings over Honolulu Harbor. The British, French and American warships answered with volleys of their own. "Tables were arranged under the marquee between the amphitheater and the palace," *The Bulletin* reported, "and chairs were used haole fashion...guests could not all sit down at once because there were too many ... probably 400 or 500 at 1 pm ... about 1,200 people were on the grounds ... after the luau the hula began, and it kept up until 11:30 pm ... the crowd was enormous probably nearly 11,000. The total cost of the party, which lasted for two weeks, was more than $50,000."[35]

The Planter's Monthly shook its editorial finger "The so called coronation of the King, with the attendant follies and extravagances has been directly damaging to the property interests and welfare of the country. It has been demoralizing in its influence and productive only of harm ... public measures of pressing importance have been neglected. The bare routine of public offices has been maintained, while nearly every measure for public advancement has had to wait the accomplishment of the coronation ceremonies."[36] *The Daily Bulletin* denounced the *hula* as "a retrograde step of heathenism and a disgrace to the age."

The opening of the new palace renewed the king's hopes that he could find expression in his yearning to assert Polynesian values. Kalākaua, 37 years old when he succeeded Lunalilo, had matured into a thicker man, with streaks of silver in his black kinky hair, mutton chop sideburns, and an arching mustache. According to one white woman, he was "... unaffected, kindly, and genial in his conduct and association with all classes, he has such a manner of kingly dignity about him, and at the same time is so jovially companionable, with that hail-fellowwell-met air, and so appreciative of his listeners, that he appears to me almost an ideal man."[37]

The king did not confine his amusements to the palace. He found much pleasure at the Snuggery, his boatclub hideaway, where, according to missionary heir Lorrin Thurston, "on an underpinning of stones set in shallow water, the king had erected a single-thickness board shack, which housed several row boats and slips on the ground floor, while overhead a broad social hall stood, and several private rooms, simple but comfortable. There the king entertained in genial fashion. Liquid refreshments were freely on tap."[38] Warships from France, Russia, Austria, Argentina England, Italy and the United States anchored nearby.

A junior officer aboard the *U.S.S. Pensacola* described a marathon round of partying with a Hawaiian woman, "... four *hula* dancers entertained us all afternoon. Wines and refreshment were in order .... In the evening took Kaomealani to the entertainment at the Palace. During the evening the King and I had several drinks together. Left at about 2 and went to a friend's home were we kept it up all night. The King sent some champagne and ice cream over and then came over himself with a party of gentlemen. Guitar music, songs, champagne and dancing were in order until daylight. We then bid the girls an affectionate farewell and rode off ... in the royal carriage."[39]

Kalākaua had revived, with variations, *kilu*, a sport which was much patronized by the *ali'i* class of the ancient regime. "The King began his modern version of the game by holding the free end of a ball of twine. He would then toss the ball into a bevy of women; the woman who caught the ball was his companion for the night. The ball was passed to the next gentleman who tossed it into the bevy of women and so forth. Under the rules of the original *kilu* forfeits were pledged, the payment of which was met by a performance of a dance

... which not infrequently called for liberties and concessions that could not be permitted on the spot or in public, but must wait the opportunity for seclusion ... kings and queens were not above participating in the pleasures of this sport .... king nor queen could not plead exemption from the forfeits incurred, nor deny to another the full exercise of privilege acquired under the rules. The payment of these extreme forfeits was delayed until a convenient season ... at the request of the loser, if a king or queen, by an equivalent of land or other valuable possession. Still no fault could be found if the winner insisted on strict payment of the forfeit. The game of *kilu* was often got up as a supreme expression of hospitality to distinguished visitors of rank, thus more than making good the polite invitation of the Spanish don, 'all that I have is yours.'"[40]

At this point the monarchy seemed more in control of the affairs of Hawai'i than at any time since the reign of Alexander Liholiho. However, amidst the gaiety, the seeds of its destruction were in evidence. Kalākaua, not content to merely rule over the Kingdom of Hawai'i, decided to expand his territory and become the sovereign ruler of the entire Pacific. In 1883 he sent commissioners to the Gilbert Islands and the New Hebrides to set up Hawaiian protectorates. His overall plan, which included bringing Samoa and other island countries such as Tonga under Hawaiian rule, brought immediate consternation to the foreign offices of European powers who had already established their own jurisdictions in these islands. The effort toward "The Primacy of the Pacific" caused immediate friction over Samoa among England, the United States and Germany. Early in 1887 Kalākaua made unusual preparations to impress the Samoans with the strength of Hawai'i and then followed up by sending an ambassador to negotiate a treaty which would tie Samoa to Hawai'i politically. When that mission ended as an expensive failure, it was charged to Kalākaua's popularity account as an error of incompetence. Other state concerns, less spectacular than building a Pacific empire but no less important to the survival of the regime, began to surface. The United States Senate, being pressured by the born-again southern sugar bloc, was seriously considering the abrogation of Hawai'i's treaty of reciprocity. Surprisingly, the man who seemed to have the most to lose by such an abrogation, Claus Spreckels, was not alarmed at the prospect. The reason was that his operation was efficient enough for him to make a substantial profit in Hawaiian sugar without the advantage of a price support from America. On the other hand, it was a hard capitalistic fact that almost all other Hawaiian sugar planters would fail without the subsidy because their operations were too badly managed to survive it. Since all but Spreckels shared the common fear of bankruptcy, they formed a committee to raise money to sponsor anti-Kalākaua candidates in the coming legislative elections. Old faithful government servants, including Charles Reed Bishop and Charles H. Judd, embittered when Gibson had dismissed them from the cabinet, contributed large sums from their own monies for anti-Kalākaua campaign expenses.* With *Daily Bulletin* Editor Lorrin Thurston as their principal agitator and spokesman, the old missionary/business alliance succeeded in getting a significant number of handpicked candidates elected to the Legislature. These newly elected lawmakers mounted podiums to attack Gibson and his cabinet for "financial embarrassments due to extravagant appropriations, flagrant irregularities in awarding public works contract," and "negligence in the conduct of government affairs." They demanded the resignation of the ministry and "retrenchment for a judicious economy."

Opposition to Kalākaua and his cabinet grew. According to U.S. Minister Rollin M. Daggett, this opposition sprang from three sources: "The Annexationists composed principally of young Americans ... with no great property interests in the Islands. They do not number, perhaps, more than three or four hundred but are zealous and outspoken ... most favor the abrogation of the Treaty of Reciprocity believing that the large sugar interests, principally in the hands of Americans would be forced to seek relief from disaster in annexation. Secondly from American and European planters and property owners. Their opposition, however, is less to the form of government than to the manner of its administration. They charge the King with extravagance, and the ministry with doing less than their duty in submitting to it .... Americans who have either been relieved from service under the government, or who would be willing to accept profitable public positions held by others. This class includes what is known here as the Missionary influence."41

Public debate boiled over as the missionary/business view that Kalākaua should "reign but not rule," collided with the monarch's insistence that he maintain strict control over all aspects of the kingdom. Editor Thurston, a founding father of the Honolulu Rifles, raised his sights on the throne room at 'Iolani Palace. "And why should we not discuss the King? The King is personally and individually responsible for the continuation of the present disreputable and disgraceful condition of affairs; why should we beat around the bush?" Then he shifted to another target, "We recognize him as a man of unusual enterprise, and one who in various ways encouraged the business and industries of these Islands. He has in many respects been a benefit to the country .... But he has manifested a disposition to exercise undue influence in the affairs of the govern-

---

*In 1874 this same group used their influence and political maneuvering to defeat pro-British Queen Emma and elect Kalākaua. They called themselves "The Down-Town Party. "

ment; to control the public administration too much for his own benefit. Col. Claus Spreckels is a power in this community .... We are not
opposers of Mr. Spreckels, on principle, although we have been
opposed to some of his projects, on principle .... So long as Mr.
Spreckels continues to support Mr. Gibson, however, he cannot
expect any hearty feelings towards himself, nor can he be considered
as acting otherwise than for personal reason."[42]

Gibson rallied in defense of Spreckels: "He is simply working
in harmony with every other man who is interested in the welfare of
these islands, for their prosperity, and is endeavoring with all of his energies to see us safe over an inevitable business depression. Colonel
Spreckels is the active and stalwart friend of Hawaiian interests."[43]

By December of 1885, Spreckels had become the prime target
for sniping legislator candidates pitted against the "palace party." An
Independent Party candidate saw Spreckels as an omnipotent tree.
"One man beyond the sea. He placed himself here some years ago
like a tree and at first overshadowed a few merchants, but since that
time the tree has grown until now it overshadows the Kingdom, the
Government and the throne itself."[44]

Thurston, having become a candidate for the Legislature,
asked "Are we to act for ourselves and nurse our own laws, or are we
to be led like swine with rings in our noses, at the will of a man who
cares for nothing but his own interests?"[45]

Spreckels was able to control the cabinet, because he was
financing the government with his own private funds and because the
king and the premier both owed him small fortunes. When Kalākaua
appeared before the Legislature and pleaded that they pass a bill
authorizing him to borrow an additional two million dollars to pay
for the importation of cane workers and for public improvements,
Spreckels admonished him indirectly in a fatherly tone, saying he "...
liked the country, the climate, and the people. The people are mild,
generous and open. But they have one fault: they are extravagant.
Take my advice, practice economy, be independent, have money in
the bank, and care for nobody."[46]

It was at this point, so goes the story, that two visiting admirals—one American and one British—were extended a royal invitation for an afternoon of cards and refreshment at the Snuggery. The
Royal Hawaiian Band saluted the gold-braided guests upon their
arrival and, as the foursome settled in to play, with Kalākaua and
Spreckels as partners against the military powers, it was obvious the
monarch and the sugar baron were at odds with each other. Spreckels
was making tough demands upon Kalākaua in return for the new loan
he was about to advance. The king was reluctant to give Spreckels
long-term bases and control over the water works, the harbor, the
wharves and the electric light plant as security for the new loan. As

the lazy afternoon wore on and the euchre hands continued to favor the admirals, the royal nerves were rubbed raw. The final indignity came when Spreckels, who held three kings, an ace and a low card in his hand, turned to the admiral on his left (still concealing his cards) and remarked, "If this were poker I would have the winning hand here." The British officer challenged Spreckels, offering to bet that he held the winning poker hand. Spreckels quickly covered the bet and, when the officer turned over his cards revealing three aces, Spreckels turned over his cards, showing the three kings, declaring, "My four kings win over your aces." Perplexed, Kalākaua asked, "Where is the fourth king?"[47] Spreckels, raking in the bet, looked Kalākaua in the eye and retorted, "I am the fourth king." Kalākaua thundered out of the boathouse, fuming down the dock, catching the Royal Band unawares. When Spreckels emerged a few moments later, laughing in the royal wake, the band, having pulled itself together, was striking up "God Save the King." The white-bearded sugar magnate stopped, turned and tipped his bowler. The relationship between Kalākaua and Spreckels cooled markedly.

When Kalākaua succeeded in negotiating the needed two million dollar loan through a London financial syndicate, Spreckels was invited to share in providing those funds.[48] He agreed, but made new demands in a tone that caused Gibson to respond, "Mr. Spreckels on one or two occasions ... ventured to express himself in such a dictatorial manner to His Majesty in the presence of several members of the Assembly, saying that his views must be carried out, or he would 'fight,' and exclaiming that this meant a withholding of financial accommodation and an immediate demand for what was owing to him, that he aroused then and there a determination on the part of the native members present to resist the dictation of '*ona miliona*' (multi-millionaire) and as they themselves avowed, to see whether their chief Kalākaua or Mr. Spreckels were king .... It was through Mr. Spreckels' offensive dictatorial manner arousing the sensitive native members to indignation, that these arrangements were thrown aside at the last moment."[49]

When Spreckels and his wife hurried aboard the *Mariposa* on October 23, 1886, to begin their return voyage to San Francisco, the Royal Hawaiian Band did not play.

Upon reaching San Francisco, Spreckels granted an interview to a reporter who had come aboard the *Mariposa* with the harbor pilot. When asked to explain the reasons for his ruptured friendship with Kalākaua, Spreckels mumbled his reply, "The King has for a long time been led by gin-drinking adventurers, men who have nothing to lose and everything to gain by leading His Majesty into escapades, and upon a course of wildest dissipation. He is easily approached when sought at the drinking or gaming table. The two leading courtiers are Colonels MacFarland and Armstrong, both Englishmen, the latter an agent for Portuguese immigrants. These men have got the ear of the King and persuaded him that they could float a loan in England for him at remarkably low rates. I think the move to secure the $2,000,000 loan in England was a positive indignity to me, for I have the greatest interest in the islands and being a citizen of the United States, the country with the closest commercial relations and the most natural geographical situation for intercourse, I think that after offering the Government all the money it was judicious for them to spend, at a rate more advantageous than the loan they have accepted, the whole proceeding was a studied insult...." [50]

Without Spreckel's steady financial hand to guide it, Hawai'i's ship of state began to flounder. As it came precariously close to capsizing, American missionary/ businessmen protecting themselves took immediate advantage of Kalākaua's vulnerability by demanding political reform designed to support their monied interests and property. Lorrin Thurston, Alatau T. Atkinson, Sanford B. Dole, William A. Kinney, William R. Castle and Dr. S. G. Tucker organized the clandestine Hawaiian League, whose sworn purpose was to force the king "to be decent, and reign, not rule, or take the consequences." A meeting was held at Dole's home, where a new constitution drafted by Thurston was adopted. When their political efforts failed to change "the extravagant and corrupt policies of the unresponsible King," they reached out to others in the pro-annexation white community and formed five rifle companies, which were to be used to effect the desired constitutional change. They formed a committee to wait upon the king and force him to repeal the Constitution of 1864 and to grant whatever new constitution they authorized.

Charles Reed Bishop briefed a carefully selected audience at a Hawaiian League meeting on the eve of an uprising "This is unquestionably an important meeting, the most important meeting ever held in Honolulu. I see before me mechanics, merchants, professional men. They are not here for amusement, but because they feel that the course of affairs calls for prompt and determined action. We should discuss matters in a peaceable manner, without any threats. I came here in 1846, became naturalized in 1849, and have lived under five kings. We thought we had a liberal Constitution because these kings would not encroach upon the rights of their subjects; but we have found out during the last four years that our Constitution is defective, partly on account of bad advice to the King, but largely on his own account. The King has encroached upon our rights. We have very few mass meetings. But when we have one like this I believe it means either a new Constitution or one with material reforms, which I am sure we shall have. I came here as a Hawaiian, not for any class or clique. If it was for any class or clique, I would not come here at all."[51]

It is difficult to understand how its members could describe the Hawaiian League as a vehicle for drawing together all classes of the community, when in fact it was a segregated organization with 405 names on its roster. A large number of prominent members of the island community were included, but not one single identifiable Hawaiian or Oriental name was listed on its rolls.

Late in June, 1887, the Executive Committee of the Hawaiian League felt confident enough about the strength of its military arm to allow Thurston to proclaim "that the time is ripe to bring about a crisis." The immediate cause was indignation, real or manufactured, surrounding a bribery scandal related to the government licensing of opium sales. The Committee, uneasy about rumors the king was fortifying the palace and activating his army, decided to act at once. The curtain was about to rise on the Bayonet Constitution.

The late librarian of Hawai'i's Archives, Albert P. Taylor, described the events which followed, "The Committee went to the King armed with evidence involving him in the illegal sale of an opium franchise to a Chinese resident, for which he received $74,000, which the Committee demanded should be returned. The King demurred to the demands, but finally agreed to the new Constitution when he found that the temper of the people was far from friendly and not to be trifled with. He admitted receiving the $74,000 from the Chinese resident, and agreed to pay it back, although stating he had spent it. This caused an agreement to be drawn up by which the King surrendered the revenues accruing from the Crown Lands, and revenues from his estates to be handled by a committee in order to make restitution and avoid a public scandal. The whole proceeding was afterwards legalized by act of the Legislature. The new Constitution dubbed 'Bayonet Constitution,' because of the force used in extracting it, took from the King the right to appoint judges and justices, and the ministry was made responsible to the people, not to the King. The recall of Gibson was demanded and a new ministry requested. The King agreed to all demands. Gibson resigned and was escorted to the wharf a few days later, under guard, whence he sailed for San Francisco, where he died a year later. The king's purse was greatly depleted."It was a complete collapse of the preeminence of Kalākaua as King, and from that day his rulership declined ... "[52]

Kalākaua and his supporters continued the political fight, trying to recapture control of the Legislature, and at times went outside of the political arena to resort to armed action. Robert W. Wilcox, one of the students that Celso Moreno had taken to Italy to study military science, returned to Honolulu in 1887. The king's capitulation disenfranchised the majority of Hawaiians by restricting Hawaiian voting rights to property owners or those with cash incomes greater than most Hawaiians had.* Its promotion of the American missionary/business interests using armed force stirred up tremendous resentment among Hawaiians, who demanded that their voting rights be restored. Wilcox joined the group and immediately began plotting to overthrow the Bayonet Constitution. His activities were brought to the attention of the new white cabinet, and they acted swiftly by exiling him to California. Two years later, Wilcox reappeared in Honolulu wearing the uniform of an Italian cavalry officer. Soon he led a rebel army of 150 heavily armed men, who seized and occupied 'Iolani Palace and all government offices. The ministry countered by posting snipers on adjacent buildings and shots could be heard all during the daylight hours of July 30, 1889. Samuel Mills Damon, son of the missionary, now Minister of Finance in the "reform cabinet," attempted to negotiate with Wilcox. When he was rebuked, he called upon U.S. Commissioner Merrill for assistance. U.S. Marines from the *U.S.S. Adams* came ashore. Seven insurgents were killed and twelve fell wounded on the steps of Kalākaua's bungalow. When Wilcox was tried for conspiracy and pleaded he had acted with Kalākaua's consent, the jury made up of Hawaiians found him innocent. Kalākaua quickly disavowed any association with Wilcox. "Regarding the rumor that I am in league with the movement of Mr. Wilcox, I make this solemn declaration that these reports or rumors are not true."[53] In spite of the king's repudiation, or perhaps because of it, Wilcox became a hero to many Hawaiians. They had lost affection and respect for their beleaguered monarch.

Regarding the Wilcox verdict, missionary heir, Dr. S. E. Bishop, editorialized, "We do not think the native jury intended to commit an act of injustice, although from the point of view of the white man, and a large body of intelligent natives, they were greatly in error .... Like the ole Jacobites, to the minds of most Hawaiians, whatever is done by the King and for the King, is legitimate, and cannot be treasonable .... A race question was made to enter into the merits of the case...a majority of the natives adhere, through thick and thin, right or wrong, and a native jury votes straight on that side. Although most of us would have preferred a conviction ... still there is probably no very great regret ...."[54]

RECIPROCITY ABROGATED

In 1890 the United States Congress created a financial panic in Honolulu by passing the McKinley Tariff Act. When this bill was

---

*The Bayonet Constitution of 1887 gave the missionary/businessmen residing in Hawaii, who had not become naturalized citizens but remained resident aliens, the right to vote.

signed into law by President Harrison on October 1, it wiped out the advantage that Hawaiian sugar had been enjoying because of reciprocity. Henry N. Castle, yet another missionary heir and *The Advertiser's* newest editor, expressed his feelings in a letter to his sister. "We are plunged into the depths of despair over the McKinley Tariff Bill. There is no doubt that the situation is a very critical one ... it is doubtful whether there is a plantation on the islands, which could make any money. Probably one or two would but most of them would collapse if such a state of things continued long. Well, we will hope for the best, and try to make money in something else if sugar busts." [55]

Kalākaua, urgently in need of a respite from the throne room crisis, boarded the U.S. Flagship *Charleston* as a guest of the U.S. Government, and sailed for San Francisco. His reception upon coming ashore on December 4 was cordial, but not ostentatious. Rumors that he had come to America either to sell his kingdom to the United States, or to sign an agreement for its annexation, were whispered at dinner parties and at diplomatic receptions. These rumors soon became headline news in Ottawa, London, New York, and Washington. A *Honolulu Bulletin* reporter, digging to find the origin of these distortions, wrote, "Without being able to locate all the sources of misrepresentations it is alleged here that some are to be found in letters received from British residents and officials; while others have come through those residing in Hawai'i, who have been putting forth insinuations of an annexation policy to further, if possible, private schemes and desires for closer commercial relations between Hawai'i and the U.S." [56]

Kalākaua pleaded innocent to any intention of relinquishing his kingdom, claiming that he had come to California only to rest and to regain his health.

It seems that the Merry Monarch could not take a rest cure. After a fortnight of nonstop San Francisco partying, especially among those whites who had enjoyed royal favors during their visits to Honolulu, the king, pampered by the luxury of a private train, was whisked off to a warmer climate. Following a five-day stop on the Monterey coast at Aptos, the sea ranch of Claus Spreckels, the king found his second wind and, upon arrival in Los Angeles, dashed off a note to a friend, "A spontaneous ovation. I have never seen the like before .... Not one moment's rest. Traveling day and night. Receptions, Balls, dinners, Dinners, Masonic initiation .... Sunshine, Rain, Storm & C. it's all the same. Wonder that I am not half dead yet .... I have learnt and have seen a great deal .... Good People and all that but awfully damn cool .... Whio!" [57]

Ensconced at the Coronado Hotel south of San Diego, Kalākaua and his entourage ventured south to Mexico and later to the San Diego Opera House for performances of *Faust* and *Carmen*. Fleet

Admiral George Brown, who had been in Washington attending a State Department briefing concerning the possibility of a trade which would renew reciprocity in exchange for permanent U.S. occupation of Pearl Harbor, greeted the king at Los Angeles' Union Depot on the return trip. When they reached Santa Barbara for three days of "Receptions, Balls, dinners, Dinners," and a final Masonic initiation, Kalākaua had a stroke. Admiral Brown called for his fleet surgeon, Dr. George W. Woods, to care for the king when the party returned to San Francisco and the Palace Hotel on January 12.

Four days later David Kalākaua spoke into a crude recording device held close to his lips by Louis Glass, a technician from the Edison Phonographic Company. In a husky voice that was barely audible, the king, as though confiding in a friend, murmured, "*Aloha kāua ... aloha kāua ... Ke ho'i nei no paha mākou ma kāia hope aku i Hawai'i, i Honolulu. A ilaila 'oe e hai aku ai 'oe i ka lehulehu i ka'u mea e lohe ai ia nei.*" ("I greet you. We are returning perhaps hereafter to Hawai'i, to Honolulu. There you, tell the people my things here heard.")

On January 20, 1891, David Kalākaua died. Among those at his bedside were Claus Spreckels and Charles Reed Bishop.

Dr. Wood reported, "The heart was found greatly hypertrophied, there was evidence of slight pericarditis, and the aorta and its branches were athermanous, suggesting the possibility of capillary rupture within the cranium, as complicating the cerebral uraemic symptoms which had been before considered. The liver was contracted, and distinctly cirrhotic. Other organs could not be examined without a complete autopsy, which was opposed."[58]

Two years earlier Robert Louis Stevenson had presented Kalākaua with a mounted golden pearl and a sonnet

> The Silver Ship, my King, that was her name
> In bright islands whence your fathers came—
> The Silver Ship, at rest from winds and tides,
> Below your palace in your harbor rides:
> And the seafarers sitting safe on shore,
> Like eager merchants count their treasures o'er.
> One gift they find, one strange and lovely thing,
> Now doubly precious since it pleased a king.
> "The right, my liege, is ancient as the lyre
> For bards to give to kings what kings admire.
> Tis mine to offer for Apollo's sake;
> And since the gift is fitting, yours to take.
> To golden hands the golden pearl I bring;
> The ocean jewel to the island king.[59]

Chapter Thirteen

TO STEAL A KINGDOM
1893 - 1924

... this relic of barbarism--the Queen was rather portly, of medium height and plainly dressed. She was about 54 years of age, with a full round face, broad across the cheeks, thick lips, rather dull expression, and a countenance indicative of a severe temper and strong determination. She was darker than the ordinary native, showing evident traces of negro blood.[1]

— Lt. Lucien Young, U.S.N.

LILI'UOKALANI

Lydia Kamaka'eha Paki, born on September 2, 1838, was an excellent student, with an extraordinary gift for poetry and music. She began her education seated beside her older brother, David Kalākaua, and her younger sister, Miriam Kekauluohi Likelike, at the elite missionary-sponsored Chief's Children's School. Described by her critics as naive, superstitious, gracious and barbaric, Lili'uokalani was thought by many to be uniquely qualified to lead her people.

Editor Sereno E. Bishop, respectfully noted, "Our good Queen Lili'oukalani takes the throne under circumstances most favorable ... for a happy and prosperous reign. She enjoys in a high degree the affection of her Hawaiian subjects, and their confidence in her attachment to their welfare. Her gentle and gracious demeanor, her good sense, and fine-culture, have also commanded the high regard of the foreign community ... "[2]

Editor Bishop was a poor prophet. A severe depression was about to upset the delicately balanced economy of Hawai'i and churn up a tidal wave of fear that would rush through the missionary/business community, causing panic. The economic circumstances for a prosperous reign for the new queen were tenuous.

Three years later, Sereno E. Bishop, who had earlier replaced Damon as editor of *The Friend*, wrote, vilifying "her majesty's gentle demeanor and fine culture" in the columns of the *New York Independent* by maligning her as the "debauched Queen of a heathenish monarchy where ... the *kahuna* sorcerers and idolators, all of the white corruptionists, and those who wish to make Honolulu a center for the manufacture and distribution of opium lie together with the lewd and drunken majority of the native race."[3] Soon thereafter he published a page out of his diary spreading an ugly lie that spilled racial venom across the entire United States in an article syndicated by the *New York Herald*. Bishop slandered Lili'uokalani, helping to speed her dethronement by repeating the unsubstantiated story she, as well as her brother David Kalākaua, were the illegitimate issues of sexual unions between her mother and a black coachman.

Upon her accession to power, her longtime friend Charles Reed Bishop, who had married her *hanai* sister, Chiefess Bernice Pau'ahi, sent his congratulations and offered this advice: "In the politics and routine of the Government the Ministers have the responsibilities, annoyances and blame—and usually very little credit. Let them have them, and do not worry about them. You will live longer and happier and be more popular by not trying to do too much."[4]

Two years later Lili'uokalani ignored Bishop's advice when she made a courageous attempt to replace the Bayonet Constitution, which had been forced upon her brother by the Honolulu Rifles, with a new constitution. Although she pledged "changes in the fundamental law of the land would be sought only by methods provided in the Constitution itself," Bishop, the banker, promptly turned on her and launched a personal attack on her politics, her morals and her race. "Had the Queen been a law abiding and honest ruler—though her private character might not have been pure—the case would have been a different matter ... That she is deceitful and treacherous I believe. Her political acts and her purposes with regard to the Constitution are the strongest points against her ... Those who know what the effect would be of being governed by such a Sovereign and a legislature largely made up of impecunious and scampish natives, look upon the situation very differently to those who are non-resident and have no property or family interests here."[5] Bishop, acting as trustee for the estate of his late wife, Bernice, who died in 1884, controlled almost 11 percent of the land mass of Hawai'i's six major islands, scorned the idea of being ruled by the queen and her fellow Hawaiians.

Other influences were working toward the demise of Hawai'i's monarchy. Secretary of State James G. Blaine gave his thoughts on United States expansion to President Harrison: " ... there are only three places that are of value enough to be taken that are not continental. One is Hawai'i and the others are Cuba and Porto [sic]

Rico ... Hawai'i may come up for decision at any unexpected hour and I hope we shall be prepared to decide it in the affirmative."[6]

The Legislature of 1892 passed a bill licensing the sale of opium and another granting a franchise to establish a lottery. Missionary/business interests roared with indignation and used those relatively minor pieces of legislation to reactivate their rifle battalions and plead with United States Minister John L. Stevens to help them overthrow the queen. Stevens responded by ordering the *U.S.S.Pensacola* to Hawai'i "to guard American interests in that vicinity." He attempted to justify his gunboat diplomacy, " ... the English are getting a strong hold on the Hawaiian Islands and the new Queen is partial to the English ... the presence of a United States vessel not only operates strongly to preserve good order among the many nationalities here, but it is a standing notice to foreign nations that the United States has a special care for these islands."[7] Although the queen stated a preference for "the absence of the *U.S.S.Pensacola* now stationed here ..., " the warship remained. *

When a resolution favoring the renewal of the U.S. reciprocity treaty was presented to the Legislature by ranch heir Samuel Parker and passed, Hawai'i's minister in Washington, Henry A. Carter [husband of G. P. Judd's daughter, Sybil], asked permission to lobby for a complete reciprocity treaty with the U.S. Shortly thereafter, Parker became Lili'uokalani's Minister of Foreign Affairs and he, too, urged her to weigh the idea of "more closely cementing the friendly relations which have always existed between Hawai'i and the United States."

The Hawai'i economy plunged even further, causing the Planters Labor and Supply Company to petition for complete free trade with the United States. Stevens, with his shoulder to the wheel of annexation, pushed for "a liberal and comprehensive policy ... absolutely necessary to save these islands from grave disaster." Then, appealing to American self-interest, he added, "If the Hawaiian group should slip from our control our natural rivals would gain great naval and commercial advantage in the North Pacific ... it is our imperative duty to hold these islands with the invincible strength of the American nation ... the only permanent security will be the moral pressure of the businessman and of what are termed 'the missionary people,' and the presence in the harbor of Honolulu of an American man-of-war."[9]

When President Harrison refused to sponsor the final version of the treaty drafted by Parker, the Hawaiian Legislature ordered the U.S.Navy to leave Pearl Harbor. Claus Spreckels, back on the scene

---

* Stevens as U.S. Minister to Paraguay and Uruguay from 1870-74 called in American troops and was rebuked by the Dept. of State. In 1883 he was recalled from Sweden and Norway.[8]

as a friend and advisor to the queen, offered to mediate. "The power which holds Pearl Harbor will be the mistress of the seas in the North Pacific. The possession of Pearl Harbor has been guaranteed to the United States ... by treaty. Why not make this condition perpetual ... conferring perpetual reciprocal advantages upon Hawai'i? This should not, and, indeed need not, involve any attack upon the independence of the Islands. No one could be more opposed to their annexation to the United States than I am."10

The Hawaiian language newspaper editorialized: "That harbor is a grand prize, and it is incumbent on our statesmen to preserve it and keep it for a more valuable and desirable consideration than the United States has yet given us."11

Charles Reed Bishop was in Washington with Lorrin Thurston, new owner-publisher of *The Advertiser*, promoting negotiations for the annexation of Hawai'i to the United States. Secretary of State James Blaine warmed up to the idea, and the Secretary of the Navy relayed a message from President Harrison, "... if conditions in Hawai'i compel you to act as you have indicated, and you come to Washington with an annexation proposition, you will find an exceedingly sympathetic administration here."12

Hawai'i's Attorney General, Arthur P. Peterson, a lawyer from Massachusetts, reported to the final session of the Legislature of 1892 that the queen had signed the lottery and opium bills into law. Lili'uokalani then arrived at the Legislature to participate in the adjournment ceremony. Upon the completion of that ritual, she quickly returned to 'Iolani Palace to keep a critical appointment with her cabinet ministers. They had barely settled into their chairs when she asked for their assent to introduce a new constitution which had been demanded in a petition signed by more than two thirds of the registered votes in Hawai'i. Although her new ministers had promised their support in a meeting three days before, agreeing to confirm the necessity for a constitutional convention, none were now willing to do so. Peterson, seeking to soften the queen's embarrassment, requested a two-week delay to study the issue. Lili'uokalani, chagrined by their sudden change of heart, quickly agreed to the delay. When this meeting adjourned, the dejected queen walked upstairs to a second-floor balcony and tearfully addressed the expectant crowd below, saying, "that your wishes for a new constitution cannot be granted now, but will some future day."

The impact of financial panic, the signing of the opium and lottery bills, and the threat of a new constitution favoring the Hawaiians gave the missionary/business interests all the reasons they needed to get rid of Lili'uokalani.

Two days later, the Citizen's Committee of Safety appealed to U.S. Minister Stevens for armed help in putting down a rebellion

which, in fact, did not exist. They wrote, "Mr. Stevens, we the under-
signed ... respectfully represent that in the view of recent public
events in this kingdom, culminating in the revolutionary acts of
queen Lili'uokalani on Saturday last, the public safety is menaced
and lives and property are in peril, and we appeal to you and the
United States forces at your command for assistance. We are unable
to protect ourselves without aid, and therefore pray for protection of
the United States forces." This letter bore eight signatures. Five were
American, two were English, and one was German. No Hawaiian
names appeared.

At 3 p.m. on January 16, U. S. Minister John L. Stevens
ordered the Captain of the *U.S.S. Boston* to "...land Marines and
sailors from the ship under your command for the protection of the
United States legation and United States consulate, and to secure the
safety of American life and property."[13] United States troops landed
on Hawaiian soil over the protest of the legitimate ruler as a deliberate and flagrant act of war.

If Stevens' reason for landing U. S. troops was "to secure the
safety of American life and property," it cuts across the grain because
those troops were, according to U. S. Navy Admiral J. S. Sherrett
"...very improperly located...to protect American citizens in person
and property...unadvisable to locate the troops there; if they were
landed for the protection of the United States citizens...if they were landed
to support the Provisional Government troops it was a wise choice."[14]

No United States troops were on the streets of Honolulu to
protect American life and property. While U. S. Marines stood facing
'Iolani Palace and Ali'iolani in a ring, the Committee of Safety's
armed militia claimed possession of the police station, the Royal
Palace and the government building, containing the cabinet offices
and archives.

The queen temporarily yielded the authority under protest. "I,
Lili'uokalani, by the Grace of God and under the Constitution of the
Hawaiian Kingdom, queen, do hereby solemnly protest against any
and all acts done against myself and the Constitutional Government
of and for this Kingdom.

"That I yield to the superior force of the United States of
America whose plenipotentiary, His Excellency John L. Stevens, has
caused United States troops to be landed at Honolulu, and declared
that he would support the said Provisional Government.

"Now, to avoid any collision of armed forces, and perhaps the
loss of life, I do, under this protest, and impelled by said force, yield
my authority until such time as the Government of the United States
shall, upon the facts being presented to it, undo the action of its representatives, and reinstate me in the authority which I claim as the
Constitutional Sovereign of the Hawaiian Islands. Done at Honolulu,

this 17th day of January A.D. 1893." It was signed by Liliʻuokalani and her Minister of Foreign Affairs, Samuel Parker.

Lieutenant Lucien Young, who commanded the marines aboard the Cruiser *U.S.S. Boston*, led the landing party ashore and declared that the cause of the overthrow was more racial than political "The downfall of the monarchy was the direct and inevitable result of an attempt to arbitrarily subjugate men of the Anglo-Saxon race, whose homes and property were at stake by illegal means. The worst enemies of the native Hawaiians have been the Kalākaua family. He and his sister Liliʻuokalani, ever since their family came into power, have constantly been the center of a baleful, degrading influence, exalting immorality, drunkenness, heathenism, and race hatred, for their own selfish ends. But for this the native government and the monarchy could have retained power indefinitely, without interference or opposition from the whites."[15]

Robert Louis Stevenson, who was "filled with regret at the monarchy's downfall," felt, as Melville had 50 years earlier, that Hawaiians had been "oppressed with civilization; it drops out too much of the man ..." In a letter to a friend in London, Stevenson wrote, "A lovely week among God's best—at least God's sweetest works—Polynesians. It has bettered me greatly. If I could only stay the time that remains, I could get my work done and be happy; but the care of my family keeps me in vile Honolulu, where I am always out of sorts amidst heat and cold and cesspools and beastly haoles."[16]

Death muted Robert Louis Stevenson's icy contempt for the Americans in Hawaii. Among his unfinished works was the comprehensive outline of a proposed prose epic entitled *The South Seas*, having as its main theme "the unjust extinction of the Polynesian race by our shoddy civilization."[17]

Liliʻuokalani wrote, "I shall not claim that in the days of Captain Cook our people were civilized. I shall not claim anything more ... than has been already attested by missionary writers. Perhaps I may safely claim even less, admitting the criticism of some intelligent visitors who were not missionaries—that the habits and prejudices of New England Puritanism were not well adapted to the genetics of a tropical people, ... where else in the world's history is it written that a savage people made equal progress in civilization and Christianity in the same space of time? What people have ever been subjected to such a flood of external demoralizing influences? ... while four-fifths of the population of our Islands was swept out of existence by the vices introduced by foreigners, the ruling class clung to Christian morality ... loyally clung to the brotherly alliance made with the better element of foreign settlers, giving freely of its ... sons and daughters to cement and to prosper it ... will it also be thought strange that education and knowledge of the world have enabled us to perceive that as a race we have some special mental and physical requirements not shared by the other races which have come among us? That certain habits and modes of living are better for our health and happiness than others? And that a separate nationality, and a particular form of government ... are ... best for us? ... these things remained to us, until the pitiless and tireless 'annexation policy' was effectively backed by the naval power of the United States.

" ... It had not entered our hearts to believe that these friends and allies from the United States ... would ever ... seize our nation by the throat, and pass it over to an alien power. Perhaps there is a kind of right ... known as the 'Right of Conquest' under which robbers and marauders may establish themselves in possession of whatsoever they are strong enough to ravish from their fellows. If we have nourished in our bosom those who have sought our ruin, it has been because they were of the people whom we believed to be our dearest friends and allies. If we did not by force resist their final outrage, it was because we could not do so without striking at the military force of the United States ... the people of the Islands have no voice in determining their future, but are virtually relegated to the condition of the aborigines of the American Continent. An alien element composed of men of energy and determination control all the resources of Honolulu and will employ them tirelessly to secure their ends."[18]

On January 16, 1895, Lili'uokalani was arrested, charged with treason, and taken by police carriage to her confinement. "As I turned the corner of the block on which is built the Central Congregational Church, I noted the approach from another direction of Chief Justice Albert Francis Judd; he was on the sidewalk and was going toward my house, which he entered. In the meantime the marshall's carriage continued on its way, and we arrived at the gates of 'Iolani Palace ... We drove up to the front steps and I remember noticing that troops of soldiers were scattered all over the yard ... Staring directly at us were the muzzles of two brass field pieces, which looked warlike and formidable as they pointed out toward the gate ... Colonel J.H. Fisher came down the steps to receive me; I dismounted, and he led the way up the staircase to a large ... airy uncarpeted room with a single bed on one corner ...."[19] Later, Fisher's brother, Colonel Will E. Fisher would auction Lili'uokalani's crown jewels.[20]

"That first night of my imprisonment was the longest night I have ever passed in my life; it seemed as though the dawn of day would never come. Outside ... there were guards stationed by day and by night, whose duty it was to pace backward and forward through the hall, before my door ... The sound of their never-ceasing footsteps as they tramped on their beat fell incessantly on my ears. I was a prisoner, and did not fail to realize my position."[21]

The queen remained a prisoner in that room for nine months, occupying herself by laying out plans to present her case to the American people and by beginning her memoir.

Her captors restricted Lili'uokalani's reading material. However, when her meals were brought in, there was always a lovely bouquet of fresh flowers from the garden at Washington Place on the food tray. The stems of these flowers were carefully wrapped with the daily newspaper or other printed matter that might interest the deposed queen.

•

When Gerrit P. Judd was forced to retire from Hawai'i's political arena forty-two years earlier, Robert C. Wyllie became the ranking cabinet officer and, as such, took charge of the papers, letters and other official government records, which heretofore had been collected and held under the authority of Judd. Certainly consistent with his modus operandi for government manipulation when it involved self-interest, Judd had already purged these "official" government records of material which had cast his eleven year administration in an unfavorable light.

Although the official pamphlet of the Archives of Hawai'i dated 1984 states that "The collection owes its origins and extensive early holdings to Robert C. Wyllie ..." and adds that "These and the records which were created in later years were placed under the control of the Board of Commissioners of Public Archives in 1905," nowhere in this information-filled, four-page pamphlet is there a single mention of the name Judd. Let's attempt to put the omission of the Judd name from that pamphlet into a brighter light. When Queen Lili'uokalani was arrested on January 16, 1895, charged with treason and taken by police escort to her confinement at 'Iolani Palace, as previously described, she wrote, "As I turned the corner of the block ..., I noted the approach from another direction of Chief Justice Albert Francis Judd; he was ... going toward my house, which he entered."* Albert Francis Judd, who served as Chief Justice of Hawai'i's Supreme Court for 19 years during the most disastrous period of history for the Hawaiians, did illegally enter the private residence of the queen on January 16, 1895. Once inside, he swept all of the queen's papers into bags and surreptitiously carried them off to the fort and into a storeroom, where he claimed the bulk of them were locked away in a sealed box.

Although Lili'uokalani desperately needed the signed petitions of two-thirds of Hawai'i's registered voters calling for a new constitution—which she claims were among the burglarized docu-

*Hawai'i's Story by Hawai'i's Queen, Tuttle,p. 267.

ments—to justify her actions in attempting to replace the Bayonet Constitution of 1887, she was never permitted to see those papers again. The boxes, with the queen's papers Chief Justice Albert Francis Judd had stolen, were opened for inspection on January 6, 1924, nearly seven years after her death.

How could it be that official public records, which in all likelihood would have aided President Cleveland in his efforts to restore the monarchy, were withheld from public scrutiny for almost thirty years? Who withheld them, and how did they manage to withhold them?

Some background information may help to answer that question. The influence of the Judd family was so pervasive in Hawai'i and in Washington, D.C. in 1893, when Lili'uokalani was overthrown, and in the years which led up to 1924 that a slogan sprang up among the Judds. It stated that, "The Sun Never Sets on the Judds and the un-Judds."* How were those records suppressed? Chief Justice Albert Francis Judd kept them under lock and key at the fort until his death in 1900.** Then, his nephew, an un-Judd, George R. Carter, son of Henry P. Carter and Sybil Augusta Judd, assumed control. First, from his seat in the First Territorial Senate in 1900, then from his newly won post of Secretary of the Territory in 1901, and, finally upon his succeeding Sanford Dole as Governor of the Territory in 1903, after having been appointed by ardent annexation advocate President Theodore Roosevelt.***

In 1905 Carter's cousin, Albert F. Judd, son of the late Chief Justice, took charge by organizing the Board of Commissioners of Public Archives, under whose control were placed all public records of Hawai'i, including "the bulk" of Lili'uokalani's papers, then the archives of Hawai'i were granted official status that same year. Albert F. Judd promptly became a Commissioner on the Board and immediately became its first Secretary, holding what amounted to personal control over all the material in that Board's possession. Later he would become Chairman of the powerful Judiciary Committee of the Hawaii Senate and would be found qualified as Chief Examiner in the Postal Censorship office in Honolulu. He wrote and published *Sidelights of Labor Recruiting*, *Labor and the Laboring Class*, and was the editor of the *Hawai'i Mission*

---

*According to HMCS genealogist, Mrs. Lee Wild, the term "Un-Judd" refers to those with Judd blood but not carrying the Judd name. Mrs. Lee (Cooke) Wild is an Un-Judd.

** In 1905, Albert F. Judd, son of Albert Francis Judd, organized the Archives Commission and served as its secretary.[22]

*** Chessman, *Theodore Roosevelt* ... "It is a great misfortune [he wrote in 1894] that we have not annexed Hawai."[sic]

Centennial Book, One Hundred Years of Civilization in Hawai'i, 1820-1920.[23] In 1922, he became Chairman of the Administration Committee at Punahou School.*

His father, the late Chief Justice, had published *The First Twenty-five Years of Punahou's History 1866, Incidents in Hawaiian History, In the Supreme Court of the Hawaiian Islands, at Chambers,* and *Lunalilo, The Sixth King of Hawai'i.*

George R. Carter acted as President of the Hawaiian Historical Society in 1908, 1912, 1914, 1915 and in 1922.** In 1922, he left an extensive library collection with many first edition copies and other rare papers and exotic items to form the basis for both the Hawaiian Mission Children's School Library and the Bishop Museum Library.[24] In 1928, Bernice Judd, great-granddaughter of Dr. and Mrs. Gerrit P. Judd and daughter of Albert Francis Judd II, son of the Chief Justice who stole Lili'oukalani's papers, became the Executive Director for HMCS and served there until her retirement in 1961.[25] She was a director of the Hawaiian Historical Society from 1938 to 1961, and chief advisor and principal researcher to *Missionary Album, Sesquicentennial Edition 1820-1970.*[26] She was published by the University Press of Hawaii and was, for 33 years, the most readily available major resource for Hawaiian history in Honolulu, greatly influencing the "factual" content of hundreds of books, many documentary films, and hundreds upon hundreds of magazine and newspaper articles concerning Hawaiian history by such eminent authors as Ralph S. Kuykendall, A. Grove Day; the Australian professor Gavan Daws; the former Big Five vice president for corporate communications turned historian Edward Joesting; and the husband of Alice Louise Judd, Fredrick Simpich, who authored *Anatomy of Hawaii* and was chairman of the Hawaii Visitors Bureau while acting as Hawaii's contributing editor to the *National Geographic Magazine* during the heyday of Hawaiian statehood.[27]

What effect does this trickle-down Judd permeation have in building the world-wide image that passes as authentic Hawaiian history? To illustrate, Gerrit P. Judd IV, a history professor at Hofstra College, came to Honolulu in the middle 1950s to rid his great, great grandfather and namesake of "the missionary taint" in a biography. He spent several months with his cousin Bernice Judd at Hawaiian Mission Children's Society Library, Hawaii Historical Society, and at the Archives. The result of their effort, *Dr. Judd - Hawaii's Friend,* was promptly published by the University of Hawaii Press in 1960. Having a surplus of material in his files, G. P. Judd IV issued another

---

* Upon calling Punahou (6/91) to verify Judd's title, the author was connected to Mary Judd, Punahou's archivist.

** According to Hawai'i *Artreach* (8/91) un-Judd "C. Dudley, Pratt, Jr. was elected president of the Hawai'i Historical Society for 1991-1992."

book in 1961 entitled *Hawaii: An Informal History.* Published on the heels of Hawaii's statehood, both of these works became widely read as establishment-endorsed books of Hawai'i history.

•

Since 1828, virtually every organization having to do with collecting, researching, preserving, editing, writing and dispersing Hawaiian history has had Judds/un-Judds controlling, managing, editing, teaching or rewriting it. From a pool of more than 807 close-knit descendants, the Judd family of Hawai'i has held more than 307 positions critical to preserving, controlling and creating Hawaiian history.[28]*

•

Dr. Gerrit P. Judd, the man most responsible for putting real estate on the sellers' block in Hawai'i, made a killing in O'ahu real estate for himself and for his heirs.

Astonishingly, Judd and six of his offspring participated in a frenzy of more than twelve hundred real estate transactions on O'ahu between 1848 and 1893.**

Robert Louis Stevenson listed six objections to the Calvinist missionaries in Hawai'i; the most important was that they: "...showed a haste to get rich. Natural, because their children stayed with them and settled. The point felt in Hawaii, and justly felt, is this: The married protestant missionary makes money, he buys land, he builds houses; he dies, his son succeeds him, and the son is seen to till and sell the acres of the disinherited Hawaiians."[29]

Or as fiesty, history buff Harry S. Truman put it "History is always written by the winners...and they had to justify what was done."[30]

---

*According to long time custodian of the Judd genealogy, 93-year-old John Scott Boyd Pratt, Jr., during a phone interview on July 24, 1985, "The Judds sailed around the *Horn* in 1828 and they've been blowing their own ever since."

** See page 186 for a documented account of Judd family real estate transactions.

EPILOGUE

Hawai'i is ours. As I look back upon the first steps in this miserable business, and as I contemplate the means used to complete the outrage, I am ashamed of the whole affair.[1]

— Grover Cleveland
Letter to Richard Olney
July 8, 1898

On July 4, 1894, Chief Justice Albert Francis Judd administered the oath of office to missionary heir Sanford Ballard Dole, the first and only president of the Republic of Hawai'i.[2] Dole, a leader in the illegal plot to overthrow Lili'uokalani, and Judd, who had made it impossible for her to defend herself in a court of law, stood at attention on the raised inaugural platform amid snapping bunting, and mouthed the lyrics to Hawai'i's national anthem, "Hawai'i Ponoi," as written by David Kalākaua.

When Claus Spreckels' life had been threatened a year earlier as he fought to restore the monarchy, he fled Hawai'i. Lili'uokalani noted that departure in her diary: "While [Spreckels was] making a speech on the wharf ... to the people who flocked down to see them off, Mr. A.F. Judd's two sons who were on their way to Harvard College hooted and stomped and made all the noise they could helped by Mr. C.M. Cooke and Mr. Hosmer ... how little and how small."[3]

When Spreckels arrived in Washington to continue his plea for Lili'uokalani's restoration, Charles Reed Bishop was in that same city violating the oath he had taken in 1849 "to support the Constitution and Laws of the Hawaiian Islands," by negotiating on behalf of the Provisional Government for the annexation of Hawai'i to the United States. Bishop, upon the death of his wife Bernice in 1884, had been willed, for the term of his life, real estate holdings which amounted to about eleven percent of all the land on Hawai'i's six major islands.

Before he left Hawai'i permanently in 1894, the wealthy banker, who according to his close friend William R. Castle " ... never liked to give, and that it was only with reluctance that he made donations,"[4] established the Bernice P. Bishop Estate and the Kamehameha Schools. That act marked the beginning of what his biographer and former president of Kamehameha Schools, Harold Winfield Kent called "the greatest [philanthropy] that the Islands had ever seen."[5] Of course, Bishop had been willed the estate lands for the term of his life—not for the life of his heirs. So he merely anticipated his death by turning the management of these temporary land

holdings over to a board of missionary/busines
even to this day, reap enormous profits from their
istrations to a few Hawaiian children.

He is credited with having founded, co-foun
the Bernice P. Bishop Estate, the Kamehameha Schools
for the first building constructed on the Kamehameha ca.
from his late wife's endowment paid for everything
Hawaiian Mission Children's Society, the Hawaiian Lit
Bernice P. Bishop Museum, Oahu College [now called H
School] and the Hawaiian Historical Society. Without except.
this very day these institutions all actively perpetuate the mis.
ary/business version of Hawaiian history. Could it be otherwise w
the Binghams, the Judds, the Wilders, the Pratts, the Damons, t.
Thurstons, the Castles, the Doles, the Baldwins, the Athertons, the
Brewers, the Greens, the Richardsons, the Osbornes, the Morgans,
the Blythes, the Erdmans, Bishop, and those beholden to them , controlling the translations of kings, the private and state papers of the
queen, the archives, the museums, the libraries, the historical societies, the financial institutions, the newspapers, the courts, the
schools, the University?

In 1895, Samuel Mills Damon, whose father had introduced
Bishop to the 15-year-old Chiefess Bernice Pauahi Paki in 1847, purchased the Bank of Bishop and Company by signing an unsecured
note of $800,000 payable to Bishop. Damon had already received the
legacy of Moanalua Gardens from the will of Bernice P. Bishop, with
9,000 choice acres from the mountains to the sea. Although it has
never been proven, it is speculated among some experts in Hawaiian
land transactions that S.M. Damon's payment of $800,000 to Bishop
was actually an under-the-table payoff for Moanalua Gardens and
other Hawaiian properties.* In 1991, the Damon Estate was listed as
owning 121,659 Hawaiian acres. [6]

Why did Bishop leave Hawai'i? In a letter written from San
Francisco on the eve of his last visit to Hawai'i, he explained, "It is
my intention to return to the city [San Francisco] as soon as I can—
within six weeks at the longest ... I shall go home [to Honolulu] with
a heavy heart and perplexed mind—and so far as I am concerned it is
fortunate that I have interests here which will require a speedy return,
for I cannot bear the wear and tear of sleeplessness in that climate." [7]

"Mr. Bishop died in Berkeley, California, June 7, 1915. His
remains were cremated and shipped to Honolulu for interment. His
funeral was one of the most notable ever held in the islands, with all
royal honors ... Riding in the forefront of the funeral procession was

---

*Honolulu Advertiser 8/7/94, 24.4 percent of First Hawaiian stock is owned by Damon
Estate. First Hawaiian Bank, formerly Bank of Bishop.

eposed Queen, Lili'uokalani ... "[8] Bishop, whose well-publi-
d philantrophic activities in Hawai'i cost him considerably less
$1,000,000,[9] left an estate of approximately $9,000,000 to his
rest of kin in America, giving, at least to the Hawaiians, support
r the axiom that "bankers always take more than they give."*

Before Bishop departed Hawai'i in 1894, he had become an
American hero in the tradition of Horatio Alger. Less publicized
aspects of his personality seem to have been buried with him in 1915.
When Reverend Damon rowed Bishop ashore at Honolulu Harbor in
1846, Bishop was dead broke. He took a dollar-a-day job posting
books for the government. Utilizing finesse, ..."the grinding tyranny
of usury,"[10], subterfuge and an upwardly mobile marriage, he became
Hawai'i's very own tycoon.

In 1892 there were 4,047 millionaires in the U.S.A.[11] Barely
two hundred of those had accumulated $10 million, qualifying them
for membership in the elite group called decamillionaires. That same
year Bishop had enough cash to join the exclusive club of moguls co-
chaired by the notorious robber barons Andrew Carnegie, J. Pierpont
Morgan and John D. Rockefeller.

Mark Twain, writing about God, money and the credo of
nineteenth century decamillionaires, asked, "What's the chief end of
man?—to get rich. In what way.?—dishonestly if we can; honestly if
we must. Who is God, the one only and true? Money is God. Gold
and Greenbacks and Stock—father, son and ghost of the same—three
persons in one; these are the true and only God, might and
supreme..."[12]

Island lore weaves an account that *Madame Pele*, the mis-
chievous and volatile Hawaiian Goddess of Fire, seeking vengeance
upon Bishop for his turncoat behavior toward his Island benefactors,
stalked him across the Pacific to San Francisco where, putting her
magical powers into play, caused the earthquake of 1906. Tellers of
this fable add that the fire which followed the quake and destroyed
San Francisco, bore the unmistakable brand of *Pele*!

In 1992 one would be hard pressed to find a *haole* name more
honored in Hawai'i than that of Charles Reed Bishop. Based upon his
treasonous activities, this honorable status cries out for an objective
reappraisal.

•

In 1896 Reverend Sereno E. Bishop penned a confidential
memo to U. S. Commissioner James H. Blount: "It is constantly
urged that by the annexation of Hawai'i without the full consent of

---

* $9 million in 1892 equates to approximately $1.25 billion in 1996.
  Total cash value of trade between U.S. and Hawai'i for 1898 amounted to
$18,385,000. See Thomas Osborne, *"Empire Can Wait."*

the natives, the United States would be committing a robbery of their rights of sovereignty and independence, taking away their cherished Flag, etc. As intimated in *The Star*, such a weak and wasted people prove by their failure to save themselves from progressive extinction, and their incapacity to help or defend the denizens of Hawai'i, the consequent lack of claim to continued sovereignty. Their only claim can be to the compassionate help and protection of their neighbors. Is it not an absurdity for the aborigines, who under the most favorable conditions, have dwindled to having less than one third (now barely one fourth, probably) of the whole number of males in the Islands, and who are mentally and physically incapable of supporting, directing or defending a government, nevertheless to claim sovereign rights? *It would seem that the forty millions of property interests held by foreigners must be delivered from native misrule.* Not to do that will be wrong Is not the only question of moral rights for America to Determine, What is best for all concerned?...[13]

By 1897 the McKinley Tariff had been lifted, restoring reciprocity to Hawaiian sugar. As the market soared again, 25,000 Japanese contract laborers crowded into cramped plantation bunk houses. When President Dole signed into law a bill that placed an extraordinarily high tax on the Japanese wine, *sake,* a warship flying the Rising Sun steamed into Honolulu Harbor, giving the McKinley administration the "yellow peril" hoax it needed to annex Hawai'i as a territory of the United States.

SUMMERTIME USA 1898

JUNE 15	Six hundred U.S.Marines defeat Spanish forces at Battle of Guantanamo Bay, Cuba.
JUNE 20	Following a day-long shelling, Island of Guam surrenders to Commander, *U.S.S. Charleston.*
JULY 1	Theodore Roosevelt ankles his Rough Riders up Kettle Hill on San Juan. Day's total U.S.casualties mount to 1,600.
JULY 3	Spanish fleet attempting to run U.S. blockade is destroyed with more than 2,000 killed and wounded.
JULY 7	President William McKinley signs annexation of Hawai'i bill, previously blocked by President Cleveland.
JULY 17	Santiago's 24,000 defenders surrender to U.S.
JULY 21	Four U.S. warships bombard Nipe, in last sea battle of the war.
JULY 25	General Wesley Merritt arrives at Manila Bay with land reinforcements to support U.S. fleet.
AUG 12	U.S. armed forces take Puerto Rico, having met only token resistance.
AUG 12	Formal cession of Hawai'i to the USA as the final chapter in the history of the spirit of Manifest Destiny and expansion which earlier gave the U.S. Louisiana, the Floridas, Texas, California and Oregon.[1]

EPITAPH

Every important thing that has happened, everything that is happening goes to establish this proposition: That hard and selfish men and hard and selfish policies will control our imperialist relations; that the kind and well-meaning will be overruled. There is no intention of mildness, humanity, and justice in the forces that are now gaining ascendancy in American life ...

Whenever the basest of international principles of pilfering and freebooting are applied to gain markets, "along with these markets will go our beneficent institutions." The halo of our blessed institutions will pervade and rectify rapacity and wrong! But it will not. We shall not build beneficent institutions on ruffianism and rapacity. We are after markets, the greatest markets in the world; we do not care what we do to get them— we will cheerfully rob and kill, we will wrench their fatherland from the weak and call it ours—we admit it in cold blood, but like the praying professional murderer, we piously declare that God and humanity will bless us in it....

If this atrocious humbug found lodging in the American spleen, every conceivable thing necessary for the spread of American monopolies would be tolerated by the American people, even down to the vivisection of whole savage races for trade experiments. This might be called a dull joke; it is still too early to say whether Americans, renowned among themselves, for their biting perception of humor, will be able to see it. Our rulers have conducted their game very artfully, and the work now is to unravel the mesh in which that art has tangled us. How, from the essence of humanity, did the President extract the right to steal? [1]

— Morrison I. Swift
Imperialism and Liberty, 1899

AFTERWORD

NATIVE HAWAIIAN 1992

Richard Kekuni Blaisdell, M.D.

At a recent community meeting here on Oʻahu, a *haole* woman identified herself as a native Hawaiian because she was born in Hawaiʻi, just as her mother was a native Texan because she was born in Texas.

Gavan Daws' widely read history of Hawaiʻi, *Shoal of Time*, concludes with a chapter entitled "Now We Are All Haoles." At a dinner celebrating the publication of that work Professor Daws gave a speech entitled "Now We Are All Hawaiians." If everyone is now *haole* and anyone in Hawaiʻi is or can be called "Hawaiian" or "Native Hawaiian," then who are we Hawaiians?

Aware Hawaiians point out that the term Hawaiian is itself non-Hawaiian, as is its pronunciation. What name did the early Hawaiians use for themselves? It was not "Indians" as Captain Cook called them in 1778, but it was *kānaka maoli*. *Kānaka* means human being. *Kānaka maoli* means true or real person. Foreigners quickly misused the term *kānaka* to refer to the Hawaiian adult male. *Kānaka* soon became a derisive metaphor similar to the *haole* word *nigger*. The term *kānaka maoli* is staging a comeback as a substitute for the term Hawaiian because it was the term by which our ancestors identified themselves.

There are Hawaiians who support the concept of Hawaiʻi as an ethnopluralistic society. That is a setting in which each ethnic group is respected and has equal opportunity in socioeconomic mobility. The fault there is that the system and its rules are not the result of equal input by each ethnic group, but are instead the imposed input of the controlling Western society. That means there is "equality" only for those who play the *haole* game. Unfortunately, the *haole* game is one of money making materialism, individual exploitation of others and the destruction of the environment.

Such slanted games not only do not respect us as the indigenous people of Hawaiʻi, living in our homeland, but they degrade us as a people. Moreover they perpetuate our oppression in our daily thinking and behavior as individual native Hawaiians. Many *kānaka maoli* are so de-Hawaiianized and Westernized that they are afraid and ashamed to be *kānaka maoli*.

According to the 1990 U. S. Census, we number 138,742 souls among a population of 1.1 million. Finer tuned statewide surveys count the total Hawaiian population at 212,274.* Thus, it is probable the U. S. Census left approximately 34 percent of the 1990 Hawaiian population uncounted. This may not be surprising if you are aware that in 1960, the first year of Hawai'i's statehood, the U. S. Census Bureau listed Hawaiians under the category of *Others.*

Most of us are mixed ancestry, while fewer than 6,000 *piha kānaka* remain.** We are being suffocated by more than 860,000 non-*kānaka,* with whites from the U. S. burgeoning. We suffer the worst health profile of all island ethnic groups, the shortest lifespan and the highest rates for the major killers, heart disease, cancer, stroke and diabetes. We lead in suicide, infant deaths, teenage pregnancies and complications of pregnancy. With 12.6 percent of the population we fill 31 percent of all prison cells and our juveniles rank first in robbery, vandalism, drug abuse, gambling and runaways.

Only 45 percent graduate from high school. Just five percent of the students on Manoa campus of the University of Hawai'i are *kānaka maoli* and less than two percent of those graduate. We have the lowest incomes and highest unemployment. Most hold unskilled service jobs and only 1.6 percent of all businesses in Hawai'i are *kānaka* owned.

Until we have a deeper factual understanding of how we came to our current plight it will be difficult for us to receive redress due us. Most importantly, only when these wrongs are corrected will our *keiki* have the opportunity to acquire self-esteem necessary to enjoy the lives they deserve.

Yet, Hawai'i's two thousand year old story has not been told from our perspective, in our way by us *kānaka maoli.* Most accounts of Hawai'i's past have been written by foreigners through their eyes beginning with their "discoveries" in the Pacific during the late eighteenth century.

Michael Dougherty's *To Steal A Kingdom* recounts our history for the most part, in the words of its key participants. Because these passages are in the white man's language, most of the principals are perforce Westerners. However, his selections, arrangement and linking statements generally empathize with the feelings of us

* "The U. S. Census data serve as a useful benchmark, but the Hawai'i Health Surveillance survey data series provide finer and more useful details on the size, age distribution and related socio-economic characteristics within blood quantum levels. The U. S. Census underestimates the number of Hawaiians of less than 50 percent Hawaiian, that grouping which represents the largest, youngest and most rapidly growing segment of the native Hawaiian population." *Demographic Profile of Native Hawaiians.* 1980-1986, by Kiyoshi Ikeda, Ph.D. with assistance of David Johnson, Ph.D., Honolulu, Hawaii, Dec. 27, 1987. In 1987, the Hawai'i Health Surveillance Survey lists the total Hawaiian population at 212,274.

** Full-blooded Hawaiians

native islanders. His research provides the facts to reverse important hero/villain roles still promoted as true in our school textbooks. The author's probing raises the question of insidious control of historiography by the *haole* establishment. The result being: miseducation in our schools, misinformation by our officials and a virtual media blackout of crimes, past and present, against us *kānaka maoli*.

To Steal A Kingdom is a nightmarish walk through history with the missionary/businessman who forced Hawai'i into the whirlpool of Manifest Destiny. Curious, open and critical readers should welcome Dougherty's refreshing, timely and provocative probing of Hawai'i's past.

Richard Kekuni Blaisdell was born in Honolulu in 1925, attended Kamehameha Schools, University of Redlands and received his degree in medicine from the University of Chicago in 1947. He spent his internship at Johns Hopkins and his residency at Tulane and at Duke, where he became an instructor in pathology. He returned to the University of Chicago in 1955 as a resident and again in 1958 as an assistant professor. In 1961 he became Chief Hematologist with the Atomic Bomb Casualty Commission in Hiroshima and Nagasaki.

Dr. Blaisdell has been a professor at the John A Burns School of Medicine at the University of Hawai'i since 1966. He is a staff physician at St. Francis Hospital in Honolulu and was the Interim Director of the Center for Hawaiian Studies of the University of Hawai'i at Manoa. He has published on a range of topics.

ACKNOWLEDGEMENTS

Sincere thanks to George Chouljian,* Marion Kelly, Ruth Gurnani-Smith, Terence Barrow, Carol Silva, Katherine K. Paine, Michaelynn P. Chou, Haunani Apoliona, Mary Jane Knight, Dick Lyday, Eleanor Au, Robert C. Schmitt, Shigeo Tengan, Lee Wild, Mary Ann Akao, LeMonte McLemore, Myron Thompson, Wattie Mae Hedemann, John Scott Boyd Pratt, Jr.,* David Penn, Stella Akana, Suzanne Marquess, Barbara Dunn, Elizabeth Trupin, H. C. Nordstrom,* Neil Abercrombie, Judy McHugh, Carlos Rivas, Susan Campbell, Deborah Johansen, David Kittleson, John Kelly, Vincent Esposito,* George Cooper, Laird Koenig, Jack Teehan,* Judith Powers, Pam Huch Kekumano, Gretchen McNeese, Gwen Kelley, Deal Crooker* and to the many authors, researchers, librarians, teachers and critics who enriched the work along the way. Finally, for caustic critique that fueled my engine, thanks to Roger Rose and David Stannard.

All erroneous interpretations, errors in fact, irregularities in continuity and deficiencies in style are the sole responsibility of the author.

* Deceased

185

O'AHU REAL ESTATE TRANSACTIONS OF THE JUDD
FAMILY IN THE 1800'S

Gerrit Parmele Judd and his wife Laura Fish Judd had nine children. Two of them died as youngsters. Of the seven which remained, four were female and three were males. One, Helen Seymour, lived her life as a spinster. Elizabeth Kīna'u, the oldest, married Samuel Gardner Wilder, Laura Fish (the daughter) wed Joshua Gill Dickson. The youngest, Sybil Augusta became the wife of Henry Alpheus Peirce Carter. Charles Hastings married Emily Cutts, Albert Francis took Agnes Hall Boyd as his bride while Allan Wilkes lived his life as a bachelor.

In the period 1847-1894 these fourteen individual adults comprised the immediate Judd family. *According to the indices of Hawaii Department of Land and Natural Resources, Bureau of Conveyances the Judds and their in-laws acted as principals in no less than twelve hundred and twelve land transactions on the Island of O'ahu between 1847-1894.*

During the period 1847-1867 *Gerrit P. Judd and Laura Fish Judd were principals in no less than one hundred and twenty-one real estate transactions on the Island of O'ahu. Many of these transactions involved immediate family members.* In the last six years of his life GPJ would slow his real estate dealings to thirteen transactions on O'ahu. Eight of these transactions involved members of his immediate family as principals. *Total real estate transactions for Gerrit P and Laura F. Judd came to one hundred and thirty-five.*

Evidence to substantiate the above statements can be found in the following official records:

Grantee Index #1 1845-1869, pp. 176-190

Includes transactions by Albert F., Allan, W. A. Francis, Charles H., Helen S., Laura Fish, Judd & Chumming, Judd and Wilder. A total of 86 transactions among all Judds, a total of 49 transactions with Gerrit P. and Laura Fish as principals.

pp. 63-64   24 transactions involving Henry A. P. Carter and S.Augusta

p. 91   9 transactions for Joshua Dickson

Grantee Index #2: 1846-1869

p. 136   Samuel G. Wilder et al., 10 transactions

Grantee Index #3 1870-1884

p. 139   Boyd et al.   13 transactions

pp. 157-158   Carter, H.A.P., Sybil.   58 transactions

p. 237   Dickson, Joshua G. & Laura Fish et al.
                          36 transactions

Grantee Index #4 1870-1884

pp. 118 -119   Albert F., A. Francis, Charles H., Emily C.,
                          71 transactions, eight separate transactions with
                          G.D.J. He dies in 1873.

Grantee Index #8 1885-1894

pp. 128-129   Boyd, et al.   44 transactions

pp. 146-148   Carter H.A.P., S. Augusta   91 transactions

Grantee Index #9 1885-1894

p. 20   Dickson, Joshua G. and Laura   18 transactions

pp. 177-179   A. F. Judd, A. Francis, Agnes Boyd, Charles H.,
                          Emily Cutt and Mary M(?)   40 transactions

Grantee Index #12 1885-1894

p. 53   Wilder, Samuel G., and Elizabeth K.
                          46 transactions

Grantor Index #1 1846-1869

pp. 210-213   104 transactions with Judd's as principals.
                          60 separate transactions with GPJ & Laura Fish
                          Judd

pp. 58, 59   Boyd et al.   17 transactions

pp. 72, 73   Carter, H.A.P. & W.F.   23 transactions

Grantor Index #3 1863-1868

                     Wilder, S. G. & W. F.   11 transactions,

Grantor Index #4 1870-1884

pp. 128, 129   Boyd et al.   47 transactions

pp. 148, 149   Carter, H.A.P. & W.F.   55 transactions

  p. 231   Dickson, Joshua & Laura   18 transactions

Grantor Index #5 1870-1884

pp. 133-135   Judd's et al.   103 transactions
                      GPJ & Laura Fish   18 transactions
                      GPJ dies in 1873

Grantor Index #8   1870-1884

pp. 229-230   Wilder, E. Kīnaʻu & H.S.B.   40 transactions

Grantor Index #9 1885-1894

pp. 136-138   Boyd et al.   94 transactions
pp. 161-164   Carter, H.A.P., S. Augusta   109 transactions

Grantor Index #10 1885-1894

  p. 26   29 transactions, Dickson, Joshua & L.F. W.F.

Grantor Index # 13 1885-1894

                     Wilder, S. G. & Elizabeth K.   27 transactions

Total 1212 transactions for Judds and in-laws between 1847-1894*

* These transactions are for Oʻahu only. The Judd family also acquired thousands of acres on the islands of Hawaiʻi, Maui, Kauaʻi and Molokaiʻi.

A small sampling of choice parcels the Judds bought and sold include corners of: Merchant & Fort Streets, Punchbowl & Beretania Streets, King & Richards, Nuʻuanu & Hotel Streets, King & Merchant Streets, Nuʻuanu & Kaʻahumanu Streets, King & Maunakea Streets.

A small sample of additional areas: Nuʻuanu Valley, Manoa Valley, Fort Street, Waikiki, Kaʻaʻawa, Koaloa, Hakipuʻu Road to Punahou, Waimanalo, Kailua, Hotel Street, Church Street, Kalihi, Kapalama, Kaneohe, Liliha Street, Pauoa, Waiʻahole, Kukui Land, Ewa.

A few of the more prominent buyers and sellers the Judds dealt with included: Kamehameha III, King Kalākaua, Bernice Bishop, Charles Reed Bishop, V. K. Kaʻahumanu, Amos Cooke, Charles Brewer, Robert Lewers, James Isaac, H. Kaiana, James M. Monsarrat, Ladd & Co., Richard Armstrong, D.P.R. Isenberg, H. P. Baldwin, V. Kamamalu, James Robinson, Alexander J. Cartwright, William Kinney, Clarence MacFarlane and John H. Paty.

NATIVE HAWAIIAN POPULATION
(Estimated)
A.D. 375 - A. D. 2025

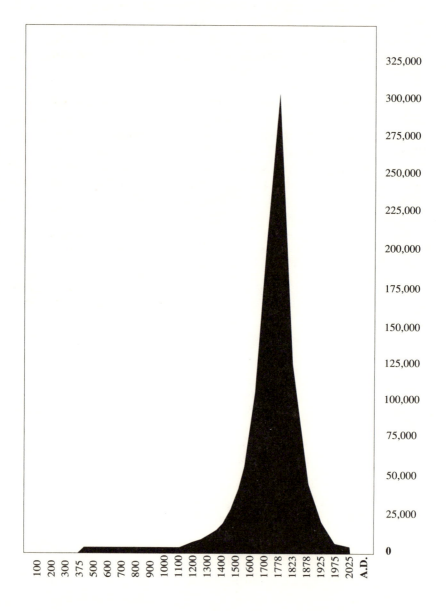

HOW HAWAIIANS FARED IN THE MAHELE

In 1850 with a Hawaiian population of 82,035, approximately 29,200 adult (heads of households) males were eligible to claim land.

Awards went to 8,750, or 30% of these eligible males. It is estimated that only 30% of the population received *kuleana,** and that 70% had their rights to land alienated at the time it was being parceled out.

CLAIMS REGISTERED	**14,295**
CLAIMS NOT ALLOWED	- 4,287
	10,008
CLAIMS REFERRED TO OTHER AWARD NUMBERS	- 808
	9,200
AWARDS TO CHIEFS	- 245
AWARDS TO FOREIGNERS	- 200
KULEANA (?) AWARDS	**8,755**

[Some of these were lesser chiefs, who received 24-acre, 15 acre and 10 acre awards as opposed to the 1, 2, and 3-acre awards of ordinary farmers. I estimate that these lesser chiefs number about 500.]

**Kuleana*: A tract of land within a larger tract of land. Report by Marion Kelly, Anthropologist, Bishop Museum, Honolulu, 1985.

MONARCHS OF HAWAI'I

Name	Birth	Accession	Death
Kamehameha I	c. 1758	1795	May 8, 1819
Kamehameha II (Liholiho)	1797	May 20, 1819	Jul 14, 1824
Kamehameha III (Kauikeaouli)	Mar 17, 1814	Jun 6, 1825	Dec 15, 1854
Kamehameha IV (Alexander Liholiho)	Feb 9, 1834	Dec 15, 1854	Nov 30, 1863
Kamehameha V (Lot Kamehameha)	Dec 11, 1830	Nov 30, 1863	Dec 11, 1872
William C. Lunalilo	Jan 31, 1835	Jan 8, 1873	Feb 3, 1874
David Kalākaua	Nov 16, 1836	Feb 12, 1874	Jan 20, 1891
Lili'uokalani	Sep 2, 1838	Jan 29, 1891*	Nov 11, 1917

*Lili'uokalani was deposed and the Hawaiian Kingdom came to an end on January 17, 1893.

APPROXIMATE ARRIVAL DATES, OTHER FOREIGNERS*

Caucasians	Beachcombers	1790
(American & European	Merchants, sea captains	1810
individuals)	Missionaries	1820
Whalers, seamen		1820
Adventurers		1840
Businessmen		1850
Plantation management		1880
Chinese		1852
(Contract Groups)		
South Sea Islanders		1865
Japanese		1868
Portuguese		1878
Norwegians		1881
Germans		1881
Galicians		1897
Okinawans		1900
Puerto Ricans		1900
Negroes		1901
Koreans		1903
Filipinos		1906
Spanish		1907
Russians		1909

* Source: Carol Silva, Archives of Hawaii, 1985.

GENERAL GLOSSARY

Australoid	Relating to an ethnic group including Australian Aborigines
Ethnographic	The descriptive anthropology of technologically primitive societies
Lapita	A distinct type of ceramic pottery found throughout Pacific islands
Melanesia	Greek for black islands
Micronesia	Greek for small islands
Mongoloids	A major ethnic division of humans characterized by yellow ish-brown to white pigmentation, course black hair, dark eyes and prominent cheek bones
Pleiades	An open star cluster in the Constellation Taurus, consisting of several hundred stars, six of which are visible to the naked eye
Polynesia	Greek for many islands
Radioactive Isotopes	Are valuable as "trace elements" in research on chemical, bio logical, medical, industrial and other processes.
Radiocarbon	Radioactive carbon, especially Carbon 14

HAWAIIAN GLOSSARY

As standardized by the missionaries early in the nineteenth century, the Hawaiian language has seven consonants (h, k, 1, m, n, p, w), pronounced as in English. The five vowels are pronounced as follows

a	*ah*, as in car
e	*eh*, as in rein
i	*ee*, as in marine
o	*oh*, as in own
u	*oo*, as in rule

In addition, there are a number of vowel combinations which resemble diphthongs

ai	*eye*, as in mile
ao, au	*ow*, as in how
ei	*eh*, as in rein
oe	*oy*, as in boy

Otherwise every letter is sounded separately Generally each word is lightly accented on the next to last syllable, but some words have no accent Others hare macrons indicating a strong accent and glottal stops representing dropped consonants

The following are some common Hawaiian words, many of which hare replaced their English equivalents among island residents

ahupua'a	land parcel, usually extending from sea to mountain
'āina	land, earth
akamai	clever, expert
ali'i	chief
aloha	love, hello, good-bye
auwē	alas
hale	house
hana	work
hao	iron
haole	white man, foreigner
hapa-haole	fraction, part-Hawaiian
hapai	pregnant, carry
heiau	place of worship
hikie'e	couch
holokū	gown, often with a train
ho'okama	adoption (as a godparent "adopts" a godchild), a supportive relationship
ho'omalimali	flattery

hoʻomanawanui	take it easy, patience
hoʻoūlu	grow, sprout, cause to increase
huhū	angry
hui	union, society syndicate
hula	dance
imu	underground oven
imua	forward, in front of
kāhili	royal standard
kahuna	expert, priest
kai	sea
kamaʻāina	native-born, old-timer
kānaka	men
kanaka	man
kāne	male, husband
kapu	forbidden, sacred
kauka	doctor
keiki	child
kiawe	algarroba (tree)
kilu	game with sexual prize
kona	leeward side of an island
koʻolau	windward side of an island
kuhina nui	premier
kuleana	a tract of land within a larger tract of land
lānai	porch, terrace
lauhala	pandanus leaf
laulau	bundle, especially of food wrapped in ti leaf
lei	necklace, usually of flowers
lokahi	unity
lomi lomi	massage
luau	feast
mahalo	thanks
mahele	division, particularly 1848 land division
maikaʻi	good, beautiful
makai	leeward
malo	loincloth
mauka	inland
mauna	mountain
mele	song, chant
menehune	dwarf, elf
moe	sleep
muʻumuʻu	gown, mother hubbard
nui	big, great
ʻoe	you
ʻohana	* (See end of glossary)
ʻōkole	posterior

'ōkolehao	liquor made from the root of the ti plant in post control times
'ōpū	stomach
pa'akikī	stubborn, hard
Pākē	Chinese
palapala	written document of any kind deed, bill, letter, etc
pali	cliff
paniolo	cowboy, Spaniard
pau	finished
picul	Oriental commercial weight, 133-1/3 lbs in China and Hawai'i
piha	full-blooded
pīkake	jasmine
pilau	stench, smelly
pilikia	trouble of any kind, great or small
pipi	beef, cattle
poha	gooseberry
poi	taro paste
pua'a	pig
puka	hole
pune'e	couch
'ukulele	stringed musical instrument, literally 'jumping flea'
'ume	attractive, alluring
wahine	woman
wiki	quick, hurry

* *'Ōhana* means extended family united in a common purpose. It frequently includes interpersonal relationship involving all persons with a lasting commitment to one another. Some components of *'Ohana* are: *Laulima*, many hands, each doing a share in a task-oriented relationship; *Kuleana*, an individuals area of responsibility; *Kōkua*, utilizing each person's unique resources in performing group tasks; *Huki-like,* pulling together, as opposed to *huki-huki*, pulling apart; *Hānai*, the system of adopting a child; *Ho'okama*, adoption of friendships whereby adults become as siblings to one another.

ABBREVIATIONS

ABCFM	American Board of Commissioners for Foreign Missions
ADM	National Maritime Museum of Britain
AH	State Archives of Hawai'i
BCR	British Consular Records
BFO	British Foreign Office
BPRO	British Public Record Office
DB	Daily Bulletin
DPI	Department of Public Instruction, AH
EB	Evening Bulletin
F	The Friend
F.O. & Ex.	Foreign Office and Executive File
FOLB	Foreign Office Letter Book, AH
HAA	Hawaiian Almanac & Annual; aka Thrum's Annual, or Hawaiian Annual
HBC	Hawai'i State Bureau of Conveyances
HG	Hawaiian Gazette
HHS	Hawaiian Historical Society
HJH	Hawaiian Journal of History
HMCS	Hawaiian Mission Children's Society
HSB	Honolulu Star-Bulletin
ID	Interior Department, AH
IDLB	Interior Department Letter Book, AH
LC	Library of Congress
MH	Missionary Herald, official organ of ABCFM, Boston
ML	Missionary Letters in HMCS
p	The Polynesian

PCA	Pacific Commercial Advertiser
PCR	Privy Council Records, AH
PP	Paradise of the Pacific
RHAS	Royal Hawaiian Agricultural Society
SIG	Sandwich Island Gazette
SIN	Sandwich Island News
SP	Saturday Press
USDS	United States Department of State
USNA	United States National Archives

BIBLIOGRAPHY

To the best of my knowledge, all of the sources actually used in this text are listed in the bibliography below. Because the material in this work was compiled and joined over a period of more than twenty years there is a possibility that a small percentage of unintentional errors of omission have occurred.

One goal of this book was to provoke a special group of readers into a scholarly reexamination of Hawaiian history. Therefore, I have included a number of bibliographical references which were not used as specific sources in this book. These references made general contributions to the quality and depth of this work. Persons seeking information regarding this period of Hawaiian history would be well served if they utilized these sources.

— M.D.

•

(ABCFM). Correspondence between American Board of Commissioners for Foreign Missions and members of the Sandwich Islands Mission. HMCS.

Adams, Henry. *History Of The United States 1800-1817*. (N.Y., 1889-91) I-3.

Adams, Romanzo. *Interracial Marriage in Hawai'i*. New York, Macmillan, 1937.

——————. The Peoples of Hawaii. Honolulu: Institute of Pacific Relations.

Adee, D. *Memories of Honolulu*. United Service. May, 1884.

Adler, J. *Claus Spreckels: The Sugar King in Hawai'i*. Honolulu, 1966.

Alexander, William D. *A Brief History of the Hawaiian People*. American Book Co., New York, 1899.

——————. "Overthrow of the Ancient Tabu System in the Hawaiian Islands," in 25 HHS Report, 38-40.

——————. *History of the Later Years of the Hawaiian Monarchy*. Honolulu, 1896.

——————. .... to S. M. Damon, House Ex. Docs. 53 Congress, 2 Sess. No. 47, LC.

Allen, Gwenfread E. *Men and Women of Hawai'i*, Vol. 8, Honolulu Star Bulletin, Inc. 1966

Allen, Helena G., *The Betrayal of Lili'uokalani*, Arthur H. Clark, Glendale, CA, 1982.

Anderson William. Journal B.R.R.O. Adm. 51/4560/203-4.

Arago, Jacques. *Narrative of A Voyage Around the World 1817-1820, Vol. II.* London, 1833.

Armstrong, W. *Around the World with a King.* Cambridge, University Press, Feb. 1904. Armstrong (Richard) to Chapman, Armstrong Letters. LC

Atkinson, Alatant. *Sketch of Recent Events.* A. M. Hewett, Honolulu, 1887.

Baldwin to Richards HMCS.

Banks, Sir Joseph. *Journal HMS Endeavor.* Mitchell Library of N.S.W.

Barclay, Glen. *A History of the Pacific From the Stone Age...* New York, 1978.

Beaglehole, J.C. *The Life of Capt. James Cook.* Stanford, 1974.

——————. ed. *Journals of Captain James Cook.* 3 Vols. Cambridge University Press for the Hakuyt Society, Cambridge, 1955-1967.

——————. Paper read before Australian Academy of Science, Canberra, May 1, 1969.

Beckwith, Martha. *Hawaiian Mythology.* The University Press of Hawai'i, Honolulu, 1976.

Beechy, F.W. *Narrative of a Voyage to the Pacific and Bherring's Straits under the Command of Captain F.W. Beechy, R.N., Vol I.* London, 1831.

Belcher, E. *Narrative of A Voyage Round the World 1836-1842.* London, 1843

Bellwood, Peter S. *The Prehistory of Polynesia.* "The Oceanic Context," Cambridge, 1979.

Besant, Walter. *Captain Cook.* MacMillan & Co., London, 1890.

Bigelow, A. *Mark Twain's Speeches.* Harper & Brothers, New York, 1923.

Bingham, Hiram. *A Residence of Twenty-one Years in the Sandwich Islands.* S. Converse, New York, 1847.

——————. Journal. Marshall & Wildes, New York, April 4, 1820.

Bingham to Parker. Letter, April 7, 1820, Parker Family Museum Collection, Waimea, Hawai'i.

Bingham to Chamberlain, July 13, 1830, HMCS.

Bishop, Asa. Ka'ahumanu to Rev. Asa Bishop at Kailua, Hawai'i, July 10, 1826,

Bishop, Artemas. *Letters*. HMCS.

Bishop, C. Journal. MS. Archives of British Columbia. (UH)

Bishop C.R. to Queen Lili'uokalani AH, March 5, 1891.

Bishop C.R. to W. D. Alexander, Alexander Collection.; HMCS Library.

Bishop, Sereno E., "The Hawaiian Queen and Her Kingdom," *Review of Reviews*, Sept. 1891; "The United States and Hawai'i," ibid., March, 1893.

Blackman, Wm. F. *The Making of Hawai'i*. Macmillan, New York, 1906.

Blaisdell, Richard Kekuni, M.D. "Ancient Hawaiians A Healthy People" by Jeanne Ambrose, *Honolulu Star-Bulletin*, September 18, 1980.

Bliss, W.R. *Paradise in the Pacific*. Sheldon & Co. New York, 1873.

Blount's Papers, Vol. VII, USNA.

Bloxam, Richard. *Voyage of H.M.S. Blonde to the Sandwich Islands in the Years 1824-1825*. London, 1826.

Boliver....to Palmerston, No. 105, PBRO, FO, 5/513. LC.

Bringhurst, Newell, *Brigham Young*, Little Brown, Boston, 1986.

Broughton, W. *Voyage of Discovery to the North Pacific Ocean, 1795-1798*. London, 1804.

Bryant & Sturgis to Capt. James Hale, Aug. 31, 1818, B&S Letter Books, Baker Library, Harvard School of Business, Cambridge.

Bryant & Sturgis to Capt. Suter, Dec 28, 1824, B&S Letter Books, Baker Library, Harvard.

Burney, James. Journal, BPRO, Adm. 51/4523/1-4

Byron, Captain, The Honorable Lord. *Voyage of HMS Blonde to the Sandwich Islands*. London, 1826.

California Journal, Sacramento, California.

Campbell, A. *Voyage Around the World, 1806-1812*. Edinburgh, 1816.

Castle, H. *Letters*. London, 1902

Castle (H.N.) to Helen Castle, Henry Northrup Castle Letters.

Castle, William R., Jr. *Hawai'i Past & Present*. Dodd, Mead & Co., New York, 1913.

Chamberlain Journal, HMCS Lib., II, 468-469 unpublished type-script.

Chamberlain, Leve. Journal MS. HMCS.

Chaney, George Leonard. *Alo'ha! A Hawaiian Salutation*. Roberts Bros. Boston, 1880.

Chappell, J. Relationships between sea-levels "o variations " & orbital perturbations during the past 250,000 years. Nature. London, 1974.

Charlton, Richard. Correspondence on the Subject of Richard Charlton's Claim to Land in Honolulu, 1845. AH.

Charlton to Palmerston. (No. 12) BPRO F.0. 58/11 USNA.

Cheever, Henry T. *The Island World of the Pacific*. Harper & Brothers. New York, 1851.

Chessman, G. Wallace. *Theodore Roosevelt and the Power of Politics*. Little Brown & Co., Boston, 1969.

Chinen, Jon J. *Great Mahele*. U.H. Press, Honolulu, 1958.

——————. *Original Land Titles In Hawai'i*. Honolulu, 1961.

Clerke, Charles. Log. British Museum, Add. MS. 8951-3.

Cleveland, Richard J. *A Narrative of Voyages & Commercial Enterprises*. Cambridge, 1842 .

Coan, Titus. *Life in Hawai'i, and Autobiographical Sketch of Mission Life and Labors*. Anson A.F. Randolph and Co. New York, 1882.

Colvin, S., ed., *The Letters of Robert Louis Stevenson*. Charles Scribner Sons, New York, 1911.

Coman, K. *History of Contract Labor in the Hawaiian Islands.* New York, 1903.

Comly to Evarts No. 113, July 15, 1880, USDS Dispatches, Hawai'i Vol. XIX, USNA.

Connell, S. Evan. *Son of Morning Star.* North Point Press, San Francisco, 1984.

Cook, James. Captain James Cook & Captain James King. *A Voyage to the Pacific Ocean.* Undertaken by the command of His Majesty, for making Discoveries in the Northern Hemisphere, to determine the Position and Extent of the West Side of North America, its Distance from Asia, and the Practicalability of a Northern Passage to Europe. Performed under the direction of Captains Cook, Clerke and Gore in the years 1776, 1777, 1778, 1779 and 1780. By order of the Lords Commissioners of the Admiralty.

Cook, James. *Cook's Voyages, Vol. I & II & III.* W.L.A. Strahan. London, 1784.

——————. Journal H.M.S. Endeavor. National Maritime Museum London.

——————. Captain Cook's Journal during his First Voyage Round the World (1768-71) W.J.L. Wharton (ed.), Elliot Stock. London:

——————. *A Voyage Towards the South Pole and Round the World... in the years 1772-5.* Vols. I & II. London.

——————. Journals II, BPRO.

——————. Journals III, BPRO.

Cooke Diary. *The Chiefs Children's School.* ed. Mary Atherton Richards, Honolulu, 1937.

"Correspondence Relating to the Last Hours of Kamehameha V." HHS Report, 6. 1898.

Cummins, J.A. Medical Report on the Last Illness and Death of Kalākaua I, King of Hawai'i. Printed on Board U.S. Flagship Charleston at Sea 1891.

(Curtis) Letter, Curtis to Hawai'i Minister of Foreign Affairs on Board U.S.S. Constitution, Dec. 1845. USNA.

Daggett to Frelinghuyqer, No. 11, USDS Dispatches, Hawai'i Vol. XX, USNA.

Dahlgren, F. *Were the Hawaiian Islands Visited by the Spaniards Before Their Discovery by Capt. Cook in 1778?* Stockholm, 1916.

Dalrymple, A. *An Historical Collection of Seven Voyages and Discoveries in the South Pacific Ocean.* (2 Vols.). Nourse, London.

Damon, Ethel M. *Samuel Chenery Damon.* HMCS. Honolulu,1966.

Davidson Janet M. *The Prehistory of Polynesia.* Samoa & Tonga, Cambridge, 1979.

Davies to Grandville, London, July 24, 1873, BPRO, Spaulding Collection, University of Michigan Library.

Daws, Gavin. *Shoal of Time.* University Press of Hawaii, Honolulu, 1968.

Dawson, Edward Walter. *The Isles of the Sea.* Betts & Co., Hartford CT, 1886.

Decker, B.G. *Atlas of Hawai'i.* Honolulu, 1982.

Delano, Amasa. A Narrative of Voyages and Travels in the Northern and Southern Hemispheres. Praeger Scholarly Reprints, 1970

Dening, G. *The Geographical Knowledge of the Polynesians in Polynesian Navigation.* Ed. I. Golson, Wellington: Polynesian Society Memoir No. 34.

Derrick, Ronald A. *Fijian Warfare.* Transaction & Proceedings of the Fiji Society of Science & Industry for the years 1940 - 1944, 2:137-146.

—————. *A History of Fiji*i. Suva,1946.

Dibble, Sheldon. *History of the Sandwich Islands.* Lahainaluna,1843. Dole Collection. AH

—————. *Memoirs of the Hawaiian Revolution.* Honolulu,1936.

Doyle, Emma Lyons. *Makua Laiana.* The Story of Lorenzo Lyons. Honolulu, 1953.

—————. "The Story of Alfred Welling Carter, 1867-1949." Parker Ranch Museum, Waimea, Hawai'i.

Edgar, Thomas. Journal. British Museum, Add. MS 37528.

Ellis, William. *Narrative of a Tour Through Hawai'i.* Fisher, Son & Jackson, London, 1827. Also the Advertiser Historical Series No. 2, Hawai'i Gazette, Ltd., Honolulu, 1917.

Ellis, William W. Journals III. AH

————————. *Authentic Narrative of a Voyage, 1776 - 1780.* 2 Vols. London, 1782.

Emerson, N. B. *Unwritten Literature of Hawai'i.* Washington, 1909.

————————. Translation of Malo, *Hawaiian Antiquities.* Honolulu, 1898.

Emma to Mrs. Pierre Jones. Queen Emma Collection. AH.

Emory, Kenneth. *National Geographic Magazine.* "The Coming of the Polynesians." December, 1974.

————————. East Polynesian Relationships: "Settlement pattern and time involved as indicated by vocabulary agreements," *Journal of the Polynesian Society*, Vol. 72, No. 2, 78-100.

Finney, Ben R. *The Prehistory of Polynesian Voyaging.* Cambridge, 1979.

————————. "New perspectives of Polynesian voyaging". In Polynesian Culture History: 1967. *Essays in honor of Kenneth P. Emory.* ed. G.A. Highland et al, Bishop Museum Special Publications No. 56, Honolulu.

Foreign Relations, 1894, II USNA

Fornander, A. *Account of the Polynesian Race.* 3 vols. London, 1878-1885.

Forster, Johann Georg. *A Voyage Around the World in his Britannic Majesty's Sloop Resolution, Vol. 1.* p. 538. London, 1777.

Forster, John Reinhold. *History of the Voyages and Discoveries made in the North.* London, 1786.

Fragments I, Family Record, House of Judd. Honolulu, 1903. HMKS.

Fragments II, H. M. Ballou, ed., *The Letters of Dr. Gerrit P. Judd 1827-1872.* Honolulu, 1911. HMKS.

Fragments III, A. F. Judd II, ed., *Pages from the Diary of G. P. Judd on the Voyage around Cape Horn in the Ship "Parthian" 1827-1828*. Honolulu, 1928. HMKS.

Fragments IV, A. F. Judd II, ed., *Pages from the Journals of Gerrit Parmele Judd and Laura Fish Judd 1830-1832*. Honolulu, 1928. HMKS.

Friend, *The Temperance Advocate and Seaman's Friend*. Newspaper, Honolulu.

Frost, Everett L. *The Prehistory of Polynesia, Fiji*. Cambridge, 1979.

——————. "Archaeological Excavations of Fortified Sites on Tareuni, Fiji." Social Sciences Research Institute, University of Hawai'i.

Fugger, Princess Hohenlohe. *The Glory of the Hapsburgs*. Dial Press. New York, 1932.

Furnas, J.C. *Anatomy of Paradise*. William Sloan Associates. New York, 1937.

Furneaux, Tobias. Journal and Log, BPRO, Adm. 55/1

Gibson, Walter M. "Gibson Diary," Archives, Mormon Church, Salt Lake City, Utah.

——————. *The Prison of Weltevreden...* J. C. Riker, New York, 1855. Gibson to Carter, Hawaiian Officials Abroad, AH.

Giffin, D. "Life of William L. Lee." MA, Vanderbilt University, 1956.

Gifford, Edward W. "Archaeological Excavations in Fiji." University of California Anthropological Records, 13:3, 1951.

——————. "Six Fijian Radiocarbon Dates," The Journals of the Polynesian Society, 64:240.

Gillis, J. A. *The Hawaiian Incident*. Libraries Press, Freeport, New York, 1897.

Gladwin. *East is a Big Bird*. Harvard University Press, Cambridge, Mass., 1970.

Goldman, Irving. *Ancient Polynesian Culture*. University of Chicago Press, Chicago, 1970.

Golovnin, Captain. "Golovnin's Visit To Hawai'i In 1818," in *Friend*. (Hono.) LI.

Golson, J. (ed.) "Polynesian Navigation." A symposium on Andrew Sharp's theory of accidental voyages, Wellington: Polynesian Society, Memoir No. 34, 1963.

Gore, John. og, BPRO. Adm. 55/120

Gould, R. *Some Unpublished Accounts of Cook's Death.* Mariner's Mirror. October, 1928, London XIV.

Gregg to Marcy, USDS Dispatches, Hawai'i, 8, USNA.

Halford, F.J. *Gerrit Parmele Judd. M.D., Surgeon and Diplomat of the Sandwich Islands.* Paul B. Haeber, New York, 1935.

Handy, E. S. Craighill & Elizabeth Green Handy, with the cooperation of Mary Kawena Pukui. *Native Planters in Old Hawai'i.* Bishop Museum Press, Honolulu, 1972.

Handy, E. S. Craighill and Mary Kawena Pukui. *The Polynesian Family System in Ka'u, Hawai'i.* Charles E. Tuttle Company, Rutland, Vermont and Tokyo, Japan, 1972.

Handy, E. S. Craighill. *Ancient Hawaiian Civilization.* Chas. Tuttle. Rutland, Vermont, 1965.

—————. "Polynesian Religions". Bishop Museum Bulletin No. 233.

Handy, Willowdean. "The Native Culture of the Marquesas." B. P. Bishop Museum Bulletin 9, Honolulu, 1923.

Harris (C.C.) to E. H. Allen. E. H. Allen Papers, BPRO 58/174, Also LC.

Harrison, Benjamin. Correspondence between Harrison & James G. Blaine, 1882 - 1893. Philadelphia, 1940.

Harrison, Samuel. *The White King.* Doubleday. New York, 1950.

Hawaiian Annual. "Hawaiian Epidemics." 1897.

Hawaiian Evangelical Association. "Proceedings." Honolulu 1863.

Hawaiian Gazette. Newspaper. Honolulu. Translated from *Ko Hawai'i Pae Aina.*

Hawaiian Spectator. Periodical, Honolulu.

Hawksmouth, J. *An Account of Voyages*, performed by Commander Byron, Captain Carteret, Captain Wallis and Captain Cook, 3rd ed., Strahan & Cadell, Vol. 1, London, 1785.

Heyerdahl, Thor. *Kon-Tiki-Across the Pacific by Raft.* Translated F. H. Lyon. Rand McNally, London, 1950.

Hitt, USDS Dispatches, Hawai'i Vol. XX, USNA.

Historical Commission, "Report of the Territory of Hawai'i, December, 1926," AH.

Holt, John D. *Monarchy in Hawai'i.* Hogarth Press, Honolulu, 1971.

Honolulu Bulletin. Newspaper. Honolulu.

Hopkins, Manley. *Hawai'i: The Past, Present and Future of its Island-Kingdom.* Appleton & Co. 2nd ed. New York,1869.

Horowitz, R. and Finn, J. *Public Land Policy in Hawai'i: Major Landowners.* Honolulu, 1967.

Ii, John Papa. *Fragments of Hawaiian History.* Translated by Mary Kawena Pukui. B.P. Bishop Museum Press, Honolulu, 1959.

Ingraham, J. Capt. *Journal of the Voyage of the Brigantine Hope.* MS LC May-Oct. 1791.

Jarves, James J. *History of the Hawaiian or Sandwich Islands.* Boston, 1843.

——————. Testimony of Judd to Henry A. Peirce. AH

——————. *Scenes and Scenery in the Sandwich Islands.* Boston, 1844.

Jennings, Jesse, ed. *The Prehistory of Polynesia.* Cambridge 1979.

Johnstone, Arthur. *Recollections of R. L. Stevenson in the Pacific.* Chatto & Windels, London, 1905.

Jones to Marshall. Marshall Manuscripts, Harvard College Library, Cambridge, Mass.

Judd, A. F. *Lunalilo, the Sixth King of Hawai'i: Contemporary Letters.* HHS Report 44. 1936.

Judd, Bernice, *Mission Album Sesquicentennial Editions 1820-1970.* HMCS, L.

Judd, Gerrit P. *Fragments II* (A series of Six Small Volumes of Excerpts from Various Judd Journals and Letters), Honolulu, 1903, AH.

——————. (Meeting with Clayton) Journal.

——————. Judd to Peirce, Jan. 1, 1845. AH.

——————. Judd to Richards, F.O. & Ex. AH.

——————. Judd to Sec. ABCCFM Sept. 26, 1831, MS. in HMCS Library.

——————. Judd to Seward, April 20, 1867, USNA.

Judd, G.P. to Dillion. Financial Dept. Letter Book, 1848-1859 AH.

Judd, Gerrit P., IV. *Hawai'i An Informal History*. Collier Books, New York, 1961.

Judd, Laura A. *Honolulu: Sketches of Life in the Hawaiian Islands*. New York, 1880.

Judd, Laura Fish. Journal 1827-1828.

——————. *The Judd Diary*, March 30, 1828.

——————. *Honolulu in 1828-1861*. Star Bulletin Press, Honolulu, 1928.

Kalākaua to James W. Robertsen, HHS.

Kaleo Ka La Hui, Newspaper.

Kamakau, Samuel M. *Kuokoa*. Bishop Museum. Honolulu,1867.

——————. *Ruling Chiefs of Hawai'i*. Kamehameha Schools Press, Honolulu, 1961.

——————. "Instructions in Ancient Hawaiian Astronomy as Taught by Kaneakahoowaha ..." (trans. from the Nupepa Kuokoa of 5 Aug. 1865, for the Maile Wreath by W. D. Alexander). Honolulu: Thrum's Hawaiian Annual, 1891.

Kaplan, Justin. *Mr. Clemens and Mark Twain*. Simon and Schuster. 1New York, 1966.

Kauikeaouli & Kīna'u, Proclamations Concerning Our Office, Oahu, July 5, 1832 HHS.

Kawaihau "Dear Sister", A.S. Cleghorn Collection AH.

Kent, Harold W. *Charles Reed Bishop: Man of Hawai'i*. Pacific Books, Palo Alto, California, 1965.

King, James. Journals III. Log and proceedings, BPRO., Adm. 55/116, 122. 'Running Journal' 1779-80, British Ministry of Defense.

Kittleson, David. *The Hawaiians, An Annotated Bibliography*. 1984.

Korn, Alfons, L. *The Victorian Visitors*. U. of Hawaii Press, 1985.

Kotzebue, Otto Van. *Voyage of Discovery, I*. London, 1809.

Kuokoa. Newspaper. Honolulu

Kuykendall, R. "Some Early Commercial Adventures of Hawai'i". HHS Report 37. 1929.

──────. *The Hawaiian Kingdom*. 3 Vols. Honolulu, 1938-1967.

Lebra, J. C. *Women's Voices In Hawaii*. U. of Colo. Press. 1991

Lecker, G. "Lahainaluna, 1831-1877". MA, UH, 1938.

Lee, John D. *Mormonism Unveiled*. Excelsior, St. Louis, 1856.

Lee, William Little. ...to Turrill HMCS Library.

Lewis, David. *We, the Navigators*. The Ancient Art of Landfinding in the Pacific. University Press of Hawai'i i. Honolulu, 1972.

──────. "Polynesian Navigational Methods". *Journal of the Polynesian Society*, 73, 364-374.

Liholiho, Alexander. ...address of Death of Kamehameha III, Dec. 15, 1854. HHS.

──────. Journal, HHS.

Lili'uokalani, Lydia. *Hawai'i's Story by Hawai'i's Queen*. Lothrop, Lee & Shepard Co., Boston, 1898.

Lili'uokalani Diary. AH.

Lind, Andrew W. *Hawai'i's People*. U. of Hawai'i Press. 1967.

Lisiansky, Urey. *A Voyage Around the World...NEVA*. London, 1814.

Loomis, Albertine. *Grapes of Canaan*. HMCS, 1951.

Lot, Kamehameha. Journal. Bishop Museum, Honolulu.

Low, Mary to Richard Smart,1931-33, Parker Collection, Waimea, Hawai'i.

Lyman, Henry M. *Hawaiian Yesterdays*. McClurg Co., Chicago, 1906.

Malo, David. *Hawaiian Antiquities*. Translated by Nathaniel B. Emerson. Bishop Museum Press, Honolulu, 1971.

——————. Hawaiian Spectator Vol. II, No. 2. April 1839. "On the Decrease of Population on the Hawaiian Islands."

Mann, Peggy. *Easter Island: Land of Mystery*. New York, 1976.

Mariner, W. *An Account of the Natives of the Tonga Islands...* J. Martin (ed.), London: John Murray, Vol. I, 1817.

Marshall, Bailey, S. "The Lost Son of Kamehameha the Great." *Paradise of the Pacific*. Magazine, Honolulu, October, 1939.

Marshall Manuscripts, Harvard College Library.

Martin, J. *Account of the Natives of the Tonga Islands.* 2 vols. London, 1817.

May, Charles. *Oceania*. Nashville, Tenn: T. Nelson. 1973.

McElroy, Robert. *Grover Cleveland The Man & The Statesman*. Harper & Bros. New York, 1923.

McKern, W. C. "Archaeology of Tonga." Bishop Museum Bulletin 60. Honolulu, 1929.

Melville, Herman. *Typee*. J. Murray, London, 1846.

——————. *Omoo*. J.M. Dent & Sons, Ltd. London, 1907.

——————. *The Whale* (or Moby Dick). J. Murray, London, 1851.

Menzies, Archibald. *Hawai'i Nei 128 Years Ago*. W.F.Wilson ed. Honolulu, 1920.

Meredith, Robert. *Around the World on Sixty Dollars*. Thomas & Thomas, Chicago.

Metraux, Alfred. "Ethnology of Easter Island." Bishop Museum Bulletin 160. Honolulu, 1944.

——————. *Easter Island; A Stone-age Civilization of the Pacific*. (Translated by Michael Bullock). Anore Deutsch, London, 1957.

Miller, Merle, *Plain Speaking, An Oral Biography of Harry S. Truman*, New York: Berkeley, 1974.

Missionary Herald. Periodical. Boston.

Molyneux, Robert. Journal, BPRO, Adm. 51/4546/152

Morgan, T. *Hawai'i: A Century of Economic Change, 1778-1876*. Cambridge, 1948.

Mumford, Lewis. *Herman Melville.* The Literary Guild of America, New York, 1929.

Munford, J., ed. *John Ledyard's Journal of Captain Cook's Last Voyage.* Corvallis, 1963.

Nellist, George I. *The Story of Hawai'i and Its Builders.* Honolulu Star Bulletin, Ltd., 1925.

New York Herald. Newspaper. Article by Reverend Sereno Bishop, Review of Reviews periodical. New York, 1891.

New York Independent. News article, "Freedom in Hawai'i at Bay."

New York Times. Newspaper.

New York Tribune. Newspaper.

Osborne, T. J. *"Empire Can Wait,"* Kent, OH, Kent St. U. Press, 1981.

Parker, Wills, E.M. *The Sandwich Islands as They Are ...* San Francisco, 1852.

PCA. *Pacific Commercial Advertiser.* Newspaper. Honolulu.

Pacific Unitarian. Newsletter. San Francisco.

Paradise of the Pacific. Magazine. Honolulu.

Peirce to Fish, No. 220, Sept. 2, 1873, USDS Dispatches, Hawai'i, Vol. XV, Report of Historical Commission, 1928, LC.

——————. Jan. 12,1875, USDS Dispatches, HI, Vol. XVII, LC.

Phillips, Kevin P. *Politics of the Rich and Poor.* Random House, New York, 1990.

Pickersgill, Richard. Journal, BPRO. Adm. 51/4546-140-1.

Planters Monthly, I. March, 1883.

Polynesian Weekly. Newspaper. Honolulu.

Pratt, John Scott Boyd, Jr. *A Record of the Descendants of Gerrit P. and Laura Judd.* HMCS L, Honolulu, 1978.

Pukui, Mary K., E. W. Haertig, M. D., and Catherine A Lee. *Nana I Ke Kumu (Look to the Source), Vol I,* Queen Lili'uokalani Children's Center, Honolulu, 1972.

Pukui, M. K. and Elbert. S. *Hawaiian-English Dictionary.* University of Hawaii Press, Honolulu, 1957.

Purves, David Laing, ed. *The English Circumnavigators.* William P. Nimmo, London, 1874.

Rains, Anthony J., Harding & Edward Jenner. *Vaccination.* Hove, East Sussex: Wayland, 1974.

Reynolds, Stephen. Journal. HMCS Library.

Robotti, Frances D. *Whaling and Old Salem.* Bonanza Books, New York, 1962.

Roggonveen, M. J. *Official Log of the Voyage of Mynheer Jacob Roggonveen in 1721-1722.* Hakluyt Society, 2nd Ser., No. 13, Cambridge, 1908.

Rosamel to LaPlace. AMAC (Paris) lles Sandwich. LC

Roth, G. K. *Fiji Way of Life.* Oxford University Press, London, 1953.

Royal Commission to Hillebrand, March 30, 1965. AH

Rush, Benjamin. *The Vices & Virtues of Polynesians.* New York, 1801.

Sacramento Union. Newsletter. (Mark Twain).

Sahlins, Marshall. "Social Stratifications in Polynesia." American Ethnological Society, 1958.

——————. *Islands of History.* University of Chicago Press, Chicago, 1987.

Samwell, David. *A Narrative of the Death of Captain James Cook.* London, 1786.

San Francisco Call. Newspaper.

Saturday Press. Newspaper. Honolulu.

Schmitt, R. " Birth and Death Rates in Hawai'i, 1848-1919." *Hawai'i Historical Review.* Jan., 1974.

Seward, Frederick W. *Reminiscences of a Wartime Diplomat.* New York, 1871.

Sharp, Andrew. *Ancient Voyagers in Polynesia.* Sydney, 1963.

——————. *Ancient Voyages in the Pacific.* Auckland, 1963.

——————. *Discovery of the Pacific Islands.* Oxford, 1960.

Shurkin, Joel N. *The Invisible Fire*. The story of mankind's triumph over the ancient scourge of smallpox. Putnam, N.Y., 1979.

Simpson, Alexander. *The Sandwich Islands: Progress & Events since ... Captain Cook*. London, 1851.

Sinoto, Yoshihiko H. *The Prehistory of Polynesia*, "The Marquesas," Cambridge, 1979.

Smallpox Epidemic: Special file. 3-10-1854. AH F.O. & Ex., 1853.

Smith, Bradford. *Yankees in Paradise*. J.B. Lippincott Co., 1956.

Smith, Theodore C. *The Life and Letters of James Abram Garfield*. New Haven, 1925.

Spaulding, T.M. "Chief Justice William Little Lee." *Honolulu Mercury II*. 346-353. March, 1930.

Stenhouse, Thos. B. H. *The Rocky Mountain Saints*. N. Y., 1875.

Stevens, Sylvester K. *American Expansion in Hawai'i, 1842-1898*. Harrisburg, 1945

Stevens to Blaine, No. 30, USDS Dispatches, Hawai'i Vol XXV, LC.

Stevens to Wiltse, enclosed in Stevens to Foster, No. 79, printed in Foreign Relations (1894). LC.

Stevenson, R. L. *Letters of RLS*. Charles Scribner's Sons, N.Y.

—————. *In The South Seas*. Hogarth Press, London, 1987.

—————. *Collected Works*. Ballads and Other Poems. Charles Scribner's Sons, XVI, New York.

Stoddard, Charles W. *Hawaiian Life*. Neely, N.Y., 1894.

—————. *Island of Tranquel Delights*. Boston, 1904.

Suggs, Charles. *Oceania*. Nashville, Tenn., 1973.

Suggs, Robert C. *The Island Civilizations of Polynesia*. New York, 1960.

—————. "The Derivation of Marquesan Culture," *Journal of the Royal Anthropological Institute*, Vol. 91, 1-10. 1961.

Synge to Russell, No. 32, Dec. 12, 1863, BPRO.

Tate, Meaze. *The United States & The Hawaiian Kingdom*, Yale, New Haven, 1965.

Taylor, A.P. *Under Hawaiian Skies*. Advertiser Pub. Co. 1926.

——————. Sesquicentennial Celebration of Captain Cook's Discovery of Hawai'i. Advertiser Publishing Co. Honolulu, 1928.

Ten Eyck, A. Ten Eyck to Buchanan (No. 52) Oct. 2, 1848, USDS Dispatches. Hawai'i, Vol. III, USNA.

Thomson, B. *The Fijians. A Study of the decay of Custom*. Heineman, London, 1908.

Thompson, W.J. "Easter Island, Report of the U.S. Nat'l Museum for Year Ending June 30, 1889". Washington, D.C.: U.S. Government Printing Office, 1889.

Thrum, T.G. *The Sandalwood Trade of Early Hawai'i*. Hawaiian Almanac and Annual, 1905.

Thurston, Lorrin A. *Memoirs of the Hawaiian Revolution*. Andrew Farrell (ed.). Honolulu, 1936.

Thurston, Lucy. *Life and Times*. Michigan. 1882.

——————. *Handbook on the Annexation of Hawai'i*. St. Joseph, 1897.

Tuggle, H. David. *Hawai'i: The Prehistory of Polynesia*. Jennings, ed. Cambridge, 1979.

Turnbull, J. *Voyage Round the World. 1800-1804*. 3 Vols. London, 1805.

Twain, Mark, (S.L. Clemens). *Letters from the Sandwich Islands*. San Francisco, 1937.

Tyerman, Daniel, & George Bennet. *Journal of Travel & Voyages ... in the South Seas*. Boston, 1832, P. 66

Vancouver, George. *A Voyage of Discovery to the North Pacific Ocean, 1790-1795*. 3 Vols. London, 1798.

Van Doren, Charles & McHenry, Robert, eds. *Webster's Guide to American History*. G. & C. Merrian Company, Springfield, Mass., 1971.

Varigny, Chas. de. *Fourteen Years in the Sandwich Islands 1855-1863*. Translated by Alfons L. Korn. University Press of Hawai'i, Honolulu, 1981. HHS.

Wales, William. *Journal H.H.S. Endeavor*. Nat'l Maritime Museum (London) Journals II.

Wager, Daniel E. *Our Country And Its People: Work On Oneida County.* Boston, 1896.

Warton, W.J.L. ed. *Captain Cook's Journal During His First Voyage Round the World.* London, 1893.

Wheeler, David. *Memoirs of the Life & Gospel Labors of...,* Society of Friends, London, 1842.

White, Henry A. "The Sugar Industry & Plantation Agencies." The 13th New Americans Conference, Honolulu, 1939.

White, J. Peter. *The Prehistory of Polynesia.* Cambridge, 1979.

Whitney, Samuel. Journal. HMCS.

Williams, T. *A Narrative of Missionary Enterprises in the South Seas.* Snow, London, 1846.

Williamson, J. Log. Ms. Adm. 55/117 PR0. AH.

Wise, John H. *Ancient Hawaiian Civilization.* Handy et al., Chas. Tuttle, Rutland, Vermont, 1965.

Wodehouse to Granville, No. 3 Confidential, BPR0, F0 58/178 LC.

Wodehouse to BFO letter. July 3, 1886, British Consular Records, AH.

Wyllie, R.C. ...Report on Mission, Cabinet. LC.

Wyllie to Thompson, Capt. HBMS (Private), F.O. & Ex. AH.

Young, Lucien. *The Boston at Hawai'i.* New York, 1899.

—————. *The Real Hawai'i.* Gibson Bros, Washington, D.C., 1900.

Yzendoorn, R. *History of the Catholic Mission in the Hawaiian Islands.* Honolulu, 1927.

Zimmerman, Heinrich. *Zimmerman's Account of Third Voyage of Captain Cook 1776-80.* Translated by Miss U. Tewsley, Alexander Turnbull Library, Government Printer, Wellington, N.Z., 1926.

NOTES

These notes give highly abbreviated references to sources. Authors, editors and others appearing in the notes will be listed in alphabetical order in the bibliography with the titles of their works. If an item has no known author, the first words of its title appear in the notes and a broader title is listed in the bibliography. In instances where periodicals or other documents are cited in the notes only by an identifying tag, the alphabetical method remains accurate in the bibliography. An identifying tag appears there, too, followed by a more descriptive title.

CHAPTER ONE: EXPLORATIONS

For background information regarding the settling of Oceania see Nelson, The Philippines, Jennings, Bellwood, White, The Prehistory of Polynesia, Emory, National Geographic 12/74; Barclay, A History of the Pacific; May, Oceania; Sharp, Ancient Voyagers.

New Guinea   1 - 3.
1.   White, *Prehistory*, p. 374.
2.   Chapell, *Papers*, 199-202.
3.   White, *Prehistory*, p. 358.
4.   Barclay, *A History of the Pacific*, p. 3.
5.   Bellwood, *Prehistory*, p. 24.
6.   Bellwood, *Prehistory*, p. 24.
7.   Suggs, *Island Civilization of Polynesia*, p. 226.
8.   May, *Oceania*, pp. 17-19.
9.   Suggs, *Island Civilizations*, p. 79.
10.   Bellwood, *Prehistory*, p. 11.
11.   White, *Prehistory*, p. 352.
12.   Bellwood, *Prehistory*, pp. 18-19.
13.   Emory, *Nat'l Geo.*, p. 743, 12/74.
14.   Jennings, *Prehistory*, p. 3.
15.   May, *Oceania*, p. 12.

Fiji   4 - 5.
16.   Barclay, *History of Pacific*, p. 18.
17.   Bellwood, *Prehistory*, p. 24.
18.   Gifford, *Archaeological Excavations*, V.C. Berkeley, p. 17.
19.   Frost, *Prehistory*, p. 79.

20. Gifford, *Six Fijian Radiocarbon Dates*, Journals of the P. Society 64:240.
21. Emory, *Nat'l Geo.*, 12/74, p. 739.
22. Barclay, *Hist. of Pac.*, p. 9.
23. Derrick, *History of Fiji*, I-18-19.
24. Gifford, *Excavations*.
25. Frost, *Archaeological Excavations of Fortified Sites on Taveuni, Fiji*, U of Hawai'i, p. 123.
26. Derrick, *A Hist. of Fiji*, I-18-19.
27. Roth, *Fiji Way of Life*, p. 47.
28. Derrick, *Fijian Warfare*, 137-146.

Tonga   6 - 7.
29. Sahlins, *Social Stratification in Polynesia*, pp. 22-37.
30. Emory, *Nat'l Geo.*, 12/74, p. 739.
31. Davidson, *Prehistory*, p. 90.
32. Davidson, *Prehistory*, p. 88.
33. Suggs, *Island Civilizations*, p. 94.
34. Davidson, *Prehistory*, p. 82.
35. Davidson, *Prehistory*, p. 82.
36. Davidson, *Prehistory*, p. 105.
37. Beaglehole, *Voyage of Resolution*, p. 275, 272.
38. Mariner, W., *Natives of Tonga*, Vol. 1.

The Marquesas   8 - 11.
39. P. Emory, *Nat'l Geo.*, p. 742.
40. Barclay, *Hist. of Pac.*, p. 15.
41. Sinoto, *Prehistory*, p. 130.
42. Barclay, *Hist. of Pac.*, pp. 15-16.
43. Sharp, *Ancient Voyages*, p. 32.
44. Heyerdahl, *Kon-Tiki*, p. 70.
45. Sharp, *Ancient Voy. in Pac.*, p. 97.
46. Emory, *Nat'l Geo.*, 12/74, p. 745.
47. Lewis, *Navigators*, p. 346.
48. Emory, *Nat'l Geo.*, 12/74, p. 743.
49. Handy, *Native Planters*, pp. 11-13.
50. Handy, Willowdean, *The Native Culture of Marquesas*, pp. 154-55.
51. Finney, *Prehistory*, pp. 332-334.
52. Lewis, *Navigators*, p. 302.
53. Barclay, *Hist. of Pac.*, p. 15.

Easter Island   12 - 14.
54. Emory, *Nat'l Geo.*, 12/74, p 743
55. Metraux, *Bishop Museum Bull.*, 1944, p. 160.
56. Barclay, *Hist. of Pac.*, p. 20.
57. Roggoveen, *Official Log*, p. 106.
58. Beaglehole, *Life of Cook*, p. 373.
59. Beaglehole, *Life of Cook*, p. 375.
60. Barclay, *Hist. of Pac.*, p. 20.
61. Metraux, *Easter Island*, p. 91
62. Barclay, *Hist. of Pac.*, p. 21.
63. Thompson, *Easter Island*s p. 92.

Hawai'i   15 - 21.
64. Tuggle, *Prehistory*, p. 186.
65. Lewis, *Journal of Polynesian Soc.*, 73, 364-374.
66. Tuggle, *Prehistory*, p. 189.
67. Lewis, *Navigators*, p. 305.
68. Finney, "New Perspectives on Polynesian Voyaging," Bishop Museum Special Pub. No. 56.
69. Lewis, *Navigators*, p. 305.
70. Goldman, *Ancient Polynesian*, pp. 51-52.
71. Wise, *Ancient Hawaiian*, pp. 83-84.
72. Emerson, N.B. "Biographical Sketch of David Malo," *Antiquities*, p. viii.
73. Malo, *Antiquities*, translated by N. B. Emerson, pp. 60-61.
74. Handy, *Ancient Hawaiians*, pp. 13-14.
75. Wise, *Ancient Hawaiian*, pp. 95-96.
76. Emory, *Nat'l Geo.*, 12/74, p. 745.
77   Handy, *Native Planters*, p 2.
78. Malo, *Antiquities*, p. 14.
79. Malo, *Antiquities*, p. 14.
80. Malo, *Antiquities*, p. 14.
81. Handy, *Polynesian Religion*, p. 360.
82. Blaisdell, SB, 9/18/80.
83. Blackman, *Making of Hawai'i,* pp. 44-45.
84. Malo, *Antiquities*, p. 74, and Handy & Pukui, *Polynesian Family*, p. 161.
85. Suggs, *Island Civilizations*, pp. 162-168.
86. Handy, *Native Planters*, p. 22.
87. Blackman, *Making of Haw.*, p. 17.

CHAPTER TWO: INVADERS

Captain James Cook   22 - 26.
1. Wharton, *Cook's Journal*, p. 66.
2. Cook, *Journals Endeavour*, p. 171.
3. Banks, *Journals I*, p. 403.
4. Cook, *Journals I*, pp. 504-5.

Second Voyage   27 - 28.
5. Wales, *Journals II*, p. 89.
6. Cook, *Journals II*, p. 252.
7. Cook, *Journals II*, pp. 321-2.
8. Forster, *A Voyage*, Vol. I, p. 538.
9. Cook, *Journals II*, p. 353.
10. Cook, *Journals II*, p. 409.

Final Voyage   29 - 41.
11. Cook, *Journals II*, p. 699.
12. Cook, *Journals III*, p. 1510.
13. Cook, *Journals III*, p. 69.
14. Beaglehole, Paper before Australian Academy of Science, Canberra, May 1, 1969.
15. Forster, *History*, p. 178.
16. Beaglehole, *The Life of Capt. James Cook ...*, p. 542.
17. Besant, *Captain Cook,* pp. 118-119.
18. Besant, *Captain Cook*, pp. 123-124.
19. Kamakau, *Kuokoa*.
20. Dibble, *Sandwich Islands*, p. 21.
21. Kamakau, *Kuokoa*.
22. King, *Journals III*, p. 525.
23. Cook, *Journals III*, 503.
24. Cook, *Journals III*, p. 490-1.
25. King, *Journals III*, p. 529.
26. King, *Journals III*, p. 530.
27. King, *Journals III*, 549.
28. Besant, *Captain Cook*, pp. 160-161-162.
29. Ellis, *Journals III*, p. 540.
30. Ellis, *A Tour Through Hawai'i*.
31. Zimmerman, *Account of Third Voyage*, p. 127.
32. Samwell, *A Narrative of the Death*, p. 51.
33. Purves, *The English Circumnavigators*, p. 137.
34. King, *Journals III*, p. 561.

CHAPTER III: KAMEHAMEHA I   1779 - 1819

Kamehameha I   42 - 43.
1. Vancouver, *A Voyage*, p. 73.
2. Vancouver, A Voyage, p. 79.
3. Menzies, *Hawai'i Nei*, pp. 23-24.

Vancouver Returns   44 - 45.
4. Bingham, *A Residence of Twenty One*, p. 81.
5. Kamakau, *Ruling Chiefs*, p. 40.
6. Ingraham, *Journal ... Brigantine Hope*, May, 1791.
7. Vancouver, *A Voyage*, p. 93.
8. Beckwith, *Mythology*, p. 8.
9. Vancouver, *A Voyage*, p. 99.

Sandalwood   46 - 49.
10. Kamakau, *Ruling Chiefs*, p. 51.
11. Arago, *Narrative* ..., p. 94.
12. Bryant, Letter to Hale.
13. Kamakau, *Ruling Chiefs*, p. 70.
14. Golovnin's visit, Friend (Honolulu), LII, (1984), pp. 50-53, 60-62.
15. Delano, Amasa, *A Narrative of Voyages and Travels* ..., pp. 391-396.
16. Adams, *Peoples of Hawai'i*, p. 5.
17. Malo, "On the Decrease of Population on the Hawaiian Islands," *Hawaiian Spectator*, Vol. II - No. 2, April, 1839.
18. "Hawaiian Epidemics," *Hawaiian Annual* 1897, pp. 95-97; also Lisiansky, Urey, *A Voyage Around the World ... NEVA*, pp. 111-112.
19. Kuykendall, *Hawaiian Kingdom*, 1778-1854, p. 90.

Ka'ahumanu   50 - 52.
20. Arago, *Narrative*, p. 94.
21. Kamakau, *Ruling Chiefs*, p. 87.
22. Kumumanao, Alexander, W. "Overthrow of the ...". in 25 HHS Report, 39-40.
23. Bingham, *A Residence*, p. 29.
24. Melville, *Typee*, p. 274.
25. Loomis, A., *Grapes*, p. 34.

CHAPTER FOUR: HIRAM BINGHAM   53 - 63.

1. ABCFM, HMCS, pp. 19-20, 17-28.
2. ABCFM, 1823, p. 94.
3. Bingham, *Journal*, April 4, 1820.
4. Alexander, *A Brief History*, p. 151.
5. Kuykendall, *Hawaiian Kingdom*, p. 171.
6. Judd, Diary, March 30, 1828.
7. Bingham, Residence, p. 203.
8. BPRO, London, Also USNA.
9. Report Historical Commission, Dec. 1926, pp. 19-20 AH
10. Bloxam, *Voyage of H.M.S. Blonde*, p. 164.
11. Bryant & Sturgis Letter Dec. 28, 1824.
12. Bingham, MLV, 1356, Nov. 23, 1831, ABCFM, Boston.
13. Judd to Sec. ABCFM Sept. 26, 1831.
14. Sahlins, *Islands of History*, p. 22.
15. Malo, *Antiquities*, pp. 214-215.
16. Bingham, 19.1 v. ABCFM, Boston, Feb. 1830.
17. Reynolds, *Journal I*, 3. HMCS Library, Aug. 1840.
18. Armstrong Papers, 18 July 1844 and 5 March, 1842 LC
19. Kotzebue, *Voyage of Discovery*, p. 281.
20. Bingham, *Residence*, p. 14.
21. Judd, L. *Honolulu: Sketches*, pp. 6, 11.
22. Kauikaiouli, *Proclamations*, July 5, 1832, HHS.
23. Holt, John D. *Monarchy*, pp. 13-14.
24. Loomis, *Grapes*, back cover.
25. Bingham, *Residence*, p. 278.

CHAPTER FIVE: JOHN PALMER PARKER   64 - 68.

1. Doyle, E. *Makua*, p. 101.
2. Bingham to Chamberlain, 13, July, 1830, HMCS.
3. Bingham, *Residence*, p. 379.
4. Cleveland, *Narrative*, p. 224.
5. Bingham to Parker Letter, April 7, 1820, HMCS.
6. Mary Low to Smart, Parker Collection.
7. Mary Low to Smart, Parker Collection.
8. Varigny, *Fourteen Years*, p. 47.
9. Low, Parker Collection.

CHAPTER SIX: HERMAN MELVILLE

Herman Melville   69 - 73.
1. Mumford, *Melville*, p. 4.
2. Melville, *Moby Dick*, p. 2.
3. Melville, *Omoo*, p. xviii.
4. Melville, *Typee*, p. 86.
5. Melville, *Typee*, pp. 151-152.
6. Melville, *Typee* , p. 228.
7. Melville, *Typee*, p. 226.
8. Melville, *Typee*, p. 241.
9. Melville, *Typee*, p. 295.
10. Melville, *Typee*, p. 245.
11. Melville, *Typee*, p. 244.
12. Melville, *Omoo*, p. 4.
13. Melville, *Omoo*, p. 196.
14. Melville, *Omoo*, p. 197.
15. Melville, *Typee*, p. 233.
16. Melville, *Omoo*, p. 328.

Whaling   74 - 76.
17. Meredith, *Sixty Dollars*, p. 79.
18. Malo, *Hawaiian Spectator*, Vol. II, No. 2, pp. 127-128.
19. F. II (October 1848). p. 9.
20. Kamakau, *Ruling Chiefs*, p. 400.
21. Kamakau, *Ruling Chiefs*, p. 400.
22. Kamakau, *Ruling Chiefs*, pp. 400-401
23. Melville, *Omoo*, p. 225.
24. Melville, *Typee*, pp. 235-236.
25. Melville, *Typee*, pp. 301-302, 305-306.
26. Wheeler, *Memoirs*, p. 171.

CHAPTER SEVEN: SAMUEL CHENERY DAMON

The Seaman's Friend   81.
1. Damon, E., *Damon,* p. 87.
2. Damon, E., *Damon,* p. 6.
3. Cheever, *Island World*, p. 214.
4. F, II (June 18, 1848), p. 17.
5. F, XI (November, 1852), p. 6.

Charles Reed Bishop   82 - 86.
6. Gregg to Marcy, March 9, 1857, No. 207 USDS Dispatches,

Hawai'i, 8, USNA.

7. Tyerman, *Journal of Voyages* ..., p. 66.
8. *Cooke Diary*, February 25, 1847.
9. F., (April, 1849).
10. F., part of a serial from September 1 to December 20, 1849.
11. F, as above.
12. F, as above.
13. F, as above.
14. F, as above.
15. P, Aug. 20, 1853.
16. F, XX (1863), p. 14.
17. Armstrong (Richard) Letters, Sept. 18, 1844.
18. P, Editorial, Sept. 20, 1845.

Mark Twain   87 - 92.

19. Twain, *Sacramento Union*, April 9, 1866
20. Twain, *Sacramento Union*, July 1, 1866.
21. Bigelow, A., ed. *Mark Twain's Speeches*, p. 121.
22. Twain, *New York Tribune*, January 9, 1873; *California Journal*, Aug. 6, 1869.
23. F, as above.
24. F, March, 1870.
25. F, dateline Philadelphia, July 4, 1876.

CHAPTER EIGHT: KAMEHAMEHA III

The Little King   93 - 96.

1. Belcher, E., *Narrative*, p. 52.
2. Rosamel to LaPlace, July 31, 1838. Vol. I.
3. Malo, *Antiquities,* pp. 212-213.
4. P, Feb. 6, 1841.
5. Baldwin to Richards, June 9, 1845, HMCS.
6. P, August 2, 1845.
7. P, as above. 8. Lecker, "Lahainaluna 1831-1877," MA, UH, 1938.

CHAPTER NINE: GERRIT PARMELE JUDD 1845

Chief Seattle   97 - 103.

1. Judd, G. P., *Fragments II.*
2. Judd, G. P., *Fragments II.*
3 . Judd, L. F., *Journal* , 1827-1828 , Dec . 9 .
4. Jones to Marshall, April 15, 1828.
5. Judd, L. F., *Journal*, March 30, 1828.
6. Judd, L. F., Journal, April 3, 1828.
7. Jarves, J., *History of the Hawaiian Islands*, p. 81.
3. Judd, L. F., *Honolulu: Sketches* , p. 46.
9 . Judd, G. P ., *Fragments II*, p . 71 .
10. Charlton to Palmerston, Nov. 12, 1839, BPRO.
11. Judd, L. F., *Honolulu: Sketches*, p. 49.
12 . Judd, G. P ., *Fragments II* , pp. 122-123 .
13 . Judd , G. P ., *Fragments II* , p . 100 .
14. Judd, G. P., *Fragments IV*, Jan. 8, 1831, p. 25.
15. Jarves, J., *Scenes & Scenery*, p. 66.
16. Charlton, R., *Correspondence 1845*, p. 180. AH
17. Judd to Richards, Nov. 2, 1843, AH.
18. Reynolds, Stephen, *Journal*, HMCS.
19. Simpson, *The Sandwich Islands*, p. 57.
20. Judd, G. P., *Fragments II*, pp. 162-163; *The Great Mahele*, pp. 146-166 .

The Mahele 1848   104 - 117.

21. Judd to Dillion Letter, May 18, 1848. AH.
22. Bishop, A. Letters, HMCS.
23. Charlton's Claim to Land, pp. 174-175. AH
24. Wyllie to Thompson Letter, April 14, 1845 AH.
25. Jarves, J. J., Testimony, March 14, 1845. AH.
26. Judd to Peirce, Jan 1, 1845. AH.
27. Ten Eyck, A. USDS Dispatches October 2, 1848, Hawai'i, Vol. III, USNA.
28. Judd, G. P., *Fragments V*, pp. 8, 10, 13, 18.
29. P, May 31, 1845.
30. Alexander to S. M. Damon, June 24, 1893, 53 Cong. 2 Sess. No. 47, pp. 639-641 LC.
31. Parker, Wills, *Sandwich Islands*, p. 10.
32. Meredith, *Around the World*, p. 114.
33. Judd, L. F., *Honolulu*, pp. 145-149.

34. Liholiho, Alexander, *Journal*, Jan. 26, 1850. HHS.
35. Liholiho, Alexander, *Journal,* April 1850. HHS.
36. Judd, L. F., *Honolulu*, p. 160.
37. Liholiho, A. *Journal*, May 1850, HHS.
38. Judd, G. P., *Journal* , June 4, 1850 .
39. Lot, Kamehameha, *Journal*, May 30, 1850.40. Buliver to Palmerston, June 9, 1850. LC.
41. Liholiho, A., *Journal*, June 1850, HHS.
42. Wyllie, Oct. 17, 18, 1850, LC.
43. Lee, W. L. to Turrill, June 1, 1851. HMCS.
44. Lee, W. L. to Turrill, Oct. 11, 1851. HMCS.
45. P, Jan. 28, 1854.
46. Judd, L. F., *Honolulu*, pp. 176-177.
47. Smallpox Epidemic. Special file, March 10, 1854. AH.
48. P, July-September, 1855.
49. Judd, G. P. to Seward, April 20, 1867. USNA.

CHAPTER TEN: THE LAST KAMEHAMEHAS

Alexander Liholiho   118 - 120.
1. Liholiho, A., *Death of Kam III*, Dec. 15, 1854. HHS.
2. Kuykendall, R., *Hawaiian*. p. 428.
3. Furnas, J., *Anatomy of Paradise*. p. 157.
4. Judd, Gerrit P. IV,. *An Informal History*. pp. 55, 74.
5. Judd Gerrit P,. *Fragments III*, p. 31.
6. Lili'uokalani, L,. *Hawai'i's Story*, p. 16.

Lot Kamehameha   120 - 123.
7. Synge to Russell, Dec. 12, 1863, BPRO.
8. Twain, M., *Letters From Sandwich Islands*. p. 185.
9. Bliss, W. R,. *Paradise*. pp. 51-52.
10. Bliss, W. R,. *Paradise*. pp. 56 57.
11. HG, Oct. 13,1869.
12. Royal Commission to Hillebrand, March 30, 1865, AH.
13. PCA, November 16, 1869.
14. *Hawaiian Gazette*. Nov. 3, 1869.
15. P, August 16,1851, Jan. 10, Aug. 7,1852.
16. Varigny, C., *Fourteen Years*. p. 143.

Honolulu Afternoon   123 - 126.
17.   Bliss, W,. Paradise. pp. 130-139.
18.   Bliss W,. Paradise, pp. 17-18.
19.   PCA, February 11, 1873, p. 4.
20.   Castle, Wm. R., Jr. *Hawai'i Past...*, p. 71.

Lunalilo   126 - 127.
21.   Davies to Greenville, July 24, 1873.
22.   Kyukendall Vol II, p. 256.

CHAPTER ELEVEN: CURIOSITY

Curiosity In His Own Land   129 - 133.
  1.   Bliss, W. R., *Paradise*, pp. 56-57.
  2.   Bliss, W. R., *Paradise*, pp. 70-71.
  3.   HG, Feb. 21, 1872.
  4.   White, H. A., *The Sugar Industry*, pp. 15-16.
  5.   Bliss, W. R., *Paradise*, p. 161.
  6.   Meredith, *Around the World*, pp. 55-58.
  7.   Castle, W. R., *Hawai'i Past*, p. 13.
  8.   Adams, R., *Interracial Marriage*, p. 8 and pp. 75-76.

Walter Murray Gibson   134 - 135.
  9.   Gibson, W., *Diary*.

Claus Spreckels   135 -139.
10.   Kyukendall op. cit., p. 222.
11.   PCA, Jan. 4, 1886.
12.   HG, Aug. 23, 1882.
13.   Emma to Mrs. Pierre Jones, Nov. 17, 1881.
14.   F, December 1858.
15.   PCA, August 30, 1886.
16.   PCA, Oct. 11, 1886.

Pearl Harbor   139 - 140.
17.   Curtis, I. W., Letter to Hawaiian Minister Dec. 1845, USNA.
18.   PCA, June 17, 1882.
19.   PCA, July 12, 1886.

CHAPTER TWELVE: DAVID KALĀKAUA

All Things to All Men   141 - 147.
1.   Stoddard, C. W., *Hawaiian Life*, p. 155.
2.   Peirce to Fish, USDS Dispatches, Sept. 2, 1873.
3.   PCA, April 18, 18874.
4.   Peirce & Fish, USDS Dispatches, Jan. 12, 1875.
5.   Comly to Evarte, USDS Dispatches, July 15, 1880.
6.   PCA, June 5, 1880.
7.   PCA, April 29, 1878.
8.   PCA, July 31, 1880.
9.   HG, Aug. 25, 1880.
10. HG, Aug. 25, 1880.
11. Harris to E. H. Allen, Sept. 27, 1880.
12. PCA, Oct. 2, 1880.
13. SP, Oct. 9, 1880.
14. SP, Oct. 2, 1880.
15. *New York Herald Review*, 1891, pp. 147-163, 227-234.
16. Castle, W., *Hawai'i Past*, p. 26.

Around the World   147 - 151.
17. Armstrong, W., *Around the World*, p. 8.
18. Harris to E. H. Allen, Feb. 12, 1881.
19. Smith, T. C., James Garfield II, pp. 1166-1168.
20. Armstrong, W., *Around the World*, p. 28.
21. Mutsuhito to Kalākaua, Jan. 22, 1882, F0 & Ex; Conroy, pp. 51-52.
22. Armstrong, W., *Around the World*, p. 130.
23. Armstrong, W., *Around the World*, p. 134.
24. Armstrong, W., *Around the World*, p. 117.
25. Armstrong, W., *Around the World*, p. 194.
26. Kawaihau, "Dear Sister", June 30, 1881.
27. Kawaihau, "Dear Sister", Aug. 11, 1881.
28. Fugger, *Hapsburg*, p. 166.
29. Hitt, USDS, Sept. 4,1881.
30. Armstrong, pp. 276-277.

Triumvirate   152 - 162.

31.   SP, Feb. 11, 1882.
32.   PCA, May 27, 1882.
33.   Wodehouse to Granville, Feb. 13, 1882.
34.   Stevenson, R. L., Letters, 1889.
35.   PCA, Feb. 20,1883.
36.   *Planters Monthly*. I., pp. 306 307.
37.   Lyman, Henry, *Hawaiian Yesterdays*. pp. 134-135.
38.   Thurston, L. A., *Memoirs*, p. 211.
39.   Atkinson, Alatant, *Sketch of Recent Events*, pp. 90 91.
40.   Emerson, N. B., *Unwritten Literature*, pp. 235-236. Also see 1898 Emerson Translation

       From Malo, *Hawaiian Antiquities*. p. 217.
41.   Daggett to Frelinghuyser, USDS, Sept. 20, 1882.
42.   HSB, July 21, 1884.
43.   PCA, July 26, 1884.
44.   HG, Dec. 29,1885.
45.   HG, Dec. 29,1885.
46.   EB, June 17, 1886.
47.   PCA, Dec. 27,1908.
48.   Wodehouse to BFO letter, July 3,1886.
49.   Gibson to Carter, Oct. 22,1886.
50.   *San Francisco Call*, Oct. 31, 1886.
51.   Kent, H., *Man of Hawai'i*. pp. 23-34.
52.   Taylor, A. P., *Under Hawaiian Skies*. pp. 442-443.
53.   PCA, July 31, 1889.
54.   F, Dec. 1889, p. 99.

Reciprocity Abrogated   162 - 164.

55.   Castle, H. N. to Helen Castle, Jan. 27,1890, Castle Letters.
56.   SB, Jan. 19, 1891.
57.   Kalākaua to J. W. Robertson, Jan. 1,1891.
58.   Cummins, J. A., *Medical Report*, 1891.
59.   Stevenson, R. L., *Collected Works*, p. 234.

CHAPTER THIRTEEN: TO STEAL A KINGDOM 1891-1898

Liliu'okalani   165 - 174.

1. Young, L., *The Boston at Hawai'i*, p. 52.
2. F, March 1891, p. 17.
3. *New York Independent*, 45, 1894.
4. Bishop, C. R. to Queen, March 5, 1891.
5. Bishop, C. R. to W. D. Alexander, Nov. 9, 1893.
6. Harrison, B. to James Blaine, pp. 173-174.
8. Allen, Helena, G., *The Betrayal of Lili'uokalani*, p. 218.
9. Gillis, J. A., *Hawaiian Incident*. p. 6.
10. PCA, March 23, 1891.
11. *Kaleo Ka La Hui*, April 10, 1891.
12. Thurston, L. A., *Memoirs*, p. 232.
13. Stevens to Wiltse, Jan. 16, 1893, App. 11, p. 208.
14. *Foreign Relations*, 1894,11, pp. 495, 585.
15. Young, L., *Real Hawai'i*, p.64.
16. Johnstone, A., *Recollections of RLS*, 1905.
17. Colvin, S., Letters of RLS.
18. Lili'uokalani, L., *Hawai'i's Queen*, pp. 368-371.
19. Lili'uokalani, L., *Hawai'i's Queen*, p. 371.
20. Nellist, G. I., *The Story of Hawai'i & Its Builders*, p. 443.
21. Lili'uokalani, L., *Hawai'i"s Queen*, p. 372.
22. Nellist, G. I., *The Story of Hawai'i & Its Builders*, p. 329.
23. Nellist, G. I., *The Story of Hawai'i & Its Builders*, p. 553.
24. HMCS, L., by phone. to M. I. Knight, 7/26/85.
25. Allen, G. E., *Men and Women of Hawaii 1966*, p. 250.
26. Judd, B., *Missionary Album. 1820-1970*, Jacket Notes.
27. Allen, G. E., *Men and Women of Hawaii 1966*. p. 464.
28. Phone interview with John Scott Boyd Pratt, Jr., 7/24/85. Also *A Record of the Descendants of G .P. & Laura Judd*, HMCS.
29. From the unpublished Robert Louis Stevenson work, *The South Seas*. Auckland Star, August 8, 1891.
30. Miller, Merle, *Plain Speaking...*, p. 137.

EPILOGUE   176 - 179.

1. Cleveland to Olney, July 8, 1898 Box 6, Richard Olney Papers, Manuscript Division LC.
2. Judd, Gerrit, P. IV, *Hawai'i*. p. 118.
3. Lili'uokalani, L., *Diary*, July 24, 1893.

4.   Kent, H. W., *Charles Reed Bishop*. p. 297.

5.   Kent, H. W., *Charles Reed Bishop*, p. 299.

6.   Decker, B. G., and students of Geography 390, Class of 1982 from Atlas of Hawai'i, DPED figures.

7.   Kent, H. W., *Charles Reed Bishop*,. p. 307.

8.   Nellist, G. 1., *The Story of Hawai'i & Its Builders*, p. 65.

9.   *Pacific Unitarian*, July 1915, p. 1.

10.   PCA, August 30, 1886, p. 1.

11.   Phillips, Kevin P., *Politics of the Rich and Poor*. p. 239.

12.   *New York Tribune*. Sept. 27, 1891.

13.   *Blount's Papers*, Vol. VII.

SUMMERTIME USA 1898
1.   Van Doren, Chas. *Webster's Guide...*, pp. 328-329.

EPITAPH FOR HAWAIIANS

1.   Van Doren, Chas. *Webster's Guide ...*, p. 329.

NATIVE HAWAIIAN POPULATION
(Estimated) A.D. 375 - A.D. 2025   p. 190.

[The figures in this chart are estimates using selected assump-
tions: Arrival of 100 Polynesians in A.D. 375 and a steady rate of
increase until a population of 300,000 was achieved in 1778.]*

Year (A.D.)	Hawaiians
375	85
600	190
700	350
800	650
900	1,200
1000	2,300
1100	4,300
1200	8,000
1300	15,000
1400	28,000
1500	53,000
1600	98,000
1700	184,000
1778	300,000
1823	134,750
1832	124,049
1836	107,354
1850	82,035
1853	71,019
1860	66,984
1866	57,125
1872	49,044
1875	46,400
1878	44,088
1884	40,014
1890	34,436
1896	31,019
1900	28,718
1910	26,041
1920	23,723
1930	22,636
1940	14,375
1950	12,245
1960	**10,502
1970	7,697
1980	***7,816
1990	****??

*According to Robert C. Schmitt, Hawai'i State Statistician, the pop-
ulation for 1778 could be as few as 250,000.

(Schmitt adds that figures for 1778 and for 1990 are too unreliable to be of any value
statistically.)

Data A.D. 375: Tuggle, H. David, *The Prehistory of Polynesia*, p. 186.

Data from A.D. 375 to 1778: Marion and John Kelly, 1977.

Computer Printout Pre-1778: Robert C. Schmitt

Computer Printout Post-1778: Evan R. Shirley

Data for 1778, 1823 and 1875 are estimates from Romanzo Colfax Adams, *The Peoples of Hawai'i*, Honolulu, pp. 8-9. Also see David Malo, "On the Decrease of Population: *Hawaiian Spectator*, Vol. II, April, 1839.

All other data up to and including 1900 based on local census as reported by Adams. Data for 1910, 1920, 1930, 1940, 1950, 1960,** from Andrew W. Lind, *Hawai'i's People*, 3rd ed. (1967), p. 28. Data for 1980, Hawai'i State Health Department. HSDH 1987 Health Surveillance Data Lists 7,816 full Hawaiians.***

**** U S Census for 1990 lists 138,742 Hawaiians in Hawaii.

In 1960 the U.S. Census eliminated the category called Hawaiian, and listed the few remaining Polynesians of Hawaiian birth under the heading *Others*.

INDEX

ABOUT THE AUTHOR

Born in Hammond, Indiana, in 1924, Michael Dougherty grew up on the same Chicago streets that produced the fictional characters Studs Lonigan and Bigger Thomas. A student in the University of Chicago Humanities Program, he departed in 1942 to serve as a private in the USMC. A survivor of thirty one months in the Pacific, he attended Lawrence College on the GI Bill and, in 1950 graduated from the University of Southern California. Shortly thereafter, he joined CBS Television as a press agent. When he left in 1960, he was director of special projects.

For a brief period he was a Foreign Service Officer functioning as a motion picture producer in South and Southeast Asia. He also served as electronic media consultant to the United States Department of State.

In 1963 Dougherty became a freelance writer and independent documentary film producer. He has principal credits in thirty- seven documentary films and has bylined more than seventy magazine pieces. *To Steal A Kingdom* is his first book.

The Journal of American History   June 1994, pg. 259

Book Review

To Steal A Kingdom. By Michael Dougherty
Waimanalo, Hawaii: Island Style Press,
Revised 1995. xvi, 246 pp. Paper $12.95,
ISBN 0-9633484-0X

From the bicentennial of Capt. James Cook's momentous voyages in the Pacific, to the centennial of Hawaii's revolution of 1893, scholars have been reassessing Western presence in the Pacific.

Michael Dougherty's *To Steal A Kingdom* covers a time frame as broad as the Pacific itself: 250,000 BC to 1924 AD. He begins with an exploration of earliest human settlements in Polynesia, proceeds to Cook's voyages and then devotes the bulk of his commentary to an indictment of American missionary/businessmen for stealing the Hawaiian kingdom from Polynesians. To cover their tracks, the thieving Americans acting through missionary Gerrit P. Judd and his descendants, controlled documentary sources upon which historians have depended.

Like the trade winds blowing...this book brings a breath of fresh air to Hawaiian studies, where missionary filial piety has been conspicuous. Voices harmonizing with Dougherty include Herman Melville, Robert Louis Stevenson, Mark Twain and Queen Liliu'okalani. They, and indigenous Hawaiians whom they championed, are the heroes of this book.

The villains are American missionary/businessmen who nearly wiped out the Hawaiian people and their culture while acquiring wealth in land, sugarcane, banking and shipping. Reverend Judd and his descendants are offered as striking examples of this villainy.

Dougherty holds that the Judd family has largely controlled the writing of Hawaiian history. He supports his claim regarding the Judd family influence on historical scholarship with enough facts and logic to make it believable. [In] its questioning of the process by which much of Hawaiian history has been written...lies the signal contribution of this important, probing work.

Thomas J. Osborne
Rancho Santiago College
Santa Ana, California   ABRIDGED